Using Chinese Classics for Intercultural Communicative Competence

Using Chinese Classics for Intercultural Communicative Competence presents new strategies and tools for integrating Mandarin language teaching with fostering intercultural competencies through contemporary, global lenses on Chinese classic texts.

Chinese classic texts are canonical works in Chinese culture published before 1911. They offer a window into deeply held cultural values which learners of the Chinese language would benefit from studying to facilitate meaningful intercultural dialogues. With chapters covering classic Chinese texts, such as *Journey to the West*, *Dream of the Red Chamber*, and *The Romance of the Three Kingdoms*, this book will demonstrate the value, importance, and feasibility of teaching Chinese classic works for ICC development in the Chinese world language classroom, and equip teachers with carefully planned, classroom-tested lesson models that demonstrate the innovative, integrative models advocated in this book.

This book will be valuable for pre- and in-service Mandarin Chinese teachers across various institutional settings at different levels, looking for ready materials and professional development resources. The book can also be used as core material for teacher training programs.

Jinai Sun is Associate Professor of Chinese Language and Culture at North Central College, Naperville, Illinois.

Xuehua Xiang is Professor of Linguistics and Applied Linguistics, Director of Chinese Program, and Head of the Department of Linguistics at the University of Illinois Chicago.

Li Ye is an esteemed instructor of Mandarin Chinese and serves as a core team leader in the Multilingual Learning Division at Adlai E. Stevenson High School in Lincolnshire, Illinois.

Routledge Studies in Chinese as a Foreign Language
Series Editor: Chris Shei
Swansea University, UK

Der-lin Chao
New York University, USA

The series will strive to produce not only scholarly books investigating aspects of Chinese language learning such as pedagogy, policy, materials and curriculum, assessment, psychology and cognition, aptitude and motivation, culture and society, media and technology and so on, but also textbooks drawing from results of this research and compiled following the pedagogical models suggested by these studies and taking into consideration the individual and social factors related to Chinese language learning uncovered by this series of research. The two strands of books published within this series complement and strengthen each other in their academic achievement and practical implication.

Teaching and Researching Chinese Second Language Listening
Wei Cai

Teaching Chinese by Culture and TV Drama
Lingfen Zhang

Reading in Chinese as an Additional Language
Learners' Development, Instruction, and Assessment
Edited by Liu Li and Dongbo Zhang

Online Chinese Learning
Exploring Effective Language Learning Strategies
Lijuan Chen

Using Chinese Classics for Intercultural Communicative Competence
A Teacher's Guide
Jinai Sun, Xuehua Xiang, and Li Ye

For more information about this series, please visit: www.routledge.com/Routledge-Studies-in-Chinese-as-a-Foreign-Language/book-series/RSCFL

Using Chinese Classics for Intercultural Communicative Competence
A Teacher's Guide

Jinai Sun, Xuehua Xiang, and Li Ye

LONDON AND NEW YORK

Designed cover image: cienpies via Getty Images

First published 2025
by Routledge
4 Park Square, Milton Park, Abingdon, Oxon OX14 4RN

and by Routledge
605 Third Avenue, New York, NY 10158

Routledge is an imprint of the Taylor & Francis Group, an informa business

© 2025 Jinai Sun, Xuehua Xiang, Li Ye

The right of Jinai Sun, Xuehua Xiang, and Li Ye to be identified as authors of this work has been asserted in accordance with sections 77 and 78 of the Copyright, Designs and Patents Act 1988.

All rights reserved. No part of this book may be reprinted or reproduced or utilised in any form or by any electronic, mechanical, or other means, now known or hereafter invented, including photocopying and recording, or in any information storage or retrieval system, without permission in writing from the publishers.

Trademark notice: Product or corporate names may be trademarks or registered trademarks, and are used only for identification and explanation without intent to infringe.

British Library Cataloguing-in-Publication Data
A catalogue record for this book is available from the British Library

Library of Congress Cataloging-in-Publication Data
A catalog record for this book has been requested

ISBN: 978-1-032-45500-6 (hbk)
ISBN: 978-1-032-45499-3 (pbk)
ISBN: 978-1-003-37727-6 (ebk)

DOI: 10.4324/9781003377276

Typeset in Times New Roman
by Apex CoVantage, LLC

Access the Support Material: www.routledge.com/9781032454993

**To our parents and our children,
the beloved storytellers in our lives.**

Contents

About the Authors   x
缘起   xii
Acknowledgments   xiii

1 **Classic Works for Developing Intercultural Communicative Competence and Language Proficiency: An Integrative Framework**   1

2 **"Sūn Wùkōng's Three Bouts with the White-Bone Demon"《三打白骨精》(Sān Dǎ Báigǔjīng): Teaching *Journey to the West*《西游记》(Xīyóujì) through Dramatic Inquiry**   19

   Appendix 2.1: Preview Packet 30
   Appendix 2.2: Enrichment Guide 34
   Appendix 2.3: Study Packet 40
   Appendix 2.4: Role-Play Project Guidelines 42
   Appendix 2.5: Mini Research Paper Guidelines 43

3 **"Dàiyù's Arrival at the Jiǎ Household"《黛玉进贾府》(Dàiyù Jìn Jiǎ Fǔ): Teaching *Dream of the Red Chamber*《红楼梦》(Hónglóumèng) through Experiential Learning**   46

   Appendix 3.1: Preview Packet 58
   Appendix 3.2: Enrichment Guide 60
   Appendix 3.3: Study Packet 63
   Appendix 3.4: Role-Play Project Guideline 66

4 "To Borrow Arrows with Thatched Boats" 《草船借箭》 (Cǎochuán Jièjiàn): Teaching *the Romance of the Three Kingdoms* 《三国演义》 (Sānguó Yǎnyì) through Question Formulation Technique — 69

Appendix 4.1: Preview Packet 84
Appendix 4.2: Enrichment Guide 89
Appendix 4.3: Study Packet 93

5 "Cháng'é Ascending to the Moon" 《嫦娥奔月》 (Cháng'é Bēnyuè): Teaching Ancient Chinese Mythology through Social Semiotics — 99

Appendix 5.1: Preview Packet 116
Appendix 5.2: Enrichment Guide 121
Appendix 5.3: Study Packet 129
Appendix 5.4: Storyboard Activity 132

6 Nézhā 《哪吒》: Teaching the Mythology of Nézhā through the *Text-to-Text, Text-to-Self, and Text-to-World* Connection-Making Strategy — 137

Appendix 6.1: Preview Packet 149
Appendix 6.2: Enrichment Guide 153
Appendix 6.3: Study Packet 155

7 "Mùlán Joins the Army" 《木兰从军》 (Mùlán Cóngjūn): Teaching the Folktale of Mulan through the Lens of Global Feminism — 161

Appendix 7.1: Preview Packet 178
Appendix 7.2: Enrichment Guide 182
Appendix 7.3: Study Packet 187

8 "Sàiwēng Lost His Horse" 《塞翁失马》 (Sàiwēng Shīmǎ): Teaching Traditional Idiom Story through the Six Thinking Hats Technique — 190

Appendix 8.1: Preview Packet 204
Appendix 8.2: Study Packet 206
Appendix 8.3: Review Idioms and Idioms in Contexts 209

9   "The Traveling Sonnet" 《游子吟》 (Yóuzǐ Yín): Teaching Classical Poetry Using Total Physical Response and Storytelling (TPRS)   213

    Appendix 9.1: Preview Packet 223
    Appendix 9.2: Enrichment Guide 225
    Appendix 9.3: Study Packet 228

Index   *232*

About the Authors

Dr. Jinai Sun is an Associate Professor of Chinese Language and Culture at North Central College in Naperville, IL. Holding a doctorate in education leadership from the Pennsylvania State University, Dr. Sun has been instrumental in directing the Chinese teacher training and student summer immersion program for the STARTALK program by the US Department of Defense since 2013. Her scholarly pursuits encompass understanding the motivation of American students in learning Chinese, devising effective teaching methodologies, and fostering cross-cultural communication skills within Chinese language classrooms. In 2019, Dr. Sun led a research team to China to delve into the cultural significance of Dream of the Red Chamber. Dr. Jinai Sun's multifaceted contributions to Chinese language education and cross-cultural understanding exemplify her unwavering commitment to academic excellence and cultural exchange. Through her research, teaching, and leadership, she continues to shape the landscape of Chinese language education and foster deeper connections between cultures.

Dr. Xuehua Xiang is Professor of Linguistics and Applied Linguistics, Director of Chinese Program, and Head of the Department of Linguistics at the University of Illinois Chicago. Dr. Xiang received her PhD in applied linguistics from the Pennsylvania State University. Her research interests span Chinese linguistics, intercultural communication, discourse analysis, and second language teaching. Her first co-authored book, *Grammar, meaning, and concepts: A discourse-based approach to English grammar*, was published with Routledge in 2018. Her second book, *Language, Multimodal Interaction and Transaction: Studies of a Southern Chinese Marketplace*, was published with John Benjamins in 2021. Dr. Xiang is interested in exploring language and culture through interdisciplinary lenses in both her research and teaching pursuits.

Dr. Li Ye, an esteemed instructor of Mandarin Chinese, serves as a core team leader in the Multilingual Learning Division at Adlai E. Stevenson High School in Lincolnshire, IL. Completing her doctoral work in curriculum and instruction at the University of Illinois at Chicago in 2009, Dr. Ye has dedicated over a decade to directing the Chinese program at SHS. Her expertise spans from introductory Chinese to advanced levels of AP Chinese Language and Culture. Beyond the classroom, she played a pivotal role as the lead teacher/trainer for the STARTALK Teacher Program at North Central College, funded by the US Department of Defense from 2017 to 2021. Dr. Ye currently serves as a pedagogical trainer for the STARTALK Teacher Program at the National Louis University – Chicago Campus from 2022 to 2024. As an ISTE-certified educator, her commitment extends to evidence-based teaching methodologies, collaborative learning, intercultural communicative competence, and innovative technology applications in teaching. Dr. Ye actively engages in local and national conferences, focusing on pedagogy and the effective integration of technology in language education, with publications centering around literacy and her doctoral work.

缘起

回忆起五年前的暑假，我和一位法语教授决定在假期互换一本我们各自语言中最重要的小说。他推荐的是雨果的《悲惨世界》而我介绍的是 Anthony Yu 所著的英文版 Monkey King。这个简单的交流成为我日后深入了解中西文学差异的起点，他后来很吃惊中国最著名的小说居然是一部儿童读物。这引发了我对中国古典文学的思索，我们从小耳熟能详的比如《三打白骨精》这样的故事到底在说什么，比起西方深刻的叩问人性的著作，我们的文学真的就是这么世俗吗？这些代代相传的经典，究竟蕴含着怎样的人文价值？

后来，在和一位酷爱中文和中国文化的美国学者司徒老先生的对话中，他解释为什么对《红楼梦》爱不释手，还分享了在小说中体验到的人情世故的例子，比如娓娓道来客套话和寒暄让他享受阅读其乐，感受到中国式人际关系的微妙。还有在疫情的时候，全家困在家里索性每晚都一起追看两集《三国演义》电视剧。渐渐地发现我儿子，一个地道的华裔"小香蕉"，从之前对日本动漫文化和二战历史的痴迷，慢慢地发生了转变，他开始赞叹中国人多么聪明，用计谋不费一兵一卒就能攻城略地，相比之下，只靠武器先进比拼的二战历史不值一提。这些经历都慢慢启发我去寻找帮助中文非母语学习者正确的打开这些中国经典故事的方式和可行性。

上次请到 *Understanding China* 一书的作者 Gary Moreau 来我们大学做讲座，他提到通过在中国生活和工作的亲身体验，发现中国人与美国人在做生意和谈判时存在许多差异。他对这些差异的根源更感兴趣，临行前，他与我分享认为这些差异源于中国的宗教和哲学思维。这启发了我在教学中开始和美国学生一起探索深层次根源的思考，不但发现差异"是什么，"更重要的探究"为什么，"而这些都是美国学生最兴趣昂然的话题。

在这几年的学习和工作中，通过不同的项目有幸结识很多学者共同探讨中国古典文学名著的重要性以及在教学中的难点。两年前，与向雪花老师和叶丽老师一拍即合，觉得有必要将我们的研究和教学经验整理成册，以帮助其他教育者更好地利用中文古典文学促进语言和跨文化能力的培养。我们通过 STARTALK 美国星谈老师培训项目和学生暑期夏令营项目不断实践并积累反馈建议，同时在自己的语言课堂上得到学生的肯定。这本书 *Using Chinese Classics and Intercultural Competence: A Teacher's Guide* 应运而生，希望为中文教育者提供一份实用的指南，帮助他们更好地运用这些古典名著提高学生中文语言水平并提升学生的跨文化理解与交流能力。

孙金爱宇
2023年12月

Acknowledgments

We would like to express our profound gratitude to those who have made this book possible.

Jinai expresses her sincere gratitude to the multitude of individuals who have played a crucial role in the completion of this book beginning with the generous support from the ASIANetwork, which facilitated the trip to China for the study of *Dream of the Red Chamber.* Special appreciation is extended to the collaboration with the Cao Xueqin Research Center in Beijing. Furthermore, Jinai acknowledges the invaluable contributions of scholars and students at Nanjing Normal University, whose expertise and resources have significantly enriched the learning experience.

Acknowledgments are also extended to the students who were integral to this project, as well as to numerous scholars and authors, including Dr. Licheng Gu, Dr. Charles Egan, Dr. Peimin Ni, Dr. Tina Lu, Dr. Brian Hoffer, and Dr. Stuart Patterson. Their valuable perspectives on the methods employed by American scholars in the study of classical Chinese literature and teaching have greatly contributed to the depth of this work.

Jinai further extends her sincere appreciation to the educators and students at North Central College STARTALK, particularly Dr. Xiaoning Chen, Mr. Yu Hangxin, Ms. Yang Yang, Ms. Dominika Szczepaniak, and Ms. Laurel Murphy. Their inspiration and feedback have played a crucial role in the development of this project. Special thanks are also reserved for Jinai's family – Shusheng Sun, Shuhua Sheng, Aaron, Scotty, Prince Kyler, and Princess Charlotte.

Xuehua thanks her students at the University of Illinois Chicago whose critical feedback and creative coursework have been a constant source of inspiration. Xuehua also thanks her colleague Duosi Meng for many conversations about teaching Chinese culture and for inspiring the student-led mini presentation activity featured in chapter 5. As always, Xuehua reserves a special thank you to her family for their love and support.

Li expresses her heartfelt thanks to her family for their unwavering support and understanding throughout the writing process. Special appreciation is extended to both Dr. Jinai Sun and Dr. Xuehua Xiang for their invaluable guidance and expertise in shaping the manuscript into its best form. Li extends her gratitude to her division director at Adlai E. Stevenson High School, Mr. Justin Fisk, for consistently supporting her exploration of new teaching approaches and providing the necessary assistance for such endeavors. She also expresses appreciation to her colleagues, Janet Wang and Tianzhou Ye, for continually inspiring her and sharing their innovative teaching strategies.

Additionally, Li would like to express her appreciation to her friend Xiaoyong Tan for encouraging her to write a book and share it with a broader audience of Chinese teacher educators. Identical appreciation is extended to Dominika Szczepaniak, a promising young Chinese language teacher, for her assistance in refining both the linguistic aspects and conceptual elements, thereby enhancing the overall quality of her writing.

Jointly we thank the series editors of *Routledge Studies in Chinese as a Foreign Language* for their valuable feedback that opened our eyes to new ways of thinking about intercultural communication. We also thank Ms. Iola Ashby and Ms. Andrea Hartill at Routledge for their support and encouragement throughout this journey. We extend our heartfelt thank you to our copyeditor, Ms. Lauren Johnson, whose skills have been instrumental to the timely completion of this project.

1 Classic Works for Developing Intercultural Communicative Competence and Language Proficiency
An Integrative Framework

1. Introduction

In this opening chapter, we lay the theoretical foundation for our book, focusing on the relevance and significance of Chinese classic stories in the context of today's globalized world. We explore how these stories can serve as powerful tools to help students simultaneously enhance their language skills and develop intercultural communicative competence (ICC). Within this framework, these classic tales act as bridges, connecting students' own cultural backgrounds with the intricacies of Chinese culture. We also integrate the principles of backward design, integrated performative assessment, and content-language frameworks to enhance the pedagogical process. Alongside highlighting the promising approach of combining ICC and linguistic development, we address the common challenges faced by educators when utilizing classic stories as language materials.

Recognizing that a substantial portion of Chinese classic stories originate from literary texts, this book serves as a platform for fostering dialogue between scholars in second language acquisition and literary studies practitioners. It's our aim to identify common ground that unites these two fields. Our readers will discover that our model can serve as a versatile tool to create teaching modules based on any classic work or authentic materials suitable for their unique educational settings. The application of this model is exemplified in the subsequent chapters, each offering case studies rooted in different literary genres.

2. Why Chinese Classic Works Matter | 中国经典故事的价值

In this section, we present six compelling reasons to consider the incorporation of Chinese classic works into your language classroom. Additionally, we encourage you to reflect on your own motivations for embracing these stories as invaluable educational resources.

2.1. *Well-Known in the Chinese-Speaking World* | 母语者耳熟能详

Chinese classic works, such as *The Romance of the Three Kingdoms* (《三国演义》 Sānguó Yǎnyì) and *Journey to the West* (《西游记》 Xīyóujì), are integral to the very fabric of Chinese culture. These stories are not mere narratives; they are a fundamental aspect of daily life for native Chinese speakers. For instance, children grow up hearing the adventures of the Monkey King (孙悟空 Sūn Wùkōng) and the moral lessons embedded in these age-old texts. This familiarity extends beyond the written word, encompassing a profound understanding of the historical, cultural, and linguistic context in which these tales were conceived.

Chinese classic literature and stories serve as a unique form of cultural capital that facilitates meaningful communication with native Chinese speakers. When American students engage with these stories and characters, they gain access to a shared cultural vocabulary that transcends language barriers. This shared cultural capital lays the foundation for establishing connections and rapport with native speakers, nurturing a deeper understanding and appreciation. Imagine an American student visiting China, sparking a conversation with a local by mentioning their favorite character from *Dream of the Red Chamber* is Dàiyù. This shared knowledge becomes a bridge for cultural exchange and a means of connecting on a personal level.

Chinese classic works are deeply ingrained in the cultural consciousness of native speakers. These stories and texts are part of their literary heritage, rendering them highly familiar with the language, themes, and nuances found within these works. For language learners, this familiarity serves as a valuable reference point and cultural context for language acquisition.

2.2. Deep Roots in the Rich Cultural Heritage | 传承中华文化基因

Storytelling is an essential means of passing cultural traditions from one generation to the next. Chinese classic texts, published before 1911, represent a timeless tapestry of narratives interwoven with Chinese culture for centuries. These literary treasures encompass a broad spectrum, from mythological legends and folklore to philosophical allegories and monumental epic novels. These texts offer windows into the collective consciousness of the Chinese people, reflecting their views on the natural world, society, and humanity's intricate interactions with their surroundings. With a history stretching back millennia, these stories have not only preserved historical perspectives and cultural values but also evolved into enduring sources of inspiration and insight across generations. This rich reservoir of literature captures the essence of Chinese intellectual, emotional, and spiritual landscapes, inviting readers to explore profound thought, emotion, and tradition that continue to resonate in modern times.

Integrating classic stories into language instruction holds the potential to enrich students' learning experiences. These timeless narratives, deeply rooted in Chinese culture and history, provide a captivating and relatable medium for language education. By incorporating classic stories into their teaching approach, Chinese language teachers can ignite students' curiosity, foster a deeper appreciation for the language, and provide insight into the traditions, values, and customs of Chinese society. Embracing the power of classic stories enables educators to bridge the gap between language learners and the vast cultural landscape of the Chinese-speaking world, fostering a comprehensive language-learning journey.

2.3. Making Abstract Cultural Concepts Tangible | 抽象的文化概念具象化

Teaching Chinese classic stories and literature offers a unique value proposition by providing concrete representations of abstract concepts. Within these timeless narratives, complex and abstract ideas come vividly to life, offering students tangible examples to grasp elusive notions. Whether delving into moral dilemmas, the nuances of human emotions, or profound philosophical inquiries, classic stories furnish students with relatable scenarios, facilitating a deeper understanding of the rich tapestry of Chinese culture. This ability to bridge the abstract and the concrete enhances students' critical thinking skills and cultural insights, making the study of Chinese classic stories a transformative educational experience.

Consider *Dream of the Red Chamber* (《红楼梦》 Hónglóumèng) as an illustration. Within the novel's intricate web of relationships, the complex love triangle involving 贾宝玉 (Jiǎ Bǎoyù), 林黛玉 (Lín Dàiyù), and 薛宝钗 (Xuē Bǎochāi) vividly illustrates the multifaceted nature of "情" (qíng, 'affection'). Bǎoyù's deep emotional connection with both Dàiyù and Bǎochāi represents a poignant exploration of conflicting emotions, desire, and the delicate nuances of love. Through these interactions and the emotional turmoil Bǎoyù experiences, students can delve into the rich layers of "情" in Chinese culture.

Chinese classic works often convey abstract concepts and moral values through vivid narratives and characters. This concrete representation of abstract ideas facilitates the comprehension of complex linguistic and cultural concepts, fostering deeper language proficiency.

2.4. Diverse Cultural Themes | 丰富多元的文化主题

Chinese classic stories consistently serve as a wellspring of inspiration worldwide and across various fields, including philosophy, history, anthropology, sociology, and the creative arts. Recent years have witnessed a resurgence of interest in Chinese mythology and classic literary works, both within China's domestic audience and among global consumers. Remarkable successes like *Ne Zha* (Jiaozi, 2019), *New Gods: Nezha Reborn* (Jiaozi, 2021), *Big Fish and Begonia* (Liang & Zhang, 2016), *Monkey King: Hero Is Back* (Tian, 2015), and *White Snake* (Wong & Jiaozi, 2019) have captivated an ever-growing global fanbase.

The enduring appeal of these classic stories can be attributed to their rich and diverse cultural themes. For example, the tale of Nézhā delves into themes such as family values and the conflicts between individualism and societal norms, as explored in chapter 6. Meanwhile, the story of Mulan joining the army provides a platform for investigating traditional gender roles in Chinese Confucian society and the development of global feminism in contemporary times, as discussed in chapter 5. Stories from epic literature offer even more diverse and interlinked narratives to explore themes that ignite students' imaginations. An excellent example is *Dream of the Red Chamber,* which explores the profound depths of affection, entangled between Confucianism, Taoism, and Buddhism, as unveiled in chapter 3.

The rapid growth of anime culture, influenced by Chinese classic stories, has provided the foreign language classroom with rich resources to engage and motivate students in the study of Chinese culture as a dynamic and evolving subject, adapting to changing socioeconomic conditions. To comprehend the modern renditions of these stories in the contemporary global context, a guided understanding of the original narratives is indispensable.

2.5. Transcultural Identification | 跨文化身份认同

Culture learning in the classroom builds on developing knowledge of cultural practices and products, awareness of cultural values, and skills to respond to and navigate situations with cultural appropriateness. In the world language classroom, with the goal of language learning for developing global citizenry (He & Xiao, 2008), cultural learning is no longer a study of a distant "target culture" but an attempt to expand one's worldviews and ability to navigate intercultural encounters. Learners develop the ability to reflect and negotiate and foster a mindset of resilience along with an enriched worldview.

Dörnyei (2006) identifies that language learners have an "ideal L2 self and more extrinsic ought-to L2 self, and actual self" regarding home and target cultures. In the context of teaching Chinese as a heritage language, He (2006) articulates a three-dimensional identity theory where self-identification is closely tied with language proficiency development. He hypothesized that students' heritage language development is dependent on continuity and coherence in the multiple communicative and social spheres that heritage students inhabit. Students learn to develop "hybrid, situated identities and stances" (p. 1). He (ibid.) particularly emphasizes the role of the classroom in supporting identity formation through ongoing interactions with others. The language classroom can enable that transformation of one's identity toward global citizenry or reify it. Chinese classic stories provide that connection between deeply held cultural values in Chinese society and the myriad, localized, individualized practices. Teaching classic stories from global perspectives can thus transform Chinese culture into concrete and dynamic themes facilitating students' own process of understanding their own identities as language learners and users, negotiating differences, and building toward coherence.

2.6. Transdisciplinary Critical Thinking | 跨领域的通识能力

In the 21st century, the world language classroom is no longer filled with quintessential methodologies narrowly applicable to the domain of language learning. The language classroom has become increasingly interdisciplinary. If language proficiency is a combination of knowledge and abilities with real-world relevance, and if language learning is for curiosity, enjoyment, personal growth, and professional development, learning a language may not be so different from learning other subject matter. In this regard, classic stories are vehicles in which teachers can incorporate various experiential learning approaches that resonate with larger educational and social contexts.

In the world language classroom, many practices involve lower-order thinking skills (LOTS), such as practicing vocabulary that involves recognizing, identifying, recalling, and reproducing, and grammar exercises that involve recognizing patterns and rule application. These LOTS activities help learners learn incrementally and process new information in manageable sizes. However, language learning that consists entirely of these practices alone does not lead to communicative skills. Classic stories as a medium can combine discrete skills toward building complex processes or higher-order thinking skills: understanding, analyzing, evaluating, and creating (Bloom, 1956).

The cognitive strategies employed in world language learning, such as fragmenting, reconstituting, synthesizing, and generalizing, are similar to those used in literary analysis. The difference lies in the shift from micro to macro levels, where literature allows readers to engage with language on multiple dimensions, connect with characters, participate in the plot, and experience new emotions. World language learning has taken an experiential turn too as teachers embrace project-based learning and content-language integrated learning. The educational climate is facilitative to merging language learning with general education learning goals.

Therefore, focusing on literature in language classrooms is not a return to the same old approach but an opportunity to adopt a transdisciplinary stance that responds to new developments in education.

3. Teaching Chinese Classics in the 21st Century in the World Language Classroom

As classic stories originate from classic literature, in this section, we review how literature has been approached in the world language classroom and discuss how our integrative approach both connects with and differs from the previous models.

Carter and Long (1991) describe three main approaches to teaching literature: the cultural model, the language-based model, and the personal growth (enrichment) model. Since then, integrated approaches have emerged, combining elements from these models to provide more relevant approaches to teaching literature in the modern foreign language setting.

1) The Cultural Model

This model exposes students to the background of a text to examine the ideas and concepts behind it, helping students explore the different cultures and patterns of thought. However, it is often lecturer-led and does not prioritize language work, making it unsuitable for most foreign language teachers. Nevertheless, exposing foreign language learners to cultural and content-based stimuli enables them to understand and appreciate different cultures and ideologies.

2) The Language-Based Model

This approach is common in the English-as-a-second-language classroom and focuses on specific linguistic features of texts, such as vocabulary and grammatical structures. While it allows teachers to target language elements through activities, explicit attention to linguistic elements, without integrating them with macro-level discourse, can create a disconnection between students, the text, and the text's literary purpose. The mechanical analysis of the text as a study tool may overshadow the appreciation of the text itself. Instead, the aim should be the comprehension of the story, with grammatical explanations and vocabulary work supporting that goal.

3) The Enrichment Model

This model emphasizes the personal enjoyment and emotional growth that students can derive from engaging with literary texts. It combines linguistic development with an appreciation for literature, encouraging student interaction with the text. Students are not passive recipients of knowledge but are encouraged to think critically and express their thoughts and opinions. Through these activities, students establish personal and meaningful connections with the text, while the teacher acts as a facilitator of learning.

4) Integrated Approaches

Integrated approaches combine elements from the three main models, offering linguistic, methodological, and motivational benefits. By using a wide range of authentic texts, learners are exposed to various text genres and difficulties of the target language. Literary discourse sensitizes readers to reading processes, and literary texts prioritize the enjoyment of reading. An integrated approach seeks to make literature accessible and beneficial for learners' linguistic development.

In an integrated approach, activities accompanying literary texts fall into two categories: linguistic analysis of the text and language activities that use the text as a springboard for discussion and writing. These activities draw on techniques from the communicative approach, including opinion sharing, critical discussion, problem-solving, role-play, and creative writing.

The adoption of an integrated approach that combines literary texts with communicative techniques marks a departure from the traditional language-focusing method. In the past, literary texts were primarily exercises for grammatical analysis, but now they are explored within the context of reader-response theory and humanistic approaches. The inclusion and presentation of literary texts in course books are crucial, as well as the way these texts are approached and treated.

The integrative approach we advocate and demonstrate in this book connects the aforementioned integrative approach to literary text with a dual focus on language as a vehicle for storytelling and stories as a medium for engaging students with critical thinking and cultural learning. What is unique in our model is the incorporation of ICC skills into the content-language integration. Section 4 will elaborate.

4. Connecting Classic Stories with Intercultural Communicative Competence

Intercultural communicative competence (ICC) has become an important goal in the world language classroom. We argue that there is a reciprocal relationship

4.1. What Is Intercultural Communicative Competence?

Intercultural communicative competence (ICC) is the ability to effectively and appropriately communicate in intercultural situations based on a combination of attitudes, knowledge, skills, and critical cultural awareness. Through ICC, individuals demonstrate awareness, sensitivity, curiosity, empathy, and an understanding of the perspectives of others (as outlined in the works of Byram, 1997, 2021; Deardorff, 2006).

4.2. Four Domains for Intercultural Communicative Competence Development

Within the context of language classroom instruction, Byram has outlined four key domains for developing ICC. The following definition, along with accompanying can-do verbs and illustrative examples, is drawn from the works of Byram (1997, 2021), Deardorff (2006), and Borghetti (2011). Language educators can utilize these resources to shape their learning objectives and create Can-do statements.

Knowledge encompasses a profound comprehension of social groups and their cultures, which comprise practices, products, and perspectives, both within one's own country or region and within the interlocutor's setting. This also entails an understanding of the broader dynamics of interaction at both individual and societal levels (Byram, 1997, 2021).

Can-Do Verbs	Can-Do Examples
illustrate, explain, describe, identify, demonstrate, differentiate . . .	– I can explain how 《游子吟》 (Yóuzǐyín, 'The Traveling Sonnet') reflects the values and emotions associated with love, longing, and filial piety in Chinese culture. (chapter 9) – I can describe fully the relationship between 贾宝玉 (Jiǎ Bǎoyù) and 林黛玉 (Lín Dàiyù). (chapter 3) – I can describe fully the story of 《三打白骨精》 (Sāndǎbáigǔjīng, 'Three Bouts with the White-Bone Demon') and explain the perspectives and values illustrated in Sāndǎbáigǔjīng and the impact of 《西游记》 (Xīyóujì, *Journey to the West*) as a whole on Chinese traditional culture and on global popular culture. (chapter 2) – I can describe fully the story of 《嫦娥奔月》 (Cháng'é Bēnyuè 'Cháng'é Ascending to the Moon') and explain the moon's symbolism in Chinese culture for a sense of unity and the cycle of life. (chapter 5) – I can describe the impact of 《山海经》 (Shānhǎijīng, *The Guideways for the Mountains and Seas*) as the source of Chinese creation mythology. (chapter 5)

8 *Intercultural Communicative Competence & Language Proficiency*

The **skill** for interpretation and correlation involves the skill to interpret a document or event originating from another culture, elucidate it, and establish connections with documents or events from one's own culture and a third culture (Byram, 1997, 2021).

Can-Do Verbs	Can-Do Examples
listen, observe, discover, notice, interpret, analyze, evaluate, relate, view the world from others' perspectives . . .	– I can relate the themes of love, longing, and filial piety in 《游子吟》 (Yóuzǐyín, 'The Traveling Sonnet') to my own experiences and emotions, fostering empathy and understanding. (chapter 9) – I can apply the lessons learned from 《游子吟》 (Yóuzǐyín, 'The Travelling Sonnet') to discuss and offer potential solutions to similar issues of love, longing, and filial piety that I encounter in my own life. (chapter 9) – I can relate Nézhā's experiences of being labeled as an evil child, being always supported by parents, being misunderstood by villagers, and striving to change his own fate to experiences that I have encountered in my life, to those that I have read from other texts, and/or to those that are happening in my own world and the wider world. (chapter 6) – I can analyze the different perspectives and values that led to Nézhā's unique experience to help me think through similar issues that I encounter and offer solutions. (chapter 6)

Attitudes, in the plural, refer to qualities such as curiosity and openness, as well as a willingness to suspend disbelief regarding other cultures and one's own beliefs (Byram, 1997, 2021).

Can-Do Verbs	Can-Do Examples
Openness: withhold judgment, open to intercultural learning and to people from other cultures, view differences as a learning opportunity **Respect:** value other cultures and cultural diversity **Curiosity and Discovering**: tolerate ambiguity and uncertainty **Empathy**: be able to see the world from others' points of view	– When reading Hónglóumèng, I can withhold judgment on the characters and appreciate the different interpretations of love and karma within the story while understanding the characters as individuals with distinctive perspectives, values, and behaviors. (chapter 3) – When describing the plot of Nézhā, I can withhold judgment about the treatment of Nézhā by different characters in the episodes and keep an open mind about the differing perspectives and values that motivate various practices in the story. (chapter 6) – When describing 《赤壁》 (Chìbì) and 《草船借箭》 (Cǎochuán Jiè Jiàn), I value and appreciate the wisdom exemplified in the stratagems applied during the battles and further develop an appreciation for the resources that I have and show more sympathy to those who do not. (chapter 4)

Critical cultural awareness denotes the capability to critically assess values found in one's own culture and in other cultures and countries. This evaluation is based on a systematic process of reasoning (Byram, 1997, 2021).

Can-Do Verbs	Can-Do Examples
Identify, interpret, evaluate, be aware . . .	– I am aware that across different cultures and time periods, people's practices, perspectives, and values remain similar though differences exist. (chapter 5) – I am aware of the different perspectives and values that different parties of the battles hold. (chapter 4) – I am also aware of the advantages and disadvantages that both I and others have in terms of "favorable timing, geographic location, and human factors" when it comes to achieving success. (chapter 4) – I am aware of the different perspectives and values that Táng Sēng and Sūn Wùkōng hold. I have become more aware of my own ideological perspectives and values as similar or different from those of others. (chapter 2)

Byram (1997, 2021) emphasized that the core of ICC development lies in critical cultural awareness, encompassing the evaluation of not only the cultures of others but also our own culture. This pivotal element forms the nexus connecting the other three fundamental factors: language, attitude, and skills. In the context of world language education, the focus is as much on "us" as it is on "them." Thus, the acquisition of knowledge should extend beyond mere cultural facts to encompass an understanding of the cultural biases inherent in an individual's interactions, significantly shaped by their personal experiences and surroundings (Moeller & Osborn, 2014).

4.3. How to Implement Intercultural Communicative Competence

As illustrated in Figure 1.1, the "window, mirror, and sliding door" metaphors (Bishop, 1990) provide teachers with a straightforward framework to enhance learners' ICC competence. In our curriculum and instructional approach, the materials we present to our students should fulfill the role of a "window." This "window" serves as a portal for curious and open-minded learners to apply their interpretive skills, allowing them to acquire knowledge about cultures different from their own. It enables them to investigate the practices, products, and perspectives of these diverse cultures.

Following the phase of learning from observing cultures through the "window," when students turn inward and reflect on their own culture, similar to looking at themselves in a mirror, a fundamental question arises: How do their own cultural practices, products, and perspectives relate to those of another culture? Are they provided with tools, such as the connection-making strategy (text-to-text, text-to-self, and text-to-world, discussed in more detail in chapter 6), to facilitate their

Figure 1.1 The "window, mirror, door" metaphors based on concepts from Bishop (1990) with image generated by Canva Dall-E).

understanding of the connections between their own culture and the one they have observed through the window? This introspective process holds the potential to reveal previously undiscovered insights and broaden their comprehension.

Subsequently, when students decide to venture through the "sliding door" and immerse themselves in the world of people from different cultures, they should be well-prepared with the knowledge acquired by looking out of the "window" and through the self-reflection "mirror" process to better understand themselves. This preparation equips them with the skills needed to build relationships, manage differences, and meditate effectively. This transformation distinguishes students as "intercultural speakers," setting them apart from native speakers and showcasing their ability to navigate and bridge cultural divides.

The sliding door phase can come before the mirror phase as well. Learners can learn from real-world interactions with people from other cultures and then reflect on their own practices and beliefs (Byram, 1997, 2021).

> Bishop's (1990) theory on diverse curriculum emphasizes the importance of having books that reflect children's own experiences. Books serve as mirrors, showing students their own reflections. Yet books can also act as windows, allowing them to see different worlds and compare them to their own. The concept of a sliding glass door takes it further, enabling learners to step into those worlds.

The "window, mirror, sliding door" metaphors effectively guide learners on their ICC development journey. Are there additional strategies or tools that can support and inspire students in this process? When students connect their current or past knowledge to language learning and discover more connections, their motivation to enhance both language and ICC skills grows. The connection-making strategy (Keene & Zimmerman, 1997) (text-to-text, text-to-self, text-to-world), a tool for the skill of "relating," is well-suited for this purpose. Learners adeptly share personal experiences or anecdotes when using the Text-to-Self connection with the material at hand. They also draw from diverse subjects and sources such as books and social media. The text-to-text approach allows students to link what they learn in language class with information acquired elsewhere. Finally, the text-to-world strategy encourages learners to relate their classroom learning to events in local or global contexts. Among the four ICC enhancement conditions proposed by Byram (1997, 2021) – language, skills, attitudes, and critical cultural awareness – the connection-making strategy stands out as a highly practical and user-friendly method for the skill of "relating," as exemplified in forthcoming chapters.

4.4. Chinese Classic Stories as the Medium for Intercultural Communication Competence

In this section, we will articulate our integrative framework where classic stories can stimulate the interests of students in the language classroom. As it currently stands, although ICC frameworks have taken center stage in the Chinese language classroom and the goals and tools have been well articulated, the curricular medium for ICC implementation remains everyday language use primarily geared toward study abroad opportunities where students are immersed in the intercultural communicative contexts. For the majority of students in the Chinese language classroom, the opportunity to study abroad is rare. The Chinese language classroom in urban settings is also increasingly mixed-levels, with an increase in heritage language students from a range of Chinese dialectal heritage backgrounds and a range of pre-existing and regular experiences with Chinese culture. In addition, Chinese culture itself has combined a complex range of cultures (from the domestic in China to diaspora communities abroad) into a heterogeneous group.

What these communities have in common are the shared classic stories that are passed down from generation to generation. As we described before, classic stories encode rich cultural values that adapt and change in time and space. For these reasons, classic stories are an ideal medium through which we engage students in cultural studies and develop ICC competencies. In our approach, classic stories, carrying deeply held cultural values, are both the "content" that students study (that is, students are to become familiar with these stories and can describe them coherently and discuss them critically) and the vehicle by which students develop ICC goals (in this regard, selected cultural and intercultural themes are also the "content" that students study and develop critical understanding of). When developing storytelling skills and ICC skills, students also develop language skills (see Figure 1.2).

As Figure 1.2 illustrates, Chinese classic stories serve as a valuable bridge for students, helping them establish connections between their own culture and the Chinese culture represented in these stories. The process of learning Chinese classic stories also aids in the development of students' ICC and language proficiency. As students engage with these stories, they gain profound insights into the values woven into the narratives, forming a solid knowledge foundation for their ICC growth.

To comprehend these stories, students need to employ their interpretation skills to grasp both the essence and the finer details. They must also connect the stories and their underlying values to their existing knowledge base through the connection-making

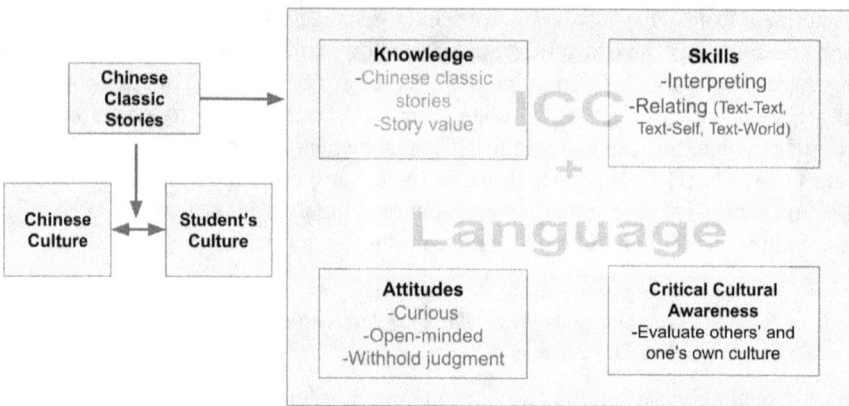

Figure 1.2 Integrative model for using classic works to foster ICC, building upon Byram's (1997) model of ICC.

strategy, which involves students relating the text to other texts, to themselves, and to the world around them. It is essential for students delving into Chinese classic stories to maintain a sense of curiosity and open-mindedness as they uncover the intricacies within each narrative. The discussion and instruction surrounding these stories impart a singular attitude: one of withholding judgment.

Furthermore, throughout this learning process, students are given the opportunity to evaluate not only Chinese culture but also their own. The overarching lesson they glean is that every individual resides within a cultural framework while navigating different cultures and experiencing different cultures from one's own unique perspective. When students engage with the four domains of their ICC skills, they simultaneously enhance their language proficiency, given that the majority of instructional time is conducted in the Chinese language and the input and output tasks are communicative in Chinese.

5. Implementing: Common Challenges and Our Strategies

Incorporating classic stories into the language classroom for ICC presents a unique opportunity to explore both Chinese culture and timeless narratives while enhancing students' language proficiency and ICC skills. Content-based instruction, also known as content-based language teaching and content language integrated Learning, encompasses a spectrum of pedagogical approaches employed in bilingual and world language classrooms. Its objective is to teach not only the language but also academic content across various disciplines, such as STEM, the arts, and the humanities (Brinton et al., 2003; Busse, 2011; Dalton-Puffer, 2011). The integration of content and language in the language classroom introduces specific challenges, which we will discuss in the context of using classic stories to foster ICC skills and language proficiency.

5.1 Common Challenges

Linguistic complexity: One primary challenge of implementing a content-based language teaching approach is the inherent linguistic complexity found in authentic materials. This complexity often exceeds the traditional "i+1" measure of comprehensible input (Krashen, 1987, 1988), which can deter educators from using authentic texts. In typical language curricula, students are introduced to everyday situations in a topical-situational framework, beginning with basic scenarios like greetings, ordering food, and using public transportation, gradually progressing to more abstract topics. These situational topics follow a lexical-structural syllabus, prioritizing high-frequency words and simpler structures. This approach is prevalent at both beginner/intermediate and advanced levels (Richards, 2001).

Authentic language, such as classic stories found in books, comics, television shows, movies, and anime series, is not tailored for language learning. The vocabulary and grammatical structures in authentic texts are determined by the author's intent to communicate with readers rather than to facilitate language learning. Consequently, even advanced learners may struggle with authentic literature due to unfamiliar vocabulary, rhetorical complexity, structural intricacies, and implicit cultural nuances. This challenge is especially pronounced when using Chinese classic stories, as many of them employ archaic language, historical references, and complex sentence structures from Classical Chinese, which can be intimidating for beginners and intermediate learners.

Cognitive Challenges: Classic stories may contain elements or themes that are culturally sensitive or difficult to comprehend from a modern perspective. These materials operate under the assumption that readers possess a pre-existing knowledge of the social and cultural contexts embedded within the narrative. This demand for cultural literacy can be particularly pronounced when exploring classic stories. Take, for instance, the epic novel *Dream of the Red Chamber*. Within its pages, a vast ensemble of characters weaves intricate relationships and undertakes a labyrinthine journey through the cultural tapestry of ancient China. While students may readily connect with universally relatable scenes, the finer nuances of character interactions and the profound social significance of seemingly ordinary behaviors can elude comprehension without the foundational understanding of the historical, philosophical, and sociocultural underpinnings. This cognitive challenge requires educators to navigate a delicate balance, ensuring that students are equipped with the cultural context necessary for a deeper understanding of these stories, without compromising the essential time allocated for language proficiency development.

Mixed Learning Outcomes: In a Chinese language classroom in the United States, where students come from diverse linguistic backgrounds, including Mandarin Chinese, English, and various heritage languages, content in a content-language integrated classroom can encompass literature, films, the arts, or other academic disciplines, such as classic stories. Students are required to comprehend the content, employ the target language for understanding, and exhibit their language and ICC skills. Classic literature, often characterized by depth and complexity, serves as a multifaceted educational tool, nurturing not only language proficiency but also a wide range of cognitive and cultural objectives. While language acquisition remains a central focus, classic literature simultaneously invites exploration of historical contexts, literary analysis, critical thinking, and intercultural competence. In this context, learning outcomes function as a compass guiding educators in their mission to equip students with a comprehensive understanding of classic literature within a world language framework.

Student Engagement: Captivating students' interest and fostering their appreciation for classic stories entails navigating a multifaceted challenge. The sheer length and complexity of many classic narratives can, at first glance, seem daunting to students. To surmount this initial obstacle, it becomes imperative to select appropriate excerpts or abridged versions thoughtfully, ensuring that the core essence of the story remains intact while making it more accessible to learners. Additionally, the constraints of classroom time add an additional layer of complexity to the teaching process. Educators must delicately balance language instruction, cultural exploration, and narrative analysis within the limited time available. To overcome these hurdles, it is essential to employ creative and engaging teaching methods that not only spark students' initial interest but also sustain their enthusiasm throughout their journey of delving into these rich and multifaceted narratives. By doing so, educators can cultivate a deeper appreciation for classic stories while keeping students actively engaged in their learning experience.

5.2. *Our Strategies* | 经典故事的正确打开方式

Now we outline the key design principles distinguishing our integrative framework from others and also showcase our integrative framework for teaching classic stories for the concomitant goals of development of ICC and advanced language proficiency. While the lesson samples in each chapter in this book are ready for use as they are, by elucidating the conscious decisions behind the lessons, we hope to familiarize teachers with the design process, leading to the design of new lessons with other genres and stories or other interdisciplinary methodologies.

5.2.1. *Scaffolding Activities*

Implementing a content-based language teaching approach presents several key strategies to tackle the linguistic complexity inherent in authentic materials. One approach involves carefully selecting and scaffolding authentic texts, such as classic stories from adapted children's books, short stories, comics, television shows, YouTube videos, and movies. Educators can choose materials that align with students' ages and language proficiency levels, gradually introducing linguistic complexity as learners progress. Additionally, providing pre-reading activities, front-loading information, glossaries, and simplified versions of the text can assist in making authentic content more accessible. To address the challenge of unfamiliar vocabulary, educators can incorporate vocabulary-building exercises and explicitly teach idiomatic expressions and cultural nuances found in the text. Furthermore, fostering a deeper understanding of cultural references and historical contexts can enhance students' comprehension of intricate texts, particularly those rooted in Classical Chinese. By employing a thoughtful combination of scaffolding techniques, language-focused instruction, and cultural context, educators can make content-based language teaching with authentic materials more effective and engaging for learners at various proficiency levels.

5.2.2. Translanguaging Support

In the realm of classic stories and language instruction, leveraging translanguaging theory offers an innovative approach to address cognitive challenges. Translanguaging acknowledges that multilingual individuals draw upon their entire linguistic repertoire, rather than isolating languages, to facilitate learning. In this context, students can use their native language or other languages they are proficient in to bridge gaps in comprehension, decode intricate sentence structures, and understand cultural nuances present in Classical Chinese texts. Encouraging students to apply their multilingual capabilities through code-switching, metalinguistic awareness, and cross-linguistic connections allows for a deeper understanding of the content. This not only makes the cognitive process of learning Classic Chinese literature more accessible but also fosters a richer appreciation of the language's historical and cultural context. Translanguaging thus provides a powerful cognitive strategy that aligns with the cognitive complexities of mastering the intricacies of Classical Chinese, ultimately enhancing the overall language learning experience in this unique educational setting.

5.2.3. Interdisciplinary Approaches with Clear Ending Goals

Research findings underscore the significance of this approach, indicating that learners build meaning by leveraging their prior knowledge as a gateway to acquire new knowledge. This insight holds particular relevance for language students. Implementing interdisciplinary approaches with clear ending goals when teaching Chinese classic novels provides students with a comprehensive understanding of the literary works. By intertwining various disciplines, such as history, philosophy, and sociology, educators can contextualize the novels within the broader tapestry of Chinese culture and society. Strategies include defining clear educational outcomes, leveraging a macro-micro curriculum design to merge thematic content with linguistic awareness, and crafting assessments that gauge students' understanding of both cultural insights and language proficiency. These strategies align with the backward design approach, ensuring that students are guided toward the predetermined goals. This interdisciplinary framework empowers learners to appreciate classic literature in a holistic manner, forging a profound connection between language proficiency, intercultural competence, and the timeless narratives of Chinese literary tradition.

5.2.4. Relatedness and Real-Life Application

Creating connection and real-life application in the teaching of Chinese classic novels is essential to engage students and make the content more relatable. One effective strategy involves drawing parallels between the themes, characters, and narratives in the classic stories and contemporary issues or personal experiences. This connection fosters a sense of relevance and immediacy, encouraging students to explore how the lessons from these timeless tales can be applied in their own lives. Additionally, incorporating interactive activities and discussions that invite students to express their thoughts, emotions, and reflections regarding the text's impact on their understanding of culture and human nature helps bridge the gap between classic literature and modern-day relevance. Furthermore, by encouraging students to connect classic stories to current global events, they develop a deeper understanding of the enduring nature of the themes explored in these novels. This approach not only enriches the students' appreciation of the classics but also equips them with valuable insights they can carry into real-life intercultural interactions and communication.

6. Summary

Aligning with these existing frameworks on meeting the challenges of a content-language integrated approach, our integrative model puts a dual-focus on the content itself – to us, the content is both classic stories and cultural themes that have salient values for intercultural inquiries. In our model, it is the simultaneous consideration of *cultural values/intercultural values* and *classic stories* as literary works that guides our selection of specific story texts and determines the social and historical contexts to relate the stories to. During the classic story learning, teachers actively build background knowledge needed to understand the story and facilitate cultural discussions, drawing connections between the story and contemporary Chinese society. Introducing supplementary materials, such as videos, images, and artifacts, can enhance learners' cultural awareness and deepen their appreciation for the story's significance. Careful curriculum planning also helps to strike a balance between exposing students to the richness of traditional Chinese literature and ensuring that the language is accessible and comprehensible. Providing vocabulary support, context explanations, and simplified versions of the stories can help address this challenge. In our approach, we use simplified language while retaining advanced vocabulary and offer access to the original literature taking advantage of the vast online classic libraries, even bilingual versions, available. Backward design principles help to foreground ICC goals and language proficiency goals that guide the amount of information and the types of information to be front-loaded for students. We elaborate on these strategies in the following chapters.

7. How to Use This Book

We aim for this book to be a valuable resource for educators looking to integrate Chinese culture into their teaching. Its structure and content offer multiple ways to utilize it effectively:

1) Integrative Framework for Language and Intercultural Communication: The book follows an integrative framework aimed at building students' intercultural communicative competence through engagement with canonical Chinese cultural sources. Each of the eight chapters provides sample lesson plans that foster these perspectives. The sample lesson plans articulate ICC and language learning goals, curricular modeling, assessment and pedagogy highlights, and more. Teachers can use these lessons to guide students in reflecting on narratives, characters, and themes central to Chinese culture, making it come alive through experience-based learning. The book thus helps educators leverage these texts to enhance linguistic and intercultural competence.
2) Ready-Made Teaching Examples: The chapters contain mature teaching examples extracted from existing curricula, including advanced-level film classes, literature classes, and intermediate-to-advanced language classes. Educators can directly incorporate the lesson plans, presentation slides, and assignments into their courses, either by creating comprehensive lessons or by supplementing their current materials. This book offers a wealth of practical teaching cases and materials, making the integration of Chinese culture into the curriculum straightforward.
3) Versatile Use as an Activity Guide: Beyond traditional teaching, the book can serve as an activity guide, facilitating efficient and effective use of cultural activities. Educators can draw inspiration from the book's content to design interactive and engaging cultural activities that align with their specific teaching objectives.
4) Theoretical and Practical Resources: The book serves as a comprehensive resource that combines theory with practice, helping teachers understand the theoretical underpinnings of their teaching objectives and instructional arrangements. This theoretical foundation can enhance educators' capacity to provide a deeper, more meaningful cultural education.
5) Downloadable Materials: For convenience, the book also allows for the direct download of ready-made materials, simplifying the process of incorporating cultural content into your teaching. These materials are adaptable to a variety of courses and instructional contexts.

We hope this book is a versatile tool for educators, offering a structured approach to integrate Chinese culture into various educational settings while also providing adaptable materials and theoretical insights to enrich students' learning experiences.

References

Bishop, R. S. (1990). Mirrors, windows, and sliding glass doors. *Perspectives, 6*(3), ix–xi.
Bloom, B. S. (1956). *Taxonomy of educational objectives: Cognitive and affective domains.* New York: David McKay.
Borghetti, C. (2011). How to teach it? Proposal for a methodological model of intercultural competence. In A. Witte & T. Harden (Eds.), *Intercultural competence: Concepts, challenges, evaluations* (pp. 141–160). Frankfurt am Main: Peter Lang.
Brinton, D. M., Snow, M. A., & Wesche, M. B. (2003). *Content-based second language instruction.* Boston, MA: Heinle & Heinle.
Busse, V. (2011). CLIL: Content and language integrated learning. *System,* 123–125.
Byram, M. (1997). *Teaching and assessing intercultural communicative competence.* Bristol, UK: Multilingual Matters.
Byram, M. (2021). *Teaching and assessing intercultural communicative competence: Revisited.* Bristol, UK: Multilingual Matters.
Carter, R., & Long, M. N. (1991). *Teaching literature* (Longman Handbooks for Language Teachers). London, UK: Longman.
Dalton-Puffer, C. (2011). Content-and-language integrated learning: From practice to principles? *Annual Review of Applied Linguistics, 31,* 182–204.
Deardorff, D. K. (2006). The identification and assessment of intercultural competence as a student outcome of internationalization at institutions of higher education in the United States. *Journal of Studies in International Education, 10*(3), 241–266.
Dörnyei, Z. (2006). Individual differences in second language acquisition. *AILA Review, 19*(1), 42–68.
He, A. W. (2006). Toward an identity theory of the development of Chinese as a heritage language. *Heritage Language Journal, 4*(10), 1–28.
He, A. W., & Xiao, Yun. (Eds.) (2008). *Chinese as a heritage language: Fostering rooted world citizenry.* Honolulu: NFLRC/University of Hawaii Press.
Jiaozi. (Director). (2019). *Ne Zha* (哪吒之魔童降世) [Film]. Chengdu Coco Cartoon.
Jiaozi. (Director). (2021). *New Gods: Ne Zha* Reborn (新神榜：哪吒重生) [Film]. Light Chaser Animation Studios.
Keene, E. O., & Zimmerman, S. L. (1997). *Mosaic of thought: Teaching comprehension in a reader's workshop.* Portsmouth, NH: Heinemann.
Krashen, S. D. (1987). *Principles and practice in second language acquisition.* Hoboken, NJ: Prentice-Hall International.
Krashen, S. D. (1988). *Second language acquisition and second language learning.* Hoboken, NJ: Prentice-Hall International.
Liang, Xuan, & Zhang, Chun. (Directors). (2016). *Big Fish & Begonia* (大鱼海棠) [Film]. Horgos Coloroom Pictures.
Moeller, A. J., & Faith Osborn, S. R. (2014). A pragmatist perspective on building intercultural communicative competency: From theory to classroom practice. *Foreign Language Annals, 47,* 669–673.
Richards, J. (2001). *Curriculum development in language teaching* (Cambridge Professional Learning). Cambridge, MA: Cambridge University Press.
Tian, Xiaopeng. (Director). (2015). *Monkey King: Hero Is Black* (西游记之大圣归来) [Film]. Gaolu Donghua.
Wong, Amp, & Jiaozi. (Directors). (2019). *White Snake* (白蛇:缘起) [Film]. Light Chaser Animation Studios.

2 "Sūn Wùkōng's Three Bouts with the White-Bone Demon"《三打白骨精》(Sān Dǎ Báigǔjīng)

Teaching *Journey to the West*《西游记》(Xīyóujì) through Dramatic Inquiry

- **Language Proficiency Level:** Intermediate high to advanced low;
- **ICC Developmental Goals:** Open to different perspectives and values;
- **High School/AP Theme:** Global challenges – diversity issues; personal and public identities – beliefs and values;
- **Suggested College Course:** Chinese communication and composition;
- **Suggested Instructional Time:** Three lessons, about one instructional hour each, followed by a stand-alone week-long project.

1. Introduction

This chapter serves as the first of eight sample modules, demonstrating concrete lessons that employ the integrative model advocated in this book. The lessons outlined here are designed to introduce students to the timeless Chinese epic《西游记》(Xīyóujì, *Journey to the West*). This classic novel, first published in 1592 and attributed to 吴承恩 (Wú Chéng'ēn), stands as one of Asia's most renowned and beloved stories. *Journey to the West* ranks among China's "Four Great Classic Novels," drawing deep inspiration from folk religion, mythology, and philosophy.

Teaching classic Chinese literature presents the challenge of making its content relatable to foreign language students, often unfamiliar with the text. While Chinese classical literature may seem initially distant to students, our experience reveals that they respond enthusiastically to the novel's themes of teamwork and self-cultivation. Furthermore, the plethora of pop-cultural adaptations of *Journey to the West* allows us to kindle immediate interest among both heritage and non-heritage Chinese students, fostering advanced proficiency and global intercultural awareness.

2. Contextualizing the Topic

The lessons outlined in this chapter originate from a college-level Chinese foreign language course titled "Chinese Composition and Communication." This advanced-level, 16-week required capstone seminar is typically taken by students pursuing a Chinese major during their fourth year of study. The course follows a two-part structure, transitioning from the study of ancient classical to modern literature.

In the initial part of the course, students explore Chinese myths, legends, philosophical parables, an essay on appreciating Tang Dynasty poetry, and excerpts from novels like *Journey to the West* and *Dream of the Red Chamber*. This eight-week survey of classical literature culminates in a one-week midterm unit on *Journey to the West*. During this week, the novel and its historical and cultural context are introduced. The focus then turns to a close examination of a specific episode of 《孙悟空三打白骨精》 (Sūn Wùkōng Sān Dǎ Báigǔjīng, "Sūn Wùkōng's Three Bouts with the White-Bone Demon"). Throughout this unit, we place the episode's plot within the larger narrative, connecting it to other themes present in the novel. We chose "Sān Dǎ Báigǔjīng" for two major reasons. First, while it conveys dramatic and profound philosophical themes, it can be presented as an independent episode without requiring extensive background knowledge of the broader narrative. Second, it has been widely illustrated and adapted in various forms, from children's books to popular films. The richness of this episode, coupled with the abundance of related resources, makes it an excellent introduction for students new to the novel.

The specific lesson unit we present here employs the approach of dramatic inquiry (see section 3 and section 4.4) to scaffold activities. Dramatic inquiry encourages students to delve into the ethical and interpersonal dynamics of the story. We commence the unit by viewing a children's cartoon that simplifies and introduces the story of "Sān Dǎ Báigǔjīng." Subsequently, we explore scenes from the more advanced movie *Monkey King 2*, which delves into the multifaceted conflict between several characters in the story: Táng Sēng, a Buddhist monk on a sacred pilgrimage to India; Sūn Wùkōng, the Monkey King protecting Táng Sēng on the journey west; and Báigǔjīng, the White-Bone Demon determined to devour Táng Sēng. In this episode, Sūn Wùkōng destroys the body of the White-Bone Demon three times to save Táng Sēng's life, despite Táng Sēng's religious principles forbidding killing. By emphasizing the tension between Táng Sēng and Sūn Wùkōng, this lesson aims to teach students how to identify and mediate conflicts when faced with two or more opposing points of view. Students engage in debates surrounding the seemingly irreconcilable perspectives held by Táng Sēng and Sūn Wùkōng, fostering critical analysis of their own beliefs and values. The goal of this lesson unit is not to lead students to a conclusion about right versus wrong but to withhold their initial judgment, attempting first to understand the reasoning behind each character's stance. The open-ended ethical questions they grapple with motivate them to formulate their opinions thoughtfully in Chinese.

3. Methodology Highlight: Dramatic Inquiry

Dramatic inquiry is an interactive process that brings the lesson content into the classroom through drama and creative dialogue, role-playing activities, and informed imaginative contexts. Dorothy Heathcote (1983), a pioneer of dramatic inquiry methodology, describes traditional learning as looking at a subject from an outsider's point of view, while dramatic inquiry brings the lesson subject matter to life by introducing it "here" into the classroom rather than leaving it "over there," beyond the classroom's scope. This methodology is especially useful for teaching world literature such as *Journey to the West*, as its rich content may trigger a reaction of "culture shock," overwhelming students who are unfamiliar with its themes. By allowing students to collaboratively create meaning and engage with the text by placing themselves in the characters' shoes, dramatic inquiry encourages critical thinking about the text from both their own experiences and those within the story.

In the context of this lesson unit, dramatic inquiry proves most effective when students have a solid foundation of background information about the novel and its characters. Therefore, the construction of this unit incorporates appropriate scaffolded pre-teaching materials and activities, enabling students to creatively leverage their comprehensive knowledge throughout the unit, culminating in a final role-playing activity. Details on implementing this approach are discussed in section 4.4.

4. Curricular Modeling

We provide a complete set of classroom materials along with corresponding activities that support and align with the learning outcomes, following the principles of backward design (McTighe & Wiggins, 2005).

4.1 Learning Outcomes

The learning outcomes we present here are integrated into a three-fold framework, merging language skills development with ICC skills development. Alongside the sample course context provided, "Chinese Communication and Composition," we offer sample learning outcomes pertaining to macro language functions for literary understanding, communication, and composition. These learning outcomes can be adapted to suit your course context, with a shared emphasis on their interconnectedness and applicability in classroom activities. They serve as the guiding compass for backward design and assessment.

Learning Outcomes as Part of the "Chinese Communication and Composition" Course

- Understanding of the Target Story and Literary Movements: Students are expected to read critically, think analytically, and communicate effectively both in writing and speech to comprehend the plot of the target story and its relevance to broader themes in Chinese history and societal changes.
- Identification of Literary Devices: Students should be able to identify specific literary devices employed in the texts and analyze how these devices

contribute to the meaning of a text. Additionally, they should apply similar devices in their communication and composition.
- Effective Communication: Students are expected to produce coherent written and oral work by adhering to the conventions of the target language. They should be able to present information in a descriptive form in the target language, clearly narrate the story, and identify major characters, themes, and the plot and its impact on Chinese society and culture.

The corresponding language performance goals are written in the "can do" format of "I can . . ." to make learners understand from their perspectives what they can achieve in this unit (ACTFL-NCSSFL, 2017).

Language Performance Objective (Can-Do Statements)

- I can follow the main story of "Sān Dǎ Báigǔjīng" and show some supporting details across major time frames in fictional texts. (*Interpretive*)
- I can narrate the story of "Sān Dǎ Báigǔjīng" in writing and speaking through organized paragraphs. (*Presentational*)
- I can apply the lessons learned to discuss my own experience dealing with conflicts and offer appropriate solutions. (*Interpersonal*)

The corresponding ICC development goals are written based on four aspects of ICC: knowledge, attitude, skills, and critical cultural awareness (Byram, 2008, 2021; Byram & Wagner, 2018; inter alia).

Intercultural Communicative Competence Developmental Goals

- **Knowledge:** I can describe fully the story of "Sān Dǎ Báigǔjīng," explain the perspectives and values illustrated in the story, and define the impact of *Journey to the West* as a whole on Chinese traditional culture and on global popular culture.
- **Attitude:** When describing "Sān Dǎ Báigǔjīng," I can withhold judgment about the ethical dilemmas in the episode and keep an open mind about the differing perspectives and values that motivate conflicting practices in the story.
- **Skill:** I can relate the ethical dilemma between Táng Sēng and Sūn Wùkōng to ones that I have encountered in my life, further analyze the

different perspectives and values that caused their dilemma to help me think through similar issues that I have experienced, and offer solutions.
- **Critical Cultural Awareness:** I am aware of the different perspectives and values that Táng Sēng and Sūn Wùkōng hold. I have become more aware of my own ideological perspectives and values as similar or different from those of others.

4.2 Materials for Teaching Journey to the West

A. Video Introduction to the Novel

- This concise and captivating three-to-five-minute video introduction to *Journey to the West* skillfully weaves together elements like historical context, the author's biography, and the novel's major themes. The objective is to craft an engaging overview, sparking students' interest and setting the stage for a compelling exploration of this literary masterpiece.

B. PowerPoint Presentation (in class)

- The PowerPoint presentation accompanies the introduction. The presentation includes slides summarizing key points, vocabulary, and exercises in Chinese. Engaging visuals will be used to enhance student engagement and understanding.

C. Children's book adaptation of the "Three Times Beating the White-Bone Demon" episode (Chinese)

- The full Chinese text and a set of illustrated story cards feature scenes and characters from this episode. Each picture depicts a key moment in the novel, serving as visual aids for comprehension and storytelling activities.

D. Vocabulary List

- The list of essential vocabulary words and phrases related to the novel including Pinyin, English translations, and example sentences to help students understand and use these words.

E. Comprehension Questions

- The set of comprehension questions guides students in analyzing the novel's themes, literary devices, and cultural significance. Include both closed-ended and open-ended questions.

4.3 Activities for Teaching Journey to the West

In this section, we will detail the activities and exercises that help students engage with the novel and develop their language proficiency and cultural awareness. Each activity is clearly explained with step-by-step instructions, objectives, and estimated time frames. These activities align with the learning outcomes and language performance goals outlined earlier.

This unit is divided into three lessons, approximately one hour each. The following sample lessons and activities are geared toward advanced-level college students who are serious about Chinese learning as a requirement for their major. As a college-level class, contact hours are limited and much of the learning is expected to take place outside of class. The lessons thus use flipped instruction principles, so that students can efficiently complete guided learning activities outside of class hours, aided by media technology and self-paced flexibility.

Students are given three "packets" to complete outside of class at different stages of their learning. If you pace this unit along a time frame that begins and ends with a weekend, the Preview Packet (Appendix 2.1) and the Enrichment Guide (Appendix 2.2) are best completed during the weekend preceding their first in-class lesson. As you can see from the full material sets in the Appendix, the Preview Packet contains guiding notes and vocabulary lists in both Chinese and English that introduce students to the Enrichment Guide of *Journey to the West*, especially highlighting its cultural role as a classical Chinese text. The students will also be introduced to the story through a short children's cartoon, which will begin to develop their listening comprehension.

Besides developing a background knowledge of the literary work, an important goal of the Preview Packet is to prepare students to use necessary vocabulary and grammar patterns for an initial discussion of the story in Chinese. The students are also prompted to answer some preliminary questions that mainly involve reading and comprehension of the story, giving the instructor an idea of students' basic understanding of the plot, characters, and major themes presented thus far.

Week 1: Introduction to the Novel and Characters

Activity 1: Video Introduction and Discussion (Estimated Time: 45 Minutes)

- Begin the class by showing the video introduction to *Journey to the West*.
- After watching the video, facilitate a class discussion using the following questions:
  - What did you learn about the author Wú Chéng'ēn and the historical context of the novel?
  - What themes and characters are associated with *Journey to the West*?
  - Why is this novel considered a classic in Chinese literature and culture?
- Encourage students to express their opinions and insights. Emphasize the importance of cultural awareness in interpreting the novel.
- Conclude the discussion by summarizing key points and transitioning to the next activity.

Activity 2: Storytelling with Illustrated Cards (Estimated Time: 60 Minutes)

- Distribute the illustrated story cards to students. Each card corresponds to a key scene or character in the novel.

"Sūn Wùkōng's Three Bouts with the White-Bone Demon" 《三打白骨精》 25

- Explain that key parts of the novel will be narrated using the cards. Explain that we will narrate key parts of the novel using the cards. Explain that key parts of the novel will be narrated using the cards.
- Begin storytelling, emphasizing repetition and clear pronunciation. Pause after each narrative segment to allow students to discuss the content.
- After completing the story, ask students to share their thoughts and interpretations of the narrative. Encourage them to use vocabulary and phrases from the novel.

Activity 3: Analyzing Themes and Cultural Significance
(Estimated Time: 30 Minutes)

- Discuss the themes and moral lessons conveyed in "Three Times Beating the White-Bone Demon," such as the triumph of good over evil, perseverance, and the importance of teamwork.
- Guide students in identifying literary devices such as symbolism, allegory, and character development in the selected excerpts.
- Encourage students to share their interpretations and insights into the cultural and historical context of the story.
- Facilitate a class discussion on how the story and its themes are relevant to contemporary society and the students' lives.

Week 2: Exploring Character Perspectives through Dramatic Inquiry

Activity 1: Study Packet Discussion (15 Minutes)

- Begin the lesson with a brief review of the Study Packet discussion questions.
- Encourage students to share their thoughts and insights on the questions, emphasizing the importance of understanding the characters' emotions and motivations.

Activity 2: Movie Scene Analysis (20 Minutes)

- Show a short scene from the movie *Monkey King 2* that highlights the major conflict in the story.
- Pause the scene at key moments to discuss the characters' emotions, facial expressions, and body language.
- Facilitate a class discussion about the impact of visual storytelling and how it helps convey character perspectives.

Activity 3: Role-Play Introduction (15 Minutes)

- Explain to the students that they will engage in a role-play activity where they take on the character of Sūn Wùkōng.
- Discuss the importance of understanding and empathizing with Sūn Wùkōng's perspective and emotions.
- Provide a brief overview of the scene they will be reenacting with Táng Sēng.

Activity 4: Role-Play – Convincing Táng Sēng (45 Minutes)

- Divide the class into pairs, with one student taking on the role of Sūn Wùkōng and the other as Táng Sēng.
- Allow each pair to practice and perform the scene where Sūn Wùkōng tries to convince Táng Sēng of the White-Bone Demon's true identity.
- Encourage students to fully immerse themselves in their characters, expressing the emotions and motivations as realistically as possible.
- Rotate pairs to ensure everyone gets a chance to portray Sūn Wùkōng.

Activity 5: Group Reflection and Discussion (20 Minutes)

- Bring the class back together for a reflective discussion.
- Ask students to share their experiences during the role-play, including the emotions they felt while portraying Sūn Wùkōng.
- Encourage students to discuss the challenges and insights gained from stepping into the character's shoes.
- Explore how this activity helped them see the conflict from a different perspective and whether their perceptions of the characters changed.

Activity 6: Creative Expression (20 Minutes)

- Have students choose a medium (e.g., writing, drawing, or acting) to creatively express a character's inner thoughts or emotions from the story. This could be a journal entry from Sūn Wùkōng's perspective, a drawing depicting Táng Sēng's misunderstanding, or a monologue from the White-Bone Demon.
- Allow students to share their creations with the class, discussing how their chosen medium allowed them to convey character emotions.

4.4 Implementing Dramatic Inquiry

To help teachers better contextualize its application, we now describe how we applied the dramatic inquiry technique in our classroom. This in-class dramatic inquiry activity should help facilitate discussion and critical thinking, as well as warm students up to the idea of placing themselves into the story and seeing through the characters' different points of view. This activity provides a logical progression from the preview and study guide discussion questions, so students should be able to begin connecting their own experience with those of the characters. In the class dramatic inquiry activity, students react and debate the major conflict of the story, that is, how misunderstanding causes Táng Sēng to send Sūn Wùkōng away, seemingly ending their master-disciple relationship.

After a short review of Study Packet discussion questions, the students watch a short scene from the movie *Monkey King 2*, which again reiterates the main conflict from the short story. Afterward, the students take turns role-playing as Sūn Wùkōng to convince Táng Sēng (played by the instructor) that he was telling the truth about the White-Bone Demon's true identity. The instructor sets the scene by sitting in the middle of the classroom floor while students act in the voice of Sūn Wùkōng to persuade Táng Sēng to let them stay. Students are encouraged to put themselves in the shoes of Sūn Wùkōng, feeling their own frustration and hope as they are misunderstood by Táng Sēng. This scene arouses students' emotions and their ability to see the conflict of the story from a different perspective.

4.5 Stand-Alone Project Week

Throughout the lesson unit, students have understood the conflict as depicted in the "Sān Dǎ Báigǔjīng" story within the broader context of *Journey to the West*. To further solidify students' understanding of the classic book in relation to their own lives, the week immediately following the unit is a stand-alone project week. This week is organized around the students completing a group project. The project leverages the students' ability to work as a team to collaboratively develop advanced level language skills for ICC developmental goals.

In our classes, we have used two such projects, a role-play skit (writing and performing), and a mini research paper (writing and presenting) (see appendix 2.5). Students can either be given these options as choices for better accessibility and motivation or use one topic choice only based on the specific interest and focus of the class.

The role-play skit project utilizes the dramatic inquiry approach that requires students to take on one of the characters in the story, adopting that character's ethical perspectives and values. Throughout the project week, working collectively, students write their script together, rehearse, scout sites for video-shooting, and finally record and edit their video skit.

The mini research project, however, requires students to complete a character analysis or define their own research topic about *Journey to the West*. The research guideline is written to guide students to focus on developing four aspects of ICC (knowledge, attitude, skills, and critical cultural awareness) and to consider its impact on action. It is important to hold the first hour of the project week for collaborative scaffolding and teacher guidance. The rest of the week can be small group work, with regular check-ins and feedback cycles through peer review and teacher conferences. The final products of the projects can be incorporated in the next stage of learning either as a performance in class, a "video skit watch party," or a website showcasing students' research papers. It is important to celebrate and share students' work with a wider audience to create authentic motivation as much as possible.

4.6 Assessment and Students' Feedback

To give a view of how the projects connect to the language and ICC goals designated for this unit, we describe the role-play skits that our students wrote and performed.

The students based their role-play skit on their own experiences as college students, journeying to receive their diplomas just as the characters in *Journey to the West* set out to retrieve the Buddhist scripture. The skit was divided into five scenes, reimagining the three encounters with Báigǔjīng as different struggles. The students had creative, original ideas for adapting the story to their own lives, such as writing scenes in which they had terrible food at the college's cafeteria and then had a hard time getting scholarships at Báigǔjīng financial aid office. Finally, the skit culminated in a scene in which the students received their long-awaited diplomas at graduation, only to realize that they were blank sheets of paper – as was the sutra Táng Sēng and his disciples got at the end of the novel.

This production emphasized the students' ability to work together, paralleling the novel's themes of teamwork. While the students came up with creative ways to liken the story to their own lives, they also reflected on the meaning of their four years spent as college students, writing to their audience:

谢谢你们看过我们的短剧。从大学第一年我们一起走过来，我们有过梦想，也经历过困难，感觉过怀疑，我们和《西游记》人物的想法很相似！而且，最后我们明白旅 程比目的地更重要！所以我们希望这个电影可以帮助你明白如何珍惜大学的学习和 生活，还有信任和帮助你的朋友，而且，最重要的是克服各种困难，做最好的自己， 要坚持你的梦想并且实现它。

[Thank you for watching our short play. We have come together since the first year of college. We have had dreams, experienced difficulties, and felt doubts. We are very similar to the characters of *Journey to the West*! In addition, in the end, we understand that the journey is more important than the destination! So we hope this film can help you understand how to cherish your university studies and life, trust and help your friends, and, most importantly, overcome all kinds of difficulties and be your best self. Hold on to your dream and make it happen.]

The research paper option provides flexibility for situations where in-person activities are limited. For example, during the COVID-19 pandemic when in-person instruction transitioned to remote learning, our students were not able to meet in person to plan and act out their script. As an alternative, the mini research project was able to reach similar ICC and language goals. Below is an excerpt from one such paper that our students wrote.

我学到吴承恩用他的方式写人物是有原因的。比如他用唐僧等师徒四人代表人的不同方面，这样让我们可以学习以更好地了解自己。另外，通过将人物分成相互补充的二分法，容易通过对比来理解它们。无论你学习哪个角色，他们都表达不同的人的特点。比如，悟空代表人类的头脑，他表现势不可挡的脾气和冲动。正如世界上很多人都有思想，可 是他们不能都公开表达或者行动，但是孙悟空有能力表现出这些想法。

其次，我认为唐僧代表了人类的心。他非常善良、又有同情心又有耐心。当然他对佛教 的信仰帮提高他的修养，而这样提高自我的境界是每个人都应该追求的。相反，猪八戒是 人类负面性格的代表。 猪八戒自傲、爱欺人，不但贪吃，又好色，这些和西方基督教信仰 中的"罪"差不多。但是，虽然他有很多缺点，可是从另外一个角度而言，他作为一个最不 完美的角色，不断实现自己的价值， 代表了人类可以通过帮助他人变得更好。因此， 唐僧 是自我完善的代表，而猪八戒体现了我们可以从自身的缺点中不多成长的、发展的特 点。

[I first learned that Wú Chéng'ēn writes characters the way he does for a reason. For example, he used Táng Sēng and his four disciples to represent aspects of the human spirit so that we may learn to better understand ourselves. Additionally, by placing these characters into complementary dichotomies, they become easy to understand. Regardless of the character you observe, they all express different human characteristics. Sūn Wùkōng represents the human mind. He displayed an unstoppable temper and impulsiveness. Many people in the world have thoughts that they do not overtly express or act upon, but Sūn Wùkōng has the ability to manifest them.

Second, I think Táng Sēng represents the human heart. He is kind, compassionate, and has patience. Of course, his devotion to Buddhism helped him in his own cultivation, and this kind of self-improvement is what everyone should pursue. Adversely, Zhū Bājiè represents the negative aspects of the human character. Zhū Bājiè is arrogant, deceitful, gluttonous, and lustful. These traits can be similarly perceived as "sins" through the lens of Western Christianity. Despite his many flaws, he serves his purpose as a character that shows humans can become better by helping others. Therefore, while Táng Sēng represents the self-improved state, Zhū Bājiè embodies the flaws that we can still rise above.]

(高亮亮/Jorge Navarro Jr., North Central College,
used with permission)

5. Teacher's Reflections

When we first started teaching the "Chinese Communication and Composition" context, we used the most popular available textbook for students. While the content units based on this commercial textbook were interesting, the topics were somewhat scattered and easily outdated from year to year. We also found it difficult to maintain a coherent, overarching learning goal throughout the semester, and students thus found it harder to maintain a steady level of interest and a sense that their knowledge was building cumulatively. Over time, we developed our own units on Chinese literature to build a more coherent structure in the course, highlighting historical and philosophical topics as auxiliary units. Overall, student feedback suggested that the emerging curriculum gave them a greater sense of engagement with the material and a feeling of accomplishment in learning the history and major concepts in Chinese thought through classic stories.

30   *"Sūn Wùkōng's Three Bouts with the White-Bone Demon"* 《三打白骨精》

In preparation for developing this chapter on *Journey to the West*, we interviewed several American students who have studied the novel extensively about their thoughts on the novel. In particular, we wanted to find out what the novel really means to them, both as a classical Chinese text and as a beloved story that Chinese people grew up with. The majority of the American students shared that the novel at first seemed distant from their lived experiences but the development of its themes and careful analysis of each character from a humanistic standpoint enabled them to find personal meaning from within the story. They appreciated that *Journey to the West* is a rich and powerful tool for understanding Chinese worldviews, spanning from ancient times to modern day.

Appendices: Sample Teaching Materials

Additional supplemental materials, such as PowerPoint slides, can be requested by scanning this QR code.

Appendix 2.1: Preview Packet

《西游记》预习作业 (Preview Packet)

1. 课文 Lesson Text:《三打白骨精》"Sūn Wùkōng's Three Bouts with the White-Bone Demon"

话说有个妖精叫"白骨精", 她听说吃唐僧肉能长生不老, 就在路上等唐僧到来。

这天, 唐僧师徒四人前往西天取经, 他们走了很久的路来到这座深山。唐僧饿得受不了, 就吩咐孙悟空去找些食物。孙悟空让师弟保护好师父, 就跳上筋斗云。白骨精躲在 石头后面, 看见孙悟空走了变成了漂亮的小女孩走出来, 手里还拿着装有食物的篮子。

一看见是个女孩子, 还带来饭菜, 唐僧想要拒绝, 可是猪八戒满心欢喜地迎上去 , 就在这时孙悟空摘完桃子飞回来, 要知道, 他可是火眼金睛, 立刻就看出来这个女孩子 是妖精变成的, 他大喊一声, 举起棒子打过去, 妖精被打倒, 变成烟溜走了。唐僧见出了 人命, 大惊失色, 要赶孙悟空走, 悟空苦苦哀求, 唐僧让他答应不再杀死无辜的人。

白骨精不甘心失败, 又变成小女孩的母亲, 哭喊着跑过来, 白骨精抱着女孩的尸体 大声哭起来, 唐僧见了也落下眼泪。孙悟空认出老太太又是白

"Sūn Wùkōng's Three Bouts with the White-Bone Demon" 《三打白骨精》

骨精变的，大怒，一棒把她打死。唐僧看见孙悟空又打死一个人，念起来紧箍咒，孙悟空痛得满地打滚。悟空向唐僧求饶，保证不再杀人，唐僧再次原谅他。

白骨精没抓到唐僧，决定这一次变成老头，一边拄着拐杖、一边念经，见到师徒几人，说"我来找我的妻子和女儿。"孙悟空听他胡说，大喝"妖精，你还敢骗我！"又一棒打死他。这次不管悟空怎么解释，唐僧都不再相信他了，说"我们师徒缘分已尽，你走吧！"孙悟空很无奈，再三叮嘱八戒和沙僧照顾好师父，含泪回到花果山。

白骨精又会对唐僧做什么呢？师徒四人的结局是什么？下集待续。

2. 生词 Vocabulary

1)	妖精	yāojing	evil fairy; demon spirit
2)	长生不老	chángshēngbùlǎo	immortality
3)	师徒	shītú	master and disciples
4)	受不了	shòubùliǎo	unbearable; cannot tolerate
5)	吩咐	fēnfù	to order; instruct
6)	变成	biànchéng	to transform; change
7)	躲	duǒ	to hide
8)	装	zhuāng	to pack; wrap something in a bag
9)	拒绝	jùjué	to refuse
10)	满心欢喜	mǎnxīnhuānxǐ	full of joy
11)	摘	zhāi	to pick (from above)
12)	V完	wán	to finish
13)	喊	hǎn	to shout
14)	举起	jǔqǐ	to lift
15)	大怒	dànù	furious
16)	打倒	dǎdǎo	to knock down
17)	溜走	liūzǒu	to slip away
18)	出人命	chūrénmìng	to cause human life
19)	大惊失色	dàjīngshīsè	to turn pale with fright
20)	赶	gǎn	to drive away
21)	苦苦哀求	kǔkǔāiqiú	to implore
22)	无辜	wúgū	innocent
23)	尸体	shītǐ	dead body
24)	甘心	gānxīn	willingly
25)	落下眼泪	luòxiàyǎnlèi	to shed tears
26)	打滚	dǎgǔn	to roll around
27)	求饶	qiúráo	to beg for mercy
28)	原谅	yuánliàng	to pardon; forgive
29)	抓	zhuā	to catch; capture
30)	拐杖	guǎizhàng	crutch; walking stick
31)	念经	niànjīng	to chant; recite Buddhist scripture
32)	胡说	húshuō	to speak total nonsense
33)	骗	piàn	to deceive; cheat

34)	缘分已尽	yuánfènyǐjìn	destiny is over; fate has finished
35)	再三叮嘱	zàisāndīngzhǔ	to exhort again and again
36)	无奈	wúnài	no choice; helpless
37)	照顾	zhàogù	to take care of
38)	含泪	hán lèi	tearful
39)	结局	jiéjú	ending

Other Terms to Know

1)	话说	huà shuō	the story says; once upon a time
2)	妖怪	yāoguài	monster
3)	长生不老	chángshēng bùlǎo	immortal
4)	西天取经	xītiān qǔjīng	go west and retrieve the scriptures
5)	师弟	shi di	junior disciples
6)	筋斗云	jīndǒu yún	孙悟空的 magical cloud
7)	火眼金睛	huǒyǎn jīnjīng	孙悟空的 discerning eyes
8)	金箍棒	jīn gū bàng	a magical golden staff
9)	花果山	huā huǒ shān	Mountain of Flowers and Fruits
10)	下集待续	xià jí dài xù	to be continued in the next episode

3. 练习 Exercise

a. Use Each of the Following Characters to Form Two Words

1) 命:_____;_____
2) 徒:_____;_____
3) 泪:_____;_____
4) 装:_____;_____
5) 无:_____;_____
6) 照:_____;_____
7) 躲:_____;_____
8) 保:_____;_____

b. Match and Then Translate into English

1) 抓	A. 紧箍咒
2) 变成	B. 唐僧
3) 念	C. 烟
4) 取	D. 经
5) 出	E. 人命
6) 赶走	F. 孙悟空
7) 举起	G. 金箍棒

"Sūn Wùkōng's Three Bouts with the White-Bone Demon" 《三打白骨精》

c. Write a Sentence Using the Following Four-Word Phrase Word

1) 满心欢喜
Sentence: _____

2) 大惊失色
Sentence: _____

3) 苦苦哀求
Sentence: _____

4) 满地打滚
Sentence: _____

d. Translate the Following Sentences into English

1) 白骨精变成了漂亮的小女孩走出来，手里还拿着装有食物的篮子。
Translate: _____

2) 唐僧念起来紧箍咒，孙悟空痛得满地打滚。
Translate: _____

3) 白骨精抱着女孩的尸体大声哭起来。
Translate: _____

e. Fill Out the Blank and Then Translate the Sentences

1) 孙悟空一棒___她打死。
2) 白骨精一边拄___拐杖、一边念经。
3) 白骨精哭喊___跑过来。
4) 这次不管悟空怎么解释，唐僧___不再相信他了。
5) 唐僧饿___受不了。

f. Answer the Following Questions in Full Sentences Based on the Story You Read

1) 白骨精是谁，她为什么想吃唐僧？
2) 唐僧很饿，他吩咐孙悟空做什么？
3) 妖精被孙悟空打倒以后，变成什么？
4) 孙悟空是怎么知道是白骨精变成的人？
5) 唐僧为什么念紧箍咒？
6) 白骨精都变成了是谁？
7) 如果你是孙悟空，你会怎么做？
8) 你觉得后来唐僧会原谅孙悟空吗？后面会发生什么事情？

34 *"Sūn Wùkōng's Three Bouts with the White-Bone Demon"* 《三打白骨精》

g. Watch the children's cartoon 《西游记精选故事集》三打白骨精儿童趣味动画 https://youtu.be/ByKOMcjXCJs

4. 延展 Read the Enrichment Guide

Appendix 2.2: Enrichment Guide

《西游记》 Enrichment Guide

1. 故事介绍 Introduction to Story

Journey to the West, otherwise known as 《西游记》 *Xīyóujì*, was written in the late Ming Dynasty (circa 1580 CE) by a scholar named Wú Chéng'ēn (吴承恩). The fictionalized events depicted in the novel are based on the real historic journey of a monk named Xuánzàng (玄奘) who traveled in 640 CE to retrieve sacred Buddhist scriptures from India. Xuánzàng greatly contributed to the development of Buddhism in China and is also the inspiration for Táng Sēng (唐僧), the fictional monk in *Xīyóujì* along with his fantastical disciples; a monkey named Sūn Wùkōng (孙悟空), a pig named Zhū Bājiè (猪八戒), and a sand demon named Shā Wùjìng (沙悟净). While the novel is based on Xuánzàng's true historic pilgrimage, the novel is a fictionalized account that incorporates mythology and the three teaching of Chinese philosophy and religion (三教), as well as many Chinese values and beliefs (价值观). The novel has been read as a children's comic book, historical fiction, political satire, and religious allegory.

《孙悟空三打白骨精》 ("Sūn Wùkōng's Three Bouts against the White-Bone Demon") is based on a story arc from the novel which features an antagonist named Báigǔjīng (白骨精: White-Bone Demon). In this story, Táng Sēng, Sūn Wùkōng, Sha Wujing, and Zhū Bājiè have already begun their journey to the West to retrieve the Buddhist scriptures. When they arrive at Yun Hai Xi Kingdom (云海西国), they are side-tracked by a demon disguised as an old woman. The old woman, Báigǔjīng in disguise, seeks to eat Táng Sēng to attain immortality, allowing her to escape the wheel of reincarnation (轮回). Although Táng Sēng listens to the old woman with sympathy, the demon cannot fool Sūn Wùkōng's truth-seeing eyes (火眼金睛). Sūn Wùkōng engages the demon in battle, ignoring Táng Sēng's orders. Though the White-Bone Demon escapes, Táng Sēng punishes Wùkōng for his disobedience. He chants a spell given to him by the bodhisattva Guānyīn (观音), which causes the golden band (紧箍咒) that binds Sūn Wùkōng's head to tighten painfully.

2. 人物 Characters

1) 唐僧　　　　Táng Sēng　　　Tripitaka
2) 孙悟空　　　Sūn Wùkōng　　Monkey King
3) 猪八戒　　　Zhū Bājiè　　　Pigsy
4) 沙悟净　　　Shā Wùjìng　　Sandy

"Sūn Wùkōng's Three Bouts with the White-Bone Demon" 《三打白骨精》   35

5)	白骨精	Báigǔjīng	White-Bone Demon
6)	观音	Guānyīn	Bodhisattva
7)	如来佛祖	Rúlái Fózǔ	Buddha

3. 历史 History: The Journey of Xuánzàng to India During the Tang Dynasty

In actual history, Xuánzàng was a Chinese Buddhist monk, scholar, traveler, and translator. In his youth, Xuánzàng became a monk in Luoyang and harbored a strong desire to discover the original Buddhist scriptures. In AD 629, defying the imperial decree under Emperor Taizong's rule, he secretly embarked on a perilous journey to India, facing challenges and conflicts as a fugitive. Ultimately, Xuánzàng reached the Nalanda monastery, where he studied Sanskrit and Brahmana philosophy. After spending over a decade in India, he returned to China in AD 645, leaving a significant impact on Chinese Buddhism.

4. 三教 Merge of Confucianism, Daoism, and Buddhism in Ming Dynasty Satirical Fiction

Xiyouji gives great insight into Chinese thought, particularly due to its synthesis of the three teachings (三教): Confucianism (儒家), Daoism (道家), and Buddhism (佛家). For example, the novel begins with Sūn Wùkōng's initial desire to achieve immortality under the guidance of a *Daoist* master, cultivating mystical powers like cloud-jumping (筋斗云) and his infamous 72 transformations (七十二变), which take him all the way to the Heavenly Empire, where he is given a post in the celestial bureaucracy. Many believe the novel to be a satirical portrayal of the government, as the Confucian organization of the Heavens mirrors the political state of the Ming Dynasty. Sūn Wùkōng, a mischievous character, eventually wreaks havoc in the heavens (大闹天宫) and earns himself a punishment from the Buddha himself. It is only when Táng Sēng begins his mission to retrieve the Buddhist scriptures from the West that Sūn Wùkōng is finally freed. This syncretism of the three teachings in *Journey to the West* is exemplary of the modern Chinese worldview, in which the influences of Confucianism, Buddhism, and Daoism can still be found today.

5. 教训 Life Lessons and the Arduous Journey

Although *Journey to the West* may appear as a fantasy novel, it serves as an allegory for conquering inner demons. Each disciple symbolizes an aspect of human nature, making the journey a shared experience. After overcoming 81 trials, characters evolve, acquiring virtues they lacked initially. The narrative illustrates personal growth and resilience. Although *Journey to the West* seems to be a story about fighting monsters, it actually tells people how to defeat their inner demons. Some readers have interpreted the story as an allegorical journey, taking Táng Sēng and his three disciples as representations of human nature. In the fable, Xuánzàng,

Sūn Wùkōng, Zhū Bājiè, Shā Wùjìng, and White Dragon Horse all represent the same person. In this way, Sūn Wùkōng is the human heart, Táng Sēng is the human body, Zhū Bājiè is the human emotion, Shā Wùjìng is the human nature, and Bái Lóngmǎ is the human willpower. In this sense, the journey is not headed by a single, heroic protagonist who alone has the power to achieve his aims. Instead, each disciple is necessary to the whole, making the journey a shared experience. When the long and arduous journey is complete, and the characters have overcome an astounding 81 trials, each disciple has cultivated within themselves something they lacked at the start, such as Zhū Bājiè resisting overindulgence and Sūn Wùkōng's newfound self-control.

6. 现当代社会 Relevance to Contemporary Chinese Society

With this allegory, the novel can be read as a journey of self-cultivation (修养). This interpretation is popular among readers young and old. For example, when asked about the relevance of Sūn Wùkōng to Chinese youth today, college students from Beijing responded that Sūn Wùkōng represents the transition from childhood to adulthood. In the novel, Sūn Wùkōng is rebellious and full of arrogance. Slowly, through the 81 trials, he learns how to work with others and to think before he acts. The impulsiveness of his character does not go away entirely, but in the end it is balanced with greater awareness of the consequences his actions might have on others.

7. 流行文化 Pop Culture of Journey to the West

Xiyouji has achieved legendary status in Chinese culture. Though the novel was written hundreds of years ago, its characters and themes still resonate with our lives today. With such a colorful cast of characters, it is not hard to imagine how the story has withstood the test of time, remaining a classic tale that lives on through its readers today. In China and across Asia, there are countless pop culture remakes and references to the prolific journey of Táng Sēng and his disciples, especially the heroic Sūn Wùkōng. Taking inspiration from the novel, there are TV series, films, theatrical productions, and even video games that incorporate familiar elements of the story for audiences across the globe. Each adaptation is unique in its portrayal of the story and characters, influenced in subtle ways by the time period in which they were created.

Here is a list of some notable remakes:

1) 《大闹天宫》 *Havoc in Heaven* (1965): Produced during the Cultural Revolution, this cartoon movie depicts a corrupt Celestial Court and places a Communist spin on Sūn Wùkōng's mischievous adventures in heaven.
2) 《西游记》 *Journey to the West* (1986): One of the oldest but most beloved remakes, best known for its character portrayal and is considered one of the more authentic renditions of the story.

"Sūn Wùkōng's Three Bouts with the White-Bone Demon" 《三打白骨精》 37

3) 《悟空传》 *Immortal Demon Slayer* (2017): A modern take on the story which focuses on Sūn Wùkōng's origins and adventures in the Heavenly Kingdom. This movie was applauded for its visual effects and depiction of the heroic Sūn Wùkōng.
4) 《大话西游》 *A Chinese Odyssey* (1995–2016): This three-part film series starring Steven Chow spins the traditional story of Xiyouji into a romantic tale of reincarnation, featuring Sūn Wùkōng as a human.
5) 《大话西游之爱你一万年》 *Love You a Million Years* (2017): The Hong Kong film series *A Chinese Odyssey* was so well-received that a TV drama based on the story was developed in mainland China, appealing to popular audiences with its themes of love and heroism.

8. 国际影响 International Inspirations from *Journey to the West*

1) *Saiyuki* (1978) is a popular Japanese TV series that was so popular it even broadcasted dubbed English episodes on British and Australian broadcasting corporations.
2) *Dragon Ball Z* (1984) is a Japanese media franchise inspired by Xiyouji, with the protagonist named Son Goku, the Japanese name for Sūn Wùkōng.
3) *Monkey: Journey to the West* (2007) is an opera created by British musician Damon Albarn, British artist Jamie Hewlett, and Chinese director Chen Shizheng.
4) *A Korean Odyssey* (2017) is a romantic Korean drama adaptation.
5) *The New Legends of Monkey* (2018) is an action-packed Australia–New Zealand series.
6) *American Born Chinese* (2006) is a Chinese American children's book series that uses Sūn Wùkōng to portray the struggles of a child born to Chinese immigrants.

9. 语言影响 Impact on Language

Here are some popular quotes and terms from the novel:

中文	翻译
"只要你心诚志坚,念念回首处,既是灵山。"	"Nothing in this world is difficult, but thinking makes it seem so. Where there is true will, there is always a way."
"一叶浮萍归大海,人生何处不相逢。"	"A duckweed will float to the sea in the end; people will eventually meet somewhere." (Meaning: "We will see each other again eventually" is an appropriate phrase for when you're not sure when you'll meet again.)
"跳出佛掌心。"	"To jump out of the Buddha's palm." (Meaning: In the novel, Sūn Wùkōng mistakenly believes he is powerful enough to escape the palm of Buddha. This phrase implies that there are always limits to our capabilities.)

10. 电影介绍 Film Overview and Background of *Monkey King 2*

Monkey King 2 《孙悟空之三打白骨精》 is based on a story arc from the novel, which features an antagonist named Báigǔjīng (literal meaning: White-Bone Demon). In this story, Táng Sēng, Sūn Wùkōng, Shā Wùjìng, and Zhū Bājiè have already begun their journey to the West to retrieve the Buddhist scriptures. When they arrive at Yun Hai Xi Kingdom (云海西国), they are side-tracked by a demon disguised as an old woman. The old woman, Báigǔjīng in disguise, seeks to eat Táng Sēng to attain immortality, allowing her to escape the wheel of reincarnation (轮回). Although Táng Sēng listens to the old woman with sympathy, the demon cannot fool Sūn Wùkōng's truth-seeing eyes (火眼金睛). Sūn Wùkōng engages the demon in battle, ignoring Tange Seng's orders. Though the White-Bone Demon escapes, Táng Sēng punishes Wùkōng for his disobedience. He chants a spell given to him by the bodhisattva Guānyīn, which causes the golden band that binds Sūn Wùkōng's head to tighten painfully.

As a monk, Táng Sēng believes that killing is wrong. His kindness and belief in pacifism (度化) even extend to Báigǔjīng. Sūn Wùkōng, understanding the danger in letting the Báigǔjīng live, is conflicted between obeying his master and saving Táng Sēng's life. Eventually, Táng Sēng sends Sūn Wùkōng away and attempts to lead Báigǔjīng onto a better path toward enlightenment.

The movie begins with the Buddhist monk Táng Sēng freeing Sūn Wùkōng from his 500-year-long imprisonment under the Five Elements Mountain (五行山). The bodhisattva Guānyīn then appears to announce that Sūn Wùkōng will escort Táng Sēng on his journey west to the monastery in India. To bind Sūn Wùkōng to his new master, Guānyīn gives Táng Sēng an enchanted golden circlet to place on Monkey's head which causes him pain whenever Táng Sēng chants the band-tightening spell (紧箍咒). The two begin their journey west, picking up two new disciples along the way, Zhu Bajia and Shā Wùjìng.

The company travels to the Yun Hai Xi Kingdom, a land terrorized by Báigǔjīng, a demon who eats people to gain immortality (长生不老). She takes the appearance of an old woman and lures the group into a cottage in the woods, where she tells Táng Sēng a tragic story about her life. Sūn Wùkōng uses his truth-seeing eyes (火眼金睛) and sees that the old woman is actually a demon who intends to eat Táng Sēng. The demoness escapes before Wùkōng can kill her, Táng Sēng blames Wùkōng for killing an innocent person. Táng Sēng chants the band-tightening spell, punishing Wùkōng for his misdeeds. Later, Táng Sēng and Wùkōng discuss what it means to trust what they perceive with their own eyes.

Táng Sēng and his disciples continue with their journey when suddenly they are attacked by Báigǔjīng once again. Chaos ensues, and in the battle, Sūn Wùkōng again uses his truth-seeking eyes and kills two people who were possessed by Báigǔjīng. Angry with his disciple, Táng Sēng banishes Wùkōng. Without the Monkey to protect him, Táng Sēng is then kidnapped by the demoness. Again, Táng Sēng attempts to convince Báigǔjīng to follow the path of enlightenment as the true path to immortality. Báigǔjīng refuses, admitting that the story she had told him as the old woman was true, recounting her suffering as a mortal. Due to her suffering as a mortal, Báigǔjīng refuses to change her evil ways. The disciples, Wùkōng, Bajie, and Wujing finally defeat Báigǔjīng, mortally wounding her.

Just before her death, the Buddha descends from the Heavens to take Báigǔjīng's soul and banish it for good. Táng Sēng, however, pleads with the Buddha to have mercy on the demon and to give him one last chance to save her soul from destruction. The Buddha tells Táng Sēng that to do so would require the sacrifice of his own life. Bravely, Táng Sēng orders Wùkōng to kill him. At first, Wùkōng refuses but Táng Sēng explains that in order to stay true to his vows as a monk, he must also lead a virtuous life and do well by others. Finally, Wùkōng uses his golden staff (金箍棒) to kill Táng Sēng, thus saving Báigǔjīng's soul from annihilation.

11. 词汇 *Monkey King 2* Vocabulary

1) 引入正道　　yǐn rù zhèng dào　　lead to the correct path
2) 火眼金睛　　huǒ yǎn jīn jīng　　discerning eyes
3) 相信缘分　　xiāng xìn yuán fèn　　to trust in fate
4) 放弃执念　　fàng qì zhí niàn　　to give up obsession
5) 长生不老　　cháng shēng bù lǎo　　immortality
6) 牺牲性命　　xī shēng xìng mìng　　to sacrifice one's life
7) 轮回　　　　lún huí　　　　　　　reincarnation
8) 回心转意　　huí xīn zhuǎn yì　　to change one's mind
9) 信以为真　　xìn yǐ wéi zhēn　　to accept something as true

12. 价值观 *Monkey King 2* Moral Lesson

The movie *Monkey King 2* takes a unique stance on the meaning of "good versus evil" and "right versus wrong." While Táng Sēng wants to save Báigǔjīng and Sūn Wùkōng wants to save Táng Sēng, the recurring theme of reincarnation means each character has the opportunity to lead a more virtuous life in the future. Rather than give up on Báigǔjīng, Táng Sēng shows her kindness and mercy because, as a Buddhist monk, he values benevolence. On the other hand, Sūn Wùkōng is largely unrestrained, impulsively attempting to eradicate evil without stopping to consider the larger problem at hand. Sūn Wùkōng's black-and-white view of the world is eventually influenced by Táng Sēng's ability to see the good in others, no matter their past wrongdoings.

The movie presents a nuanced perspective on good versus evil, emphasizing kindness and redemption. Táng Sēng's benevolence toward Báigǔjīng contrasts with Sūn Wùkōng's impulsive approach. The theme of reincarnation suggests opportunities for characters to lead virtuous lives in the future. The influence of Táng Sēng's compassionate view eventually impacts Sūn Wùkōng's perception of the world.

"Sūn Wùkōng's Three Bouts with the White-Bone Demon" 《三打白骨精》

Appendix 2.3: Study Packet

《西游记之孙悟空三打白骨精》 Study Packet

Read the short story again and complete the activities:

1. Speaking

Record yourself reading the story. Pay attention to your pace, word groups, tones and pronunciation. Be as fluent, accurate and natural as you can. Link to submit the recording: https://vocaroo.com/

2. Grammar

2.1. 着 (zhe) indicates a continuous action. It is added to verbs to indicate *aspect*. Other particles used to indicate aspect in Chinese are 了 (le) and 过 (guo). 着 is used when the action is expected to continue for a while. It is also used to describe a second verb with the structure **Verb 1 + 着 + Verb**

(a) 我出去一下，你帮我看着行李。

Translate: _____

(b) 手里还拿着装有食物的篮子。

Translate: _____

(c) 白骨精抱着女孩的尸体大声哭起来。

Translate: _____

(d) **Make** your own sentence in Chinese with 着:
_____

2.2. V+完 (wán) indicates a completed action. Similar to 到 (dào) and 见 (jiàn), you can also form result complements with 完. This indicates that an action is finished or completed.

(a) 我看完了那部电影。

Translate: _____

(b) 我们明天可以做完。

Translate: _____

(c) 孙悟空摘完桃子飞回来。

Translate: _____

(d) **Make** your own sentence with **V+**完:
_____

"Sūn Wùkōng's Three Bouts with the White-Bone Demon" 《三打白骨精》

2.3. 把 (bǎ) sentences allow for longer sentences in which the focus is on the result of an action. It essentially brings the object of the verb closer to the front of the sentence anyway d precedes it with a 把.

(a) 孙悟空一棒把她打死。
Translate: _____

(b) 那个女孩把篮子装好了。
Translate: _____

(c) 孙悟空把桃子摘完了。
Translate: _____

(d) **Make** your own sentence with 把:
_____

2.4. 得 (de) is used after an adjective to express advanced degree complements. The structure is follows the pattern **adjective** + 得 + **degree**.

(a) 孙悟空饿得可以吃一只猪。
Translate: _____

(b) 我不喜欢这个蛋糕，甜得受不了！
Translate: _____

(c) 我哭得眼泪像一条河。
Translate: _____

(d) I'm so busy I didn't have time to eat breakfast.
Translate: _____

(e) **Write** your own sentence with 得 to describe your life:
_____

3. Listening Comprehension

Watch the movie scene from 49:44 to 52:20, then fill in the ten blanks:

唐僧：悟空，刚才我也是(1)___，才那样做的。
悟空：你是不是以后都用这个紧箍咒管着俺老孙？
唐僧：只要你不再滥杀(2)___，小僧(3)___不在(4)___。
悟空：你为什么不相信她们是(5)___？
唐僧：我们两个人长得是很像。我们只会相信我们眼睛所看见的。就是因为这个佛祖才(6)___ 我们俩安排在一起(7)___吧。悟空，你看，这串 (to string together; measure word for string) 佛珠。紫檀来自扶南，取来南海，可是它们是被一根绳子 (rope) 串在一起的，就像你、我、八戒、悟净，把我们串在一起的是这十万八千里(8)___之路。你可能不会相信我所看见的，但我 (9)___你会相信小僧每念一声紧箍咒，我心里是跟你一样的(10)___。

悟空： 这颗 (measure word for bead) 肥肥白白的一定是八戒。

4. Short Essay

Answer the following questions in a number of organized paragraphs, using the new vocabulary words and grammatical structures you learned from this lesson.

1) 介绍一下《三打白骨精》的故事。
2) 你在别的电影或者文学作品里，有没有看到类似的人物被误解的场景？和孙悟空被 误解的场景有什么一样和不一样的地方？
3) 你被别人误解过吗？发生了什么？你有什么感受？你那时候是怎么解决问题的？
4) 你从《三打白骨精》这个故事学到什么？这个故事能帮你更好地解决问题吗？

Appendix 2.4: Role-Play Project Guidelines

Midterm Project Guideline: Role-Play Skit and Video Production

During the midterm week, your task is to collaborate on creating a play based on 《西游记之孙悟空三打白骨精》 and your personal experiences as college students. This project aims to showcase your language proficiency and your ability to engage with Chinese culture while drawing connections to your own life. By employing dramatic tools, you'll delve into the characters of Táng Sēng and his four disciples, gaining a comprehensive understanding of each character's perspective and motives. The project comprises two parts: a written script with stage directions and a final recorded video performance.

PART 1: Written Script (Chinese with some English directions; at least one page of background introduction and dialogue for each student; some roles may be split between students).

The script should include the following:

1) Background information for each character (personality, relationship, experience, etc.)
2) Introduction to 西游记 and its history
3) Connection to a basic theme of students' "journeying" to our college to achieve a goal (e.g., diplomas, a scholarship, self-improvement, etc.)
4) Should center around a conflict resembling 《三打白骨精》
5) New words and grammar (at least 4 new grammatical structures and 10 words)
6) Written reflection (8–10 sentences) on the process of writing the script and how you connected 西游记 to your own experiences

"Sūn Wùkōng's Three Bouts with the White-Bone Demon" 《三打白骨精》

PART 2: Play Performance (All in Chinese; one character role per student; the roles of Táng Sēng and Sūn Wùkōng may be split between students, as long as there is one page total of dialogue per student; if necessary, additional roles may be added).

The performance should focus on the following:

1) Thorough understanding of each character's motives and perspectives
2) Use of proper tones and vocabulary
3) Thoughtful choice of setting and stage directions
4) Careful use of time and resources

The final project will be assessed on three levels:

1) The overall production and performance of the play
2) Intercultural communicative competence
3) Proficient use of language

Appendix 2.5: Mini Research Paper Guidelines

Final Project Guideline: A Mini Research Paper

During the final week, you will embark on a scholarly exploration by developing a research topic related to one of the Four Great Novels 《四大名著》, delving into various aspects of Chinese culture, history, and philosophy as portrayed in the narrative. Your choice may revolve around the connection to a contemporary pop cultural remake of 《西游记》 or involve a detailed character study with careful analysis. This project aims to foster thoughtful ideas, fostering connections to your own perspectives while incorporating nuanced insights from Chinese culture.

Part 1: Research

1) **Background Research:** Conduct preliminary research on two to three potential topics, accumulating approximately a page of notes to represent your initial ideas. Explore the depths of each topic, considering their relevance to your interests and the themes of the chosen novel.
2) **Consultation with Laoshi:** Schedule a meeting with Laoshi to discuss your preliminary ideas. Seek guidance on refining your topic, ensuring it aligns with the project's objectives and your own academic interests.
3) **Final Topic Confirmation:** After receiving feedback and guidance, choose one main topic that resonates most with you and aligns with the project's scope. This topic will be the focal point of your research and subsequent essay.
4) **Scholarly Resources:** Identify and gather two to four scholarly resources that both support and contrast with your chosen argument. Utilize reputable academic sources to enrich the depth and credibility of your research.

"Sūn Wùkōng's Three Bouts with the White-Bone Demon" 《三打白骨精》

Part 2: Written Essay

- **Content:** Craft a comprehensive essay in Chinese, with a length of approximately two pages. Ensure that your essay provides a detailed exploration of your chosen topic, integrating insights from the novel, scholarly resources, and your own reflections.
- **Structure:** Organize your essay with a clear introduction, presenting the background and significance of your chosen topic. Develop the body of the essay to delve into the various aspects of your research, supported by evidence from both the novel and scholarly sources. Conclude with a summary that reinforces your key findings and contributions to the understanding of the chosen topic.
- **Language Proficiency:** Demonstrate a high level of Chinese language proficiency by employing precise vocabulary, proper grammar, and coherent sentence structures. Strive for clarity and eloquence in expressing your ideas.
- **Connections to Personal Views:** Weave thoughtful connections to your own views throughout the essay. Illustrate how the chosen topic resonates with your perspectives, fostering a deeper engagement with the material.
- **Consideration of Chinese Culture and Society:** Emphasize the careful consideration of perspectives and themes from Chinese culture. Analyze how cultural elements are represented in the novel and the contemporary context you're exploring.

Grading Rubric

Criteria	*Acceptable*	*Very Good*	*Excellent*
Content Knowledge and Understanding	Makes inferences about the characters and drama context with limited degree of effectiveness Demonstrates a satisfactory understanding of the character's perspective and motives	Makes inferences about the characters and drama context with a considerable degree of effectiveness Demonstrates considerable understanding of the character's perspective and motives	Makes inferences about the characters and drama context with a high degree of effectiveness Demonstrates a thorough understanding of the character's perspectives and motives
Intercultural Communication Competence	Communicates partially developed cultural perspectives Expresses the character's point of view with partially developed complexity Identifies some diversity among cultural themes, and can relate to own experiences	Communicates well considered cultural perspectives Expresses the character's point of view with some complexity Identifies and suspends judgment while critically examining cultural themes, and can compare with own perspectives	Communicates insightful, well considered cultural perspectives Expresses the character's point of view and motives with high degree of complexity Identifies and engages with cultural themes and can critically mediate between own experiences

Criteria	Acceptable	Very Good	Excellent
Language Application and Performance	Applies the elements of drama and language proficiency to establish relationships, place and time, and focus with a partially developed degree of effectiveness Is able to narrate accurately in some time frames Uses precise vocabulary and intonation to express meaning with a partially developed degree of accuracy	Applies the elements of drama and language proficiency to establish relationships, place and time, and focus with a considerable degree of effectiveness Is able to explain and narrate in most time frames Uses precise vocabulary and intonation to express meaning with a considerable degree of accuracy	Applies the elements of drama and language proficiency to establish relationships, place and time, and focus with a high degree of effectiveness Is able to explain in detail and narrate fully in all time frames Uses precise vocabulary and intonation to express meaning with a high degree of accuracy

References

ACTFL-NCSSFL. (2017). *NCSSFL-ACTFL can-do statements*. Retrieved June 1, 2022, from www.actfl.org/resources/ncssfl-actfl-can-do-statements

Byram, M. (2008). *From foreign language education to education for intercultural citizenship: Essays and reflections*. Clevedon: Multilingual Matters.

Byram, M. (2021). *Teaching and assessing intercultural communicative competence* (2nd ed.). Clevedon: Multilingual Matters.

Byram, M., & Wagner, M. (2018). Making a difference: Language education for intercultural and international dialogue. *Foreign Language Annals, 51*(1), 140–151.

Heathcote, D. (1983). Learning, knowing, and languaging in drama: An interview with dorothy heathcote. *Language Arts, 60*(6), 695–701.

McTighe, G., & Wiggins, J. (2005). *Understanding by design* (2nd ed.). Alexandria, VA: Assn. for Supervision & Curriculum Development ASCD.

3 "Dàiyù's Arrival at the Jiǎ Household" 《黛玉进贾府》 (Dàiyù Jìn Jiǎ Fǔ)

Teaching Dream of the Red Chamber 《红楼梦》 (Hónglóumèng) through Experiential Learning

- **Language Proficiency Level:** Intermediate high to advanced low;
- **ICC Developmental Goals:** Open to different perspectives and values;
- **High School/AP Theme:** Families and communities – family structure/ roles; social customs; personal and public identities – the role of the individual in society;
- **Suggested College Course:** Chinese Communication and Composition;
- **Suggested Instructional Time:** Three lessons, about one instructional hour each, followed by a stand-alone week-long project.

1. Introduction

This chapter serves as a captivating introduction to the world of 《红楼梦》 (Hónglóumèng, *Dream of the Red Chamber*), a literary masterpiece authored by the renowned 曹雪芹 (Cáo Xuěqín) during the Qing Dynasty. Within the realm of China's Four Great Classical Novels, *Hónglóumèng* holds a distinguished position, celebrated for its profound depth and complexity. Often hailed as the "encyclopedia" of Chinese culture, it unfolds its pages to reveal deep insights into the intricacies of fate, love, enlightenment, family, duty, and sociopolitical discourse.

The majority of the novel takes place in a noble mansion, the family home of a young aristocratic boy named Jiǎ Bǎoyù. It chronicles his tumultuous coming-of-age journey within the framework of feudal Chinese society, skillfully weaving between the mortal and divine realms. The narrative places a particular emphasis on the ill-fated relationship between Jiǎ Bǎoyù and his destined love, Lín Dàiyù. These two characters, connected through the threads of a past life, find themselves reunited as distant relatives living in close quarters. Their tragic love story has enchanted the hearts of Chinese readers for centuries, embodying a timeless tale of love, fate, and longing.

For American students delving into the world of *Hónglóumèng*, its episodic nature and portrayal of complex relationships offer captivating and rich insights into Chinese social norms and the intricate cosmological conceptions of love, life, and death. As they navigate the narrative, they will embark on a transformative journey into the heart of Chinese culture, history, and literature, expanding their horizons and fostering a deeper appreciation for the complexities of human sentiment interwoven within the stories of this literary masterpiece.

2. Contextualizing the Topic

In the Chinese Communication and Composition course, the semester was divided into two segments. The initial seven weeks were dedicated to the exploration of classical Chinese literature, spanning from myths and legends to iconic works like *Hónglóumèng*. The overarching objectives of the course were to enhance students' spoken and written Chinese proficiency, deepen their understanding of Chinese literary culture through comparative analysis of classical and modern narratives, and empower them to apply their newfound skills and knowledge in both Chinese and English communication contexts.

In the context of a modern Chinese literature course, students engaged in a comprehensive exploration of five key topics through various weekly exercises. These exercises encompassed vocabulary and grammar practice, short composition and translation tasks, recorded speaking practices, five-paragraph essays in Chinese, reading comprehension activities involving adaptations of Chinese classics, and aural comprehension exercises featuring audio clips from adaptations of literary works. Students were encouraged to practice speaking with the teaching assistant weekly.

During the first week of our exploration into *Hónglóumèng*, we embarked on an engaging journey with students. The week commenced with a captivating video introduction, where students were treated to a brief clip from the TV adaptation of the novel. This visual experience served as an excellent starting point for delving into the narrative. After watching the video, a lively class discussion ensued, allowing students to share their interpretations and observations. The focus of this lesson was directed toward a pivotal moment in the story: Dàiyù's arrival at the Rong Mansion. This sequence not only heightened students' interest in the narrative but also set the stage for a more profound exploration of the characters and their intricate relationships. Moreover, this week initiated the discussion of significant cultural concepts, with a particular emphasis on qíng (情 "feeling and emotion"). Students received handouts with clear definitions and explanations of Chinese cultural concepts that have deep roots in centuries of thought and practice. At the end of week one, students were equipped with a better understanding of the novel and a broader cultural awareness, nurturing their intercultural understanding and critical awareness.

Transitioning to the second week of our educational journey, our focus remained on character exploration, with an emphasis on Dàiyù. The week's activities began with a dynamic PowerPoint presentation that illuminated the intricacies of table manners and formality in traditional Chinese settings. This visual aid, complemented by engaging images, provided students with a comprehensive understanding of the social etiquette prevalent during the era of the novel. To gauge students' existing knowledge, they were prompted to share what they knew about the character Dàiyù from *Hónglóumèng*. The highlight of the second week was an experiential activity where we recreated a traditional Chinese dining scene within the classroom. The setup included a low table, cushions, and tableware to enhance the immersive experience. Each student was assigned a role, with one embodying Dàiyù, another taking on the character of Bǎoyù, and the rest assuming the roles of servants or family members. This role-play activity emphasized the importance of adhering to proper table manners, covering aspects such as using chopsticks, serving tea, and engaging in polite conversation while immersing themselves in the language and etiquette appropriate to the time and culture of the novel. After the reenactment, students engaged in a reflective group discussion, sharing their experiences and insights. This activity not only deepened their understanding of the characters but also provided an authentic feel for the cultural nuances and etiquettes of the time, further strengthening their connection with the story.

3. Methodology Highlight: Experiential Learning and Role-Play

Experiential learning, often referred to as "learning by doing," is a pedagogical approach that empowers students to apply abstract knowledge in tangible, real-world scenarios. This dynamic method, originally championed by the renowned education expert and psychologist John Dewey in 1938, places a fundamental emphasis on active engagement and the practical application of language skills in authentic, real-world contexts (Dewey, 1938).

In the domain of foreign language education, experiential learning can manifest itself both within the confines of the classroom and in external contexts. One of its most engaging and immersive forms is through role-play, offering an opportunity to actively practice and refine their language skills. It fosters authentic language use, challenges students to think on their feet, and reinforces the relevance of language in real-life situations. In this scenario (the "table etiquette" scene from *Dàiyù Jìn Jiǎ Fǔ*), students simulate the intricate world of traditional Chinese dining, applying not only their language skills but also their understanding of social customs and etiquette.

An essential facet of experiential learning, and role-play in particular, is the phase of reflection. After students have engaged in these practical, hands-on experiences, they are encouraged to contemplate their performance. What aspects of the scene went smoothly? What challenges did they confront? How can they adapt and apply the knowledge gained from these experiences to future encounters?

Embracing this methodology both fosters active student engagement and equips them with a profound understanding of the real-world applications of their language skills. It cultivates critical thinking, problem-solving abilities, and self-directed learning, enriching their educational journey and preparing them to tackle the challenges of an interconnected, globalized world. Through role-play and experiential learning, students gain not only linguistic proficiency but also the cultural competence necessary to thrive in diverse, international environments.

4. Curricular Modeling

We offer the following complete set of materials ready for use in the classroom along with accompanying activities. These materials and suggested activities support and are guided by the learning outcomes described for robust use of backward design principles (McTighe & Wiggins, 2005).

4.1 Learning Outcomes

The following learning outcomes are three-fold, integrated by situating language skills development in ICC skills development and vice versa. In addition to the sample course context used for illustration, "Chinese Communication and Composition," we also offer sample learning outcomes related to the macro language functions for literary understanding, communication, and composition. You can adapt the three sets of learning outcomes for your course context. The important, common consideration is how these learning outcomes, course-specific learning outcomes, language performance descriptors, and ICC developing goals relate to each other and are exemplified in the class activities. The learning outcomes provide the most important compass for backward design and assessment.

Learning Outcomes as Part of the "Chinese Communication and Composition" Course

- Gain a comprehensive understanding of the plot of the target story and its relevance to broader themes in Chinese history and societal changes. Students are expected to read critically, think analytically, and communicate clearly both in writing and in speech.
- Identify the specific literary devices employed in the texts and analyze how these devices contribute to the meaning of a text. Students are expected to apply similar devices in their communication and composition.
- Produce well-structured written work by adhering to writing conventions of the target language, present information in a descriptive form in the target language. Students are expected to clearly narrate the story through writing, identifying the major characters, themes, and plot of the story.

The corresponding language performance goals are written in the "can do" format of "I can . . ." to make learners understand from their perspectives what they can achieve in this unit (ACTFL-NCSSFL, 2017).

Language Performance Objective (Can-Do Statements)

- I can grasp the central storyline of *Dàiyù Jìn Jiǎ Fǔ* and discern key supporting details that span significant time frames within fictional texts, allowing me to comprehend the context and significance of the table manners scene. (*Interpretive*)

- I can articulate the narrative of *Dàiyù Jìn Jiǎ Fǔ* in both written and spoken forms, presenting it coherently through structured paragraphs. This skill enables me to effectively communicate the essence of the table manners scene. (*Presentational*)
- I can apply the lessons extracted from *Dàiyù Jìn Jiǎ Fǔ* to engage in discussions about my personal experiences dealing with seating culture, and I can offer appropriate solutions. This competence facilitates constructive interpersonal exchanges based on the insights gained from the scene. *(Interpersonal)*

The corresponding ICC development goals are written based on four aspects of ICC: knowledge, attitude, skills, and critical cultural awareness (Byram, 2008, 2021; Byram & Wagner, 2018; inter alia).

Intercultural Communicative Competence Developmental Goals

- **Knowledge:** I can provide a comprehensive description of the dynamics between Jiǎ Bǎoyù and Lín Dàiyù in the table manners scene, elucidating their behaviors and perspectives. I can effectively blend my personal viewpoints, beliefs, and opinions with the cultural values depicted in this specific context.
- **Attitude:** While exploring the table manners scene in *Hónglóumèng*, I can refrain from making hasty judgments about the characters. Instead, I can appreciate the diverse interpretations of etiquette, love, and karma within the narrative. I will perceive the characters as unique individuals with their distinct perspectives, values, and behaviors, especially in this cultural setting.
- **Skill:** I can recognize and apply my knowledge of cultural customs specifically in the context of the table manners scene.
- **Critical Cultural Awareness**: I am conscious of the distinct perspectives and values held by Lín Dàiyù and Jiǎ Bǎoyù, particularly in the context of the table manners scene. I have engaged in introspection, enhancing my understanding of my own interpretations of love and karma, allowing me to relate to these concepts as portrayed within the specific cultural context of *Hónglóumèng*.

4.2 *Materials for Teaching*

A. TV Program Clip "Introduction to the Novel" (Chinese pronunciation with English subtitles)

"Dàiyù's Arrival at the Jiǎ Household" 《黛玉进贾府》

- A short video clip from the 2010 TV program *Dream of Red Mansions*, episode 2 (about ten minutes) that presents the setting of this story, the relationship between the main characters, and the scene that depicts Bǎoyù and Dàiyù meeting for the first time.

B. PowerPoint Presentation (in class)

- A PowerPoint presentation to accompany the introduction including slides summarizing key points, vocabulary, and exercises in Chinese. Use engaging visuals to enhance student engagement and understanding.

C. Excerpt of Rewriting the Story from the Novel *Dream of the Red Chamber* (adapted from chapter 2, "Dàiyù's Arrival at the Jiǎ Household," of the original novel in Chinese)

- The full Chinese text and a list of essential vocabulary words and phrases related to the novel including Pinyin, English translations, and example sentences to help students understand and use these words.

F. Props or Costumes Representing Characters and Settings

- Using visual aids or props to illustrate Chinese customs and traditions mentioned in the novel.

G. Handout with Explanations of "缘分" (yuánfèn, 'love karma'), "还" (huán, 'return karmic debt'), "情" (qíng, 'feeling and emotion'), and "规矩" (guījǔ, 'formality')

- Providing students with explanations of these cultural concepts to enhance their understanding of the context.

H. Comprehension Questions

- A set of comprehension questions that guide students in analyzing the novel's themes, literary devices, and cultural significance. Include both closed-ended and open-ended questions.

4.3 Sample Activities for Teaching Hónglóumèng

In this section, we will detail the activities and exercises that help students engage with the novel and develop their language proficiency and cultural awareness. Each activity is clearly explained with step-by-step instructions, objectives, and estimated time frames. These activities align with the learning outcomes and language performance goals outlined earlier.

Week 1: Introduction to the Novel and Characters

Activity 1: Video Introduction and Discussion (Estimated Time: 20 Minutes)

- Begin the class by reviewing a short clip of the scene in the TV show *Dream of Red Mansions*.

- After watching the video, facilitate a class discussion to encourage students to share their understanding and observations.
- Explain that today's lesson will focus on a pivotal moment in the story: Dàiyù's arrival at the Jia household.
- Provide a brief overview of the novel and its importance in Chinese literature.

Activity 2: Storytelling with Adapted Children's Book
(Estimated Time: 60 Minutes)

- Begin storytelling, emphasizing repetition and clear pronunciation. Pause after each narrative segment to allow students to discuss the content.
- After completing the storytelling, ask students to share their thoughts and interpretations of the narrative. Encourage them to use vocabulary and phrases from the adapted story.
- Conclude the discussion by summarizing key points and transitioning to the next activity.

Activity 3: Cultural Concept Exploration: Explicit Teaching
(Estimated Time: 15 Minutes)

- Summarize the key takeaways from the lesson, emphasizing the cultural concepts explored.
- Provide handouts with definitions and explanations of the Chinese cultural concepts rooted in centuries of thought and practice in the stories.
- Discuss concepts like 缘分 (yuánfèn), 规矩 (guīju), 情(qíng), and 还(huán) and their relevance in *Hónglóumèng*.
- Encourage students to reflect on how understanding these concepts enhances their intercultural understanding and critical intercultural awareness.

Activity 4: Connecting to Contemporary Life (Estimated Time: 20 Minutes)

- Present real-life scenarios or contemporary examples where the concept of yuánfèn and huán might apply, such as chance encounters or meaningful connections.
- Ask students to reflect on these scenarios and discuss how these concepts can be applied to their own lives.
- Encourage students to share personal experiences related to yuánfèn and huán or moments of unexpected connection.

Activity 5: Character Exploration Activity (Estimated Time: 20 Minutes)

- Assign each student a main character role from the novel excerpt. Include character descriptions to help students understand their roles and relationships.
- Provide role-play scenarios based on the novel passage, where characters interact with each other, and yuánfèn and qíng plays a role in their interactions.

- Encourage students to establish connections between themselves and certain characters in the novel. This exercise aims to help students empathize with the characters and gain a deeper understanding of the emotions they experience.

Week 2: Exploring Stories through Role-Play

Activity 1: PowerPoint Presentation about Table Manners and Formality
(Estimated Time: 15 Minutes)

- Prepare a PowerPoint presentation to accompany the scene of Dàiyù's arrival and family dining in chapter 2. Include slides summarizing key points, vocabulary, and exercises in Chinese. Use compelling visuals to enhance student engagement and understanding.
- Compare seating culture in the West to that in the East, including the Confucian influence on Chinese formality of guījǔ.
- Conclude the discussion by applying it to real-world contexts. Help students learn not only about the cultural norms of the novel but also how to adapt and apply our understanding of etiquette and relationships in contemporary settings.

Activity 2: Experiential Activity "Dàiyù at the Dining Table"
(Estimated Time: 30 Minutes)

- Set up a traditional Chinese dining scene in the classroom, including a low table, cushions, and tableware (if available).
- Assign roles to students, with one student as Dàiyù, another as Bǎoyù, and others as servants or family members.
- Guide students in reenacting a dining scene from the novel, emphasizing appropriate table manners with guījǔ, such as how to hold chopsticks, serve tea, and engage in polite conversation.
- Encourage students to immerse themselves in their roles and follow the cultural norms of the time. Encourage them to use the language and etiquette appropriate to the time and culture.
- After the role-play activity, have a group discussion about the students' experiences. Encourage students to reflect on how they felt in their assigned roles and what they learned about the characters and the story.

Activity 3: Research and Presentation

- Encourage students to research and present on other Chinese cultural concepts and their representation in classic literature.
- Evaluate students based on their active participation in role-play activities, their ability to identify cultural concepts in the text and role-play, and their reflections on how these concepts relate to contemporary life.
- Encourage students to suspend judgment, appreciate diverse interpretations of etiquette and love karma, and perceive the characters as unique individuals with distinct perspectives. This aspect of the lesson broadens our intercultural horizons and promotes open-mindedness.

4.4. Implementing Experiential Learning: Role-Play

To apply the theory of experiential learning in a foreign language setting, this lesson utilizes role-play. Role-play is a form of experiential learning that provides students with an opportunity to apply their skills and knowledge in a safe but realistic environment. For this role-play-based activity, students are first equipped with sufficient understanding of the characters or perspectives that they are meant to represent. Then, once this has been achieved, the students are guided by the instructor to engage with their roles in a variety of simulated scenarios. Role-play can be implemented through improvisation or by using a more structured "scripted" approach (Lee, 2015). Because of the complexity of content within this lesson, the more structured method of role-play has been shown to be the most effective way of integrating the content with applied learning. In this structured role-play activity, the instructor provides support by pre-teaching vocabulary and workshopping with students to design a script based on the assigned scenario.

The scenario reenacted for this lesson is based on Dàiyù's first meal with the Jiǎ family. This scene provides a meaningful context for students to explore table manners and dining conventions in a cultural setting. Dàiyù, an outsider in Rong Mansion, must quickly adapt her behavior to show respect for the Jiǎ family elders. Through role-playing this scene, students can explore how family values and societal traditions in China affect the everyday occurrence of sharing a meal with others, while practicing contemporary dining conventions in a simulated setting. After the role-play activity, the instructor can encourage students to discuss and reflect on their own understanding of the different roles one might fill in a social setting and how they can integrate their understanding of language and culture into future real-world applications. In this way, the role-play activity is set apart from the use of dramatic inquiry in the previous chapter. While dramatic inquiry encourages student's creative use of language and unique interpretation of the novel's themes, this role-play activity is less abstract and focuses instead on social identities and cultural norms in a day-to-day setting. In this way, the real-world application of this role-play scene is what makes it a great example of experiential learning.

4.5. Stand-Alone Project Week

Throughout the lesson unit, students will have built up their knowledge of *Hónglóumèng*, familiarizing themselves with the story's crucial themes and main characters. The stand-alone project ties this knowledge together through the creation of a role-playing exercise. Encouraging the students to use their language skills and cultural knowledge in tandem, this role-play project allows students to practically apply their skills in a complex simulation based on one of three scenes in the novel. The three scenes available to students are 一见钟情 (Yījiàn Zhōngqíng, 'Fall in Love at First Sight'), 黛玉葬花 (Dàiyù Zàng Huā, 'Dàiyù Buries Flowers'), and 钗玉婚礼 (Chāi Yù Hūnlǐ, 'Chāi and Yù's Wedding', also known as 黛玉之死 [Dàiyù Zhī Sǐ, 'The Death of Dàiyù']). In context with the broader course, students will have spent time studying the chapters from which these scenes are taken. This allows students to revisit topics that were of particular interest to them throughout the course and reinforces their understanding of the situation as it occurs in the novel. Touching on various aspects of Chinese cosmology, such as reincarnation, karma, love, and fate, this role-play project gives students the opportunity to deepen their understanding of the novel's key cultural concepts.

5. Assessment and Student Feedback on *Hónglóumèng* Experiential Learning

The experiential learning lesson plan for *Hónglóumèng* was designed to immerse students in the world of this classic work, with a particular focus on the significant moment of Dàiyù's arrival in the story. This approach aimed to foster a deeper connection to the characters and themes of the novel. Students engaged in role-play activities and a midterm project to explore the narrative more deeply, followed by a final writing project where they could express their insights.

The feedback from students who participated in these activities was overwhelmingly positive, showcasing the effectiveness of the experiential approach. Here are some key points from the student feedback:

Immersive Experience: Students greatly appreciated the immersive nature of the role-play activities. They highlighted that it allowed them to step into the shoes of the characters, making the story come alive in a way that traditional classroom discussions couldn't achieve. This immersive approach was not only engaging but also educational, as it allowed them to understand the cultural norms and etiquette of the Qing Dynasty.

Cultural Understanding: Students noted that the physicality of the experience, such as enacting a traditional Chinese dining scene, helped them gain a deeper understanding of the cultural norms and etiquette of the time. This experiential learning approach gave them insights into how people sat, ate, and interacted during that era, providing a richer cultural context for the narrative.

Exploring Relationships and Emotions: The midterm *Hónglóumèng* role-play project provided students with a unique opportunity to explore the relationships between the characters and the emotions they experienced in key episodes. Students appreciated the freedom to use their interpretations, which allowed them to develop a profound understanding of the characters and the cultural and social nuances embedded in the narrative.

In the students' final written review, they were encouraged to write about their greatest takeaways from *Hónglóumèng*. Their responses reveal how deeply the stories and characters impacted them, and they were able to convey their insights and personal connections to the text. The following excerpts provide great insight into their experiences and the tangible impact of the experiential learning approach:

Student A: "我在大学四年级的时候读了《红楼梦》，它对我的人生有深远的影响。作为一名美国学生，这本书让我第一次接触到中国古典文学，并很快产生了深刻的共鸣…"
[My encounter with *Dream of the Red Chamber* during my senior year of college has had a profound influence on my life. As an American student, this book introduced me to Chinese classical literature for the first time and quickly resonated with me.]
Student B: "对我来说，这部作品最有影响力的地方就是在明朝和清朝"三教合流"的趋势下，它把道家、儒家和佛家思想融合在具体的故事中，帮助我

开始理解中国的哲学和价值观，而且让我大开眼界，开始来从三种不同的思想中明白人生意义。《红楼梦》虽然是一部古典名著，却依然能穿越时空，引领我们每个人学会如何过更好自己的一生。"

[The novel's most impactful aspect, in my view, is its incorporation of Daoist, Confucian, and Buddhist philosophies within the story. It helped me begin to grasp Chinese philosophy and values, expanding my perspective on life.]

Student C: "最终，经过在道家的自由与儒家的规矩两种相反的思想之间长期的挣扎，宝玉最终选择了皈依佛门。虽然宝玉对自己的身份或者财富都没兴趣，但是他从小到大认为情感依恋是他一生中最重要的方面。可悲的是，当宝玉失去了一生命中的挚爱，他就认为佛家是他唯一的应对方法。"

[What struck me the most about this work is its portrayal of Bǎoyù's journey as he grapples between the opposing philosophies of Daoism and Confucianism, eventually embracing Buddhism. Despite his disinterest in wealth and status, he considers emotional attachment the most significant aspect of life. Sadly, it's when he loses his true love that he turns to Buddhism as his only solace.]

Student D: "对我而言，《红楼梦》是一部非常有价值的、给人警示的作品。正如我们看到的，宝玉的结局是他自己行为的结果，从小到大他从一个极端走向另一个极端，没有平衡不同处境的方法和思想。我认为宝玉受苦是因为他从来没有学会如何控制自己的欲望，比如，他很小的时候生活无忧无虑，直到家族开始衰败，他不得不去考取科举、可最终他还是无法妥协，一直处在选择和放弃两个极端，面对着极大的幸福和极大的悲伤。这让我意识到人们不但应该学会平衡我们的愿望和责任，而且还要学习融合三种哲学思想，这样我们才能综合儒家入世的积极态度和责任心、道家无拘无束的出世态度以及佛教超脱的境界来对抗痛苦。"

[To me, *Dream of the Red Chamber* is a profoundly valuable and cautionary work. Bǎoyù's fate, as we witness, is a result of his own actions, oscillating from one extreme to another throughout his life. This journey has taught me that people need to learn to balance desires and responsibilities, as well as to integrate the three philosophical ideologies – Confucianism, Daoism, and Buddhism – to navigate life's ups and downs.]

6. Teacher's Reflections

In contemplating the challenge of effectively conveying complex stories in the target language and maintaining students' immersion in the narrative, we've come to recognize the paramount importance of this facet in our teaching journey. It's not merely about rendering stories accessible; it's about infusing them with meaning and value for our students. Throughout our teaching experience, we've unearthed various methods to aid students in grasping the narrative, discerning its significance, and embracing the underlying values.

Primarily, the incorporation of visual literacy strategies has emerged as a potent tool. The integration of visual aids – including images, videos, and illustrations – within the storytelling process has proven immensely impactful. These visual elements not only enhance students' comprehension but also captivate their engagement, forging a deeper connection with the narrative. Visuals serve as a bridge, rendering intricate narratives more digestible and fostering a profound understanding of the story's core essence and values.

Furthermore, the pivotal step is linking these stories with key culture concepts to establish a robust educational foundation. These concepts provide the cultural context that enriches the narrative and imparts profound cultural significance. To accomplish this, it's imperative to delve into and spotlight elements such as yuánfèn and qíng and the factors that contribute to falling in love, encompassing personality, fate, and social status. The alignment of the narrative and the experiential learning experience with these cultural concepts creates a bridge for students, enabling them to relate to the story, thus eliciting a profound resonance.

Ultimately, it's this connection and resonance that empowers students to find the story not only comprehensible but also personally meaningful. While experiential learning necessitates additional preparation for both students and instructors, various methods exist to assist educators in either substituting or supplementing traditional learning activities with authentic classroom experiences. To begin, the lesson content should be appropriately complex and culturally relevant yet adaptable to the classroom setting. The content should, above all, possess the potential to nurture students' real-world communication skills. This can be achieved by ensuring that the selected learning episode directly relates to students' daily lives. Moreover, the experiential activity should harmonize with the content. Potential experiential activities within the classroom encompass forms like debates, role-playing, or interactive games. Ideally, these activities will necessitate students' physical, cognitive, and emotional involvement.

This continuous expedition of making intricate narratives more tangible, infusing them with cultural wisdom, and nurturing a profound connection between students and the story is a perpetual exploration. It consistently evolves as we uncover novel strategies to enrich the language and cultural learning experience in our classroom.

Appendices: Sample Teaching Materials

Additional supplemental materials, such as PowerPoint slides, can be requested by scanning this QR code.

"Dàiyù's Arrival at the Jiǎ Household" 《黛玉进贾府》

Appendix 3.1: Preview Packet
《红楼梦》预习作业 (Preview Packet)

1. 课文 Lesson Text

中国古典小说之巅峰

当提到中国古典文学时，人们往往会说"唐宋诗词，明清小说"。这句话表达了在两千多年的中国文学发展中，唐宋时期的诗歌达到了成熟的高度，而明清时期的小说则显得最出色，尤其是《三国演义》、《水浒传》、《西游记》和《红楼梦》，被誉为中国的"四大名著"。这些小说无论是在艺术手法还是在思想深度上，这些作品都代表了中国古典小说的巅峰，为我们提供了理解中国传统社会的机会。

　　古典小说中最有名的一部《红楼梦》，是清朝曹雪芹用了二十年的时间写的，去世时还不到五十岁。《红楼梦》一共有一百二十回，主要讲述了两个悲剧：一个是贾宝玉和林黛玉相爱却不能结婚的爱情悲剧，另一个是他们生活的贵族家庭从繁荣走向衰亡的时代悲剧，曹雪芹通过小说向我们展示了对生命和人性的思考。在文学的艺术元素上，诗歌、音乐、绘画，这些文学元素都在小说中有精彩的描绘。

　　小说中的主要人物宝玉和黛玉是表兄妹，两人彼此深爱。宝玉心地善良，蔑视世俗，而宝玉的反叛精神只有黛玉能理解。黛玉聪明漂亮，但体弱多病又多愁善感。后来宝玉被父母欺骗结婚，娶了另一个表妹薛宝钗。黛玉知道以后伤心离世，这个贵族家庭也很快地衰落，在故事结尾宝玉也出家当了和尚。

　　"黛玉葬花"是全书中一场最有象征意义和情感深度的重要场景。有一天黛玉看到园子里的花儿被风吹落，她不愿意看到美丽洁净的花被人踩，于是把花埋起来，然后写了一首非常感人的《葬花吟》，其中最有名的诗句："一朝春尽红颜老，花落人亡两不知。"展现了她对生命的敏感，对美好的追求，以及对无常命运的深刻认知。

　　总体来说，《红楼梦》不仅是一部"百科全书"式的文学之作，更是一部让读者人跨越时空产生共鸣的生命之书。透过曹雪芹的文字，我们看到了作者对于爱情、人性和生命的真诚追求和思考，这使得这部作品成为不朽的经典之作。

改编自《新编中文课外阅读丛书》文章

2. 生词 New Words

1)	四大名著	sì dà míngzhù	Four Great Classical Novels
2)	古典	gǔdiǎn	classical
3)	唐宋	Táng Sòng	Tang and Song (dynasties)
4)	出色	chūsè	outstanding
5)	艺术手法	yìshù shǒufǎ	artistic techniques
6)	思想深度	sīxiǎng shēndù	depth of thought
7)	巅峰	diānfēng	summit
8)	传统社会	chuántǒng shèhuì	traditional society
9)	耗时	hàoshí	spent time

10)	爱情悲剧	àiqíng bēijù	tragedy of love
11)	贵族家庭	guìzú jiātíng	aristocratic family
12)	衰亡	shuāiwáng	decline
13)	思考	sīkǎo	contemplate
14)	艺术元素	yìshù yuánsù	artistic elements
15)	表兄妹	biǎo xiōng mèi	cousin
16)	蔑视	mièshì	disdain
17)	反叛精神	fǎnpàn jīngshén	rebellious spirit
18)	体弱多病	tǐruò duōbìng	physically weak and often sick
19)	伤心离世	shāngxīn líshì	depart in sorrow
20)	衰落	shuāiluò	decline
21)	出家	chūjiā	become a monk/nun
22)	象征意义	xiàngzhēng yìyì	symbolic significance
23)	生命之书	shēngmìng zhī shū	book of life
24)	真诚追求	zhēnchéng zhuīqiú	sincere pursuit
25)	描绘	miáohuì	depict
26)	敏感	mǐngǎn	sensitive
27)	深刻	shēnkè	profound
28)	共鸣	gòngmíng	resonance
29)	透过	tòuguò	through
30)	曹雪芹	Cáo Xuěqín	author of *Dream of the Red Chamber*

3. 练习

a. 生词 Vocabulary: Translate the Following Words and Find the Root of Each Team

1) 文章/ 文化/ 文艺/ 文明/ 文字
2) 悲剧/ 喜剧/ 戏剧/ 京剧/ 电视剧
3) 封建社会/ 现代社会 / 社交
4) 蔑视/ 轻视/ 重视/ 近视
5) 反叛/ 反对/ 反义词
6) 古典文学/ 现代文学

b. 短语 Paraphrase: Please Explain the Following Words in Chinese

1) 出色:_____
2) 世俗:_____
3) 功名;_____
4) 体弱多病:_____
5) 多愁善感:_____

c. 回答问题 Reading Comprehension

1) 中国最有名的古典小说都有哪些？
2) 《红楼梦》的作者是谁？故事讲述了什么故事？

3) 林黛玉和贾宝玉的性格特点是什么？
4) 林黛写了《葬花吟》，你认为这样的情节代表了什么？
5) 《红楼梦》为什么这么有名？

Appendix 3.2: Enrichment Guide

《红楼梦》 Enrichment Guide

1. 故事介绍 Background

Dream of the Red Chamber (《红楼梦》 *Hónglóumèng*), penned by a man named Cáo Xuěqín (曹雪芹) during the Qing Dynasty (1644–1911), is a revered classical work celebrated for its vibrant portrayal of 18th-century Chinese life. The narrative unfolds the trials and tribulations of an elite family, influenced profoundly by Confucianism, Daoism, and Buddhism. The novel is a literary masterpiece, known as one of China's "four great classical novels" (四大名著 sì dà míngzhù). *Dream of the Red Chamber* has enchanted Chinese readers for centuries, often referred to as the "encyclopedia" of Chinese culture. Its pages reveal culturally rich insights into the intricacies of fate, love, enlightenment, family, duty, and sociopolitical discourse of its time.

The storyline primarily follows Bǎoyù, detailing his upbringing and interactions with various characters, notably women. The novel begins with the supernatural origins of Bao-yu as a magical stone, initially unused by the goddess Nüwa in repairing the sky. Born with a piece of jade (a magical stone) in his mouth due to the interventions of a Buddhist monk and a lame Daoist priest, Bǎoyù is destined to experience the pleasures of the mundane, mortal world or "red dust."

The basic narrative involves the conflict between Bǎoyù and his family, particularly regarding his laziness and academic shortcomings. The plot also unfolds a complex love story, with Bǎoyù anticipating marriage to Dàiyù, while his family arranges a union with the more robust Bǎochāi. Unexpected events transpire on Bǎoyù's wedding day, leading to Dàiyù's heartbreak and eventual demise. The novel weaves a series of family tragedies, but Bǎoyù eventually fulfills his families wishes by succeeding in the civil examinations and fathering a son with Bǎochāi. In the end, the Jiǎ family's fortunes, though initially fallen, experience a resurgence.

This lesson, we will discover the impact of *Dream of the Red Chamber* on Chinese literature, as well as explore how the novel's characters and themes can even connect to our lives today.

2. 历史背景 Historical Background

While the novel is commonly known as 《红楼梦》 (*Hónglóumèng, Dream of the Red Chamber*), the original 18th-century manuscript bore the title 《石头记》 (*Shítoujì, Story of the Stone*). In fact, multiple titles are associated with various versions of the manuscript, which were initially written and circulated in installments. The author, Cáo Xuěqín, composed the first 80 chapters over two decades, sharing them within his social circle. The complete novel was posthumously published

"Dàiyù's Arrival at the Jiǎ Household" 《黛玉进贾府》 61

after Cáo Xuěqín's death in the 1760s, and his authorship remained largely unknown to scholars until the 20th century. Many consider *Dream of the Red Chamber* a loose autobiography of Cáo Xuěqín's life, mirroring his own family's rise to prominence and subsequent fall from imperial favor.

3. 人物介绍 Introduction of Characters

Characters in *Dream of the Red Chamber* are richly depicted, with over 400 named individuals and around 40 main characters. The "Twelve Beauties of Jinling," particularly Lín Dàiyù and Xuē Bǎochāi, form a love triangle with the central male protagonist, Jiǎ Bǎoyù.

1) Bǎoyù (宝玉), born with a jade stone, represents the sole male heir of Rong Manor, resisting societal norms. The novel revolves around his coming-of-age, navigating familial expectations, and ultimately choosing love over duty.
2) Dàiyù (黛玉), characterized by fragility and emotion, shares a past life connection with Bǎoyù, where he was a stone and she a wilting flower. Their reincarnated selves, unaware of this bond, become entangled in a tragic love story.
3) Bǎochāi (宝钗), Bǎoyù's betrothed and Dàiyù's opposite in many aspects, suffers from an excess of yang energy. The novel explores their contrasting characters and the consequences of their forced marriage.

4. 文化主题 Key Cultural Themes

Dream of the Red Chamber is often hailed as a comprehensive repository of ancient Chinese culture, encapsulating the essence of Chinese aesthetics and worldview. Serving as the apex of China's diverse literary tradition, the novel seamlessly incorporates various forms of Chinese literature, including diverse genres of poetry. Its profound cultural significance extends to shedding light on virtually every facet of both elite and popular culture. From family life, social roles, and values to religious practices, attitudes, amusements, food, medicine, clothing, and architecture, the novel provides an intricate panorama of Chinese societal norms. The cultural themes woven into the narrative further enhance its depth. Here are some examples:

1) **情 (qíng, 'love and senitment'):** This theme intricately explores the multifaceted aspects of love and desire, encapsulating the richness and complexity of emotions. The term "qíng" encompasses a spectrum of meanings, ranging from objective truth to the depth of sentiment and passion, contributing to the nuanced portrayal of relationships within the narrative.
2) **缘分 (yuánfèn, 'love karma'):** The concept of yuánfèn illuminates the narrative with the notion of serendipitous encounters and connections that transcend mere coincidence or destiny. Linked to the principles of karma and past incarnations, yuánfèn shapes relationships and events, portraying a sense of predestined interconnection that goes beyond the characters' immediate understanding.

3) 还 (huán, 'return karmic debt'): Symbolizing the concept of return and repayment, huán is particularly evident in the character Dàiyù's poignant expression of karmic debt through tears. This emotional repayment is intricately woven into her past encounter with Bǎoyù when he existed as a magical stone. The theme of huán adds a layer of complexity to the characters' fates, emphasizing the cyclical nature of cause and effect.
4) 规矩 (guījǔ, 'social etiquette and norms'): It refers to social etiquette and norms. The novel meticulously portrays the intricacies of societal expectations, manners, and codes of conduct prevalent in ancient Chinese society. Guījǔ serves as a guiding principle that shapes the characters' behavior, highlighting the delicate balance between individual desires and societal expectations. This exploration adds a layer of realism to the novel, showcasing how societal rules influence characters' decisions and relationships, contributing to a deeper understanding of the cultural fabric woven into the narrative.

By grounding the narrative in these cultural concepts, the novel not only provides a rich cultural tapestry but also invites readers to contemplate the universal themes of destiny, reciprocity, and the complexities of human emotion that transcend cultural boundaries.

5. 文学手法 Literary Devices Employed by Cáo Xuěqín

Dream of the Red Chamber poses a challenge even for native Chinese speakers due to its intricate plot and characters. The novel's richness lies in hidden symbolism behind seemingly trivial daily life details.

1) Poetry is a prominent literary device, with each poem foreshadowing key plot points. For instance, Dàiyù's flower burial poem symbolizes her "pureness" and anticipates her tragic fate.
2) Homophones are utilized, associating scenes with characters. The mention of snow (雪 xuě) in a poem typically relates to Xuē Bǎochāi. Bǎoyù's surname, Jiǎ (贾), serves as a homophone for "fake" (假 jiǎ), potentially hinting at the Jiǎ family's corruption or the novel's illusory nature.

6. 翻译 English Translations of Dream of the Red Chamber

English translations of *Dream of the Red Chamber* have been instrumental in bringing Cáo Xuěqín's Chinese literary masterpiece to a global readership. Various translators have undertaken the challenge of capturing the richness and nuances of the original work. For instance, David Hawkes' translation, known as *Story of the Stone*, is celebrated for its meticulous attention to linguistic intricacies, maintaining the elegance of the Chinese prose. Another notable translation by Yang Xianyi and Gladys Yang strives for clarity and accessibility, making the narrative more approachable for English-speaking audiences. In recent years, David Lattimore's translation has added a contemporary perspective to this classical piece. The nuances of Chinese culture, including Confucian and Daoist influences, often present challenges in translation. These translations not only serve as linguistic bridges but also as cultural ambassadors, facilitating a cross-cultural exchange that allows readers to delve into the profound themes and intricate storytelling of *Dream of the Red Chamber*.

7. 阅读视角 Diverse Perspectives on the Novel: A Multifaceted Exploration

Dream of the Red Chamber unfolds as a literary mosaic, offering a multitude of traditional interpretations – whether seen as a poignant love story, a satirical political commentary, or an autobiographical narrative. Significantly, it pays homage to women, with the term "Red Chamber" encapsulating the essence of the women's quarters in a traditional familial context. At its essence, the novel delves into the fundamental theme of a quest for identity and the pursuit of purpose in life. From the vantage point of Chinese Communist interpretations, the narrative serves as a critique of "feudal" society, unraveling the intricacies of societal structures. Beyond its cultural representation, the novel serves as a reflection of Chinese aesthetics and worldviews, embodying the culmination of China's diverse literary tradition, which spans various forms of poetry. Its overarching cultural value is profound, casting light on elite and popular culture, covering family life, social roles, values, religious practices, attitudes, amusements, food, medicine, clothing, and architecture. Furthermore, it astutely underscores the disparity between theoretical ideals and practical realities in Chinese social life, adding nuanced layers to its societal critique.

Appendix 3.3: Study Packet

《红楼梦》学习作业 (Study Packet)

1. 课文录音 Recording

a. Sample: https://voca.ro/1ggHESvA6kZN
b. Student's recording link

2. 生词练习 Vocabulary

a. Please Translate the Antonyms

1) 蔑视 vs. 尊重 _____
2) 反叛 vs. 顺从_____
3) 揭露 vs. 掩盖_____
4) 结尾 vs. 开始_____
5) 悲剧 vs. 喜剧_____
6) 衰亡 vs. 繁荣_____

b. Make Sentences with the Following Words

1) 古典:
2) 成熟:
3) 彼此:

4) 多愁善感：
5) 衰落：

c. 语法 Grammar: Please Make Sentences with the Following Sentence Structures

1) 在 . . . 时，(when . . .)
2) 不论 A 还是 B，都 . . . (No matter A or B, they're all . . .)
3) 一个是 . . .，另一个是 . . . (One is . . ., the other is . . .)
4) 并不是 . . .，而是 . . . (not . . ., but . . .)

d. 翻译 Translation: Please Translate the Following Chinese Sentences into English

1) 在两千多年的中国文学发展中，唐宋时期的诗歌最成熟，明清的小说最出色。
2) 不论是在艺术手法还是在思想深度上，《四大名著》都代表了中国古典小说的最高峰，为我们提供了理解中国传统社会的机会。
3) 《红楼梦》主要讲述了两个悲剧：一个是贾宝玉和林黛玉相爱却不能结婚的爱情悲剧；另一个是他们生活的贵族家庭从繁荣走向衰亡的时代悲剧。

e. 课外阅读 Reading Comprehension: Read the Stories and Watch TV Drama Clip, and Then Answer the Following Questions

第一回：宝玉出生

女娲补天的时候，剩下了一块石头，丢在了山下。这块石头很伤心，因为它觉得自己没有用。一天，有两位神仙从山下经过，一边休息一边谈论人间的美好。石头听了很好奇，他也想去人间看一看。神仙告诉石头："人间的事情都不完美，你还是要去吗？"石头回答："我一定要去！"神仙就把它带走了。

贾家是京城有名的"四大家族"之一。贾母有两个儿子和一个女儿。她的孙子出生的时候嘴里面有一块玉，所以叫"宝玉"。宝玉的妈妈、奶奶、姐姐都很疼爱他，他的爸爸是当官的，所以对他很严厉。宝玉又聪明又善良，可是他很贪玩，不喜欢学习。

Vocabulary: https://quizlet.com/_6eirki
Video clip: www.youtube.com/watch?v=virK4GUMM_w&t=61s (start-05:00)

Questions

1) 石头被谁丢在山下？
2) 石头为什么伤心？
3) 两位神仙在谈论什么？
4) 石头为什么想去人间？神仙答应石头的要求了吗？
5) 贾家在京城是什么地位？
6) 贾母有几个孩子？都有谁？贾母和宝玉是什么关系？
7) "宝玉"为什么叫这个名字？

"Dàiyù's Arrival at the Jiǎ Household" 《黛玉进贾府》

8) 介绍一下宝玉的性格。
9) 谁疼爱"宝玉"？谁对"宝玉"严厉？
10) 请用5句话介绍一下第一故事（什么时候，谁，在哪儿，发生什么）

第二回：黛玉进贾府

传说灵河岸上有一块三生石，它的旁边有一个绛珠草。每天石头用雨露帮助小草长大。小草说"石头用雨水帮助过我，现在他要去做人，我也要和他去人间，把我一生的眼泪都还给他。"

林黛玉聪明漂亮，却体弱多病，六岁的时候母亲因病去世。后来，贾母心疼她没人教养，接黛玉和她一起住。黛玉坐船从苏州到金陵，下船的时候已经有轿子在等她了。黛玉听母亲说过外祖母家非常有钱有地位，她从轿窗向外看，街上很繁华，过了一会儿，看见大门口站着两个石狮子，门上面写着几个字。临走的时候，爸爸告诉她不要多说话、做事要留心，黛玉一想到自己要在这个陌生的城市生活，心里越来越觉得不安和孤单。

Vocabulary: https://quizlet.com/_6ej1z9
Video clip: www.youtube.com/watch?v=virK4GUMM_w&t=61s (35:36 to the end)

Questions

1) 三生石每天做什么帮助绛珠草长大？
2) 小草为什么要跟石头去人间？
3) 为什么林黛玉要离开自己的家？
4) 林黛玉是怎样从苏州到金陵的？
5) 林黛玉从母亲那里听说过什么？
6) 林黛玉从轿窗里都看见了什么？
7) 林黛玉为什么心里会觉得不安？
8) 离开家的时候，林黛玉的爸爸告诉她什么？
9) 为什么黛玉觉得不安和孤单？
10) 请简单介绍一下林黛玉的性格。

第三回：宝黛第一次见面

黛玉吃完饭，听见仆人说："宝玉来了！"黛玉一看见宝玉，就大吃一惊，心里想："太奇怪了，好像是在哪里见过她，怎么这么眼熟？"

进来的是一位英俊的公子，穿着大红袍子，脖子上戴着一块儿玉。宝玉也发现多了一个妹妹，他知道是他的表妹、林姑妈的女儿。在宝玉眼中，黛玉有一双水灵灵的大眼睛，脸上有淡淡的忧伤，像仙女一样美丽。

宝玉坐在黛玉旁边，一边仔细地看她一边问：妹妹上学了吗？黛玉回答说：只上了一年学，认识几个字。宝玉又问，妹妹叫什么，黛玉说了自己的名，宝玉又问：字呢？黛玉回答"无字。"宝玉马上玩笑到，那就叫你"颦颦"吧，因为你常常皱眉！

Vocabulary: https://quizlet.com/_6ej1z9
Video clip: www.youtube.com/watch?v=r0RaJLBu4DM&list=PLZXpZVzkPMb4_MKVg2R2Es7BTtEZQfCDx&index=2 (11:35–14:51)

"Dàiyù's Arrival at the Jiǎ Household" 《黛玉进贾府》

Questions: https://quizlet.com/_6exohw

1) 宝玉什么时候看见黛玉？
2) 林黛玉看见宝玉的时候，有什么感觉？
3) 在林黛玉眼中，宝玉是什么样子的？穿了什么样的衣服？
4) 在贾宝玉眼中，黛玉是什么样子的？
5) 林黛玉上了几年学？
6) 林黛玉有"字"吗？
7) 宝玉为什么叫黛玉"颦颦"？

Appendix 3.4: Role-Play Project Guideline
《红楼梦》角色表演

1. Introduction and Topics

For this role-play project, your task is to perform a role-play with your classmates and present your understanding of Dàiyù and Bǎoyù's relationship. You can choose from the following episodes:

- 一见钟情 ("Love at First Sight)
- 黛玉葬花 (Dàiyù Buries Flowers)
- 黛玉之死 (The Death of Dàiyù)

2. Teamwork and Division of Responsibility

All team members are expected to work collaboratively, making equal contributions. However, specific responsibilities are assigned as follows:

- Producer: Design the story, coordinate, and participate in all aspects.
- Actors: Portray the roles of Bǎoyù and Dàiyù.

3. Requirement

- Create a script in Chinese. Avoid writing in English and translating, as it may lead to vocabulary, phrase, and sentence issues.
- Memorize the script; a well-prepared performance enhances confidence and relaxation.
- Ensure the role-play is a minimum of 5 minutes (15 sentences per student, at least 45 sentences in total).
- Incorporate a minimum of 10 new vocabulary words and 5 grammatical structures learned during this term.

4. **Timeline**

- First Scripts: Submit by 9 p.m. on Sunday, week 9 (around 40 sentences in total).
- Final Scripts: Further details to be discussed.
- Rehearsal: Schedule to be determined.
- Final YouTube link submission on BB before class on Wednesday, week 10.

5. **Rubric**

Category	D	C	B	A
Content and Scripts	Role-play is very short. Script lacks class content.	Role-play is short or lacks class content. Modest script.	Role-play is long enough. Good script with class content.	Role-play meets required length. Well-written, natural script.
Comprehensibility	Inaudible, mumbling, fast/slow speech impedes understanding.	Soft speaking, mumbling, or speed issues affect understanding.	Generally loud, clear voices, with some issues.	Consistently loud, clear voices, easy to understand.
Language	Chinese not used or consistently inaccurate. Pronunciation/grammar errors.	Chinese used with difficulties due to errors. Pronunciation/grammar errors.	Generally effective use of Chinese with some difficulties. Pronunciation/grammar errors present.	Effective use of Chinese, conveying meaning with minimal difficulties.
Staging	No presence in front of the room; role-play not memorized.	Stand in front, little setting conveyance, poor memorization.	Well-thought alignment; lapses in memorization; props may be used.	Effective use of props and stage; faultless memorization.
Teamwork and Participation	Dominant group member; others contribute little or act as props.	Dominant members; limited contributions from others.	One member has a lesser role; valuable contributions from others.	All members make equal, valuable contributions to the dialogue.
Video Presentation & Props	Poor video and sound; ineffective scenes; no props.	Adequate video and sound; somehow edited properly; no props.	Good video and sound; edited properly; used props.	Excellent video and sound; well-edited scenes; effective use of props.

References

ACTFL-NCSSFL. (2017). *NCSSFL-ACTFL can-do statements.* Retrieved June 1, 2022, from www.actfl.org/resources/ncssfl-actfl-can-do-statements

Byram, M. (2008). *From foreign language education to education for intercultural citizenship: Essays and reflections.* Clevedon: Multilingual Matters.

Byram, M. (2021). *Teaching and assessing intercultural communicative competence* (2nd ed.). Clevedon: Multilingual Matters.

Byram, M., & Wagner, M. (2018). Making a difference: Language education for intercultural and international dialogue. *Foreign Language Annals, 51*(1), 140–151.

Dewey, J. (1938). *Experience and education.* New York, NY: Macmillan Company.

Lee, S. (2015). Revisit role-playing activities in foreign language teaching and learning: Remodeling learners' cultural identity? *Electronic Journal of Foreign Language Teaching, 12*(1), 346–359.

McTighe, G., & Wiggins, J. (2005). *Understanding by design* (2nd ed.). Alexandria, VA: Assn. for Supervision & Curriculum Development ASCD.

4 "To Borrow Arrows with Thatched Boats" 《草船借箭》 (Cǎochuán Jièjiàn)

Teaching *the Romance of the Three Kingdoms* 《三国演义》 (Sānguó Yǎnyì) through Question Formulation Technique

- **Language Proficiency Level:** Intermediate low to high;
- **ICC Development Goal:** Identify and interpret the implicit value from the story "To Borrow Arrows with Thatched Boat" and relate it to the values from their own experience and other cultures;
- **High School/AP Theme:** Personal and public identity – heroes and national figures; science & technology innovations;
- **Suggested High School Course:** Chinese 4, AP Chinese Language & Culture;
- **Suggested College Course:** Chinese Communication and Composition; Explore China Through Films;
- **Suggested Instructional Time:** Twelve 50-minute lessons.

1. Introduction

This module features one of the most well-known stories 《草船借箭》 (Cǎochuán Jièjiàn, 'To Borrow Arrows with Thatched Boats') from the famous Battle of Red Cliff (赤壁, Chìbì) in 《三国演义》 (Sānguó Yányì, *The Romance of the Three Kingdoms*), one of the Four Great Classic Novels, first published in 1552 and attributed to 罗贯中 (Luó Guànzhōng). 《三国演义》 is one of the best-known and most well-loved stories across Asia and has recently begun developing new audiences around the world. The greatest contribution of 《三国演义》 in the history of Chinese literature lies in its comprehensive portrayal of historical events and complex characters, showcasing the essence of strategic warfare and political intrigue during the Three Kingdoms period. It remains a monumental work that continues to captivate readers with its enduring themes of loyalty, ambition, and the pursuit of power. 《三国演义》 has had a significant impact on modern culture, both within China and internationally. It has inspired numerous adaptations in various forms of media – such as films, television series, video games, and even board games – contributing to its long-lasting popularity and the continued exploration of

DOI: 10.4324/9781003377276-4

its rich narrative and iconic characters. Additionally, its themes of strategy, loyalty, and leadership have permeated popular culture, influencing storytelling, character archetypes, and strategic thinking in various creative works and entertainment mediums around the world.

One of the major challenges of teaching classic Chinese literature is how to spark students' interest and relate the content to foreign language students who have no previous knowledge of the text. We have found that students respond enthusiastically to the 2009 film version *Red Cliff II* 《赤壁二》, and their interest becomes even stronger when they see a connection between the themes in the film and their current lives. Additionally, Question Formulation Technique (QFT), developed by Right Question Institute, a structured method to generate and improve questions, will be demonstrated in this chapter to showcase how teachers can more efficiently engage students to learn by asking and answering the questions generated on their own. Together with the connection strategy (text-to-text, text-to-self, text-to-world; see chapter 6 for more details about this method), students are able to see how the classic works written more than one thousand years ago can still relate to themselves and guide them to develop intercultural communicative competence (ICC).

The story that we chose to further explore after watching the movie *Red Cliff II* 《赤壁二》 is 《草船借箭》 (Cǎochuán Jièjiàn, 'To Borrow Arrows with Thatched Boats'), which features the genius of the military advisor 诸葛亮 (Zhūgé Liàng). Zhūgé Liàng's success in a "mission impossible," in which he exploits favorable timing, geographic location, and human factors (天时地利人和, tiānshí dìlì rénhé) will serve as a prompt for students to discuss the following questions to help develop their ICC skills: How have favorable timing, geographic location, and human relations, that is, "天时地利人和," contributed to a notable success in your life? How have some groups of people's opportunities been limited by lacking "天时地利人和?" Inspired by Zhūgé Liàng and his way of "thinking outside the box," do you know other occurrences that feature this approach?

2. Contextualizing the Topic

The Chinese program in our high school has been developing its own thematic units for all levels for more than ten years, except for AP Chinese Language and Culture, which gives the teachers more freedom to include the latest materials. Overall, student feedback suggests that the emerging curriculum gives them a greater sense of engagement and accomplishment in learning. As a result, the number of students in our Chinese language program has been steadily increasing. The unit illustrated in this chapter is used in a high school Chinese world language course titled *Chinese Four Accelerated*, which is also a one-year dual-credit course. More than 90% of the students are heritage speakers who have Chinese learning experience before entering high school. They are placed into different levels based on their placement test results using the ACTFL Assessment of Performance toward Proficiency in Languages® (AAPPL). Two higher-level Chinese courses followed *Chinese Four Accelerated*: *AP Chinese Language and Culture* and *Chinese Six: Chinese*

Literature, Media, and Culture. The course *Chinese Four Accelerated* covers current and historical figures, customs and traditions, environment protection, teenagers' lives, and Chinese movies. Our movie unit includes three movies that help students to explore culture and history from different perspectives; specifically, the film *Ne Zha* enables students to delve into Chinese mythology, the film *Red Cliff II* showcases a part of ancient Chinese history, and *To Live* guides them to experience Chinese people's lives in modern history.

The movie unit chose *Red Cliff II* for two main reasons. First, it provides students with comprehensive insight into the historical background, political struggles, heroic figures, and war strategies of China's Three Kingdoms period. Second, *Red Cliff II* vividly portrays the well-known story of "To Borrow Arrows with Thatched Boats." This story also provides an excellent opportunity for students to discuss the concepts of "thinking outside the box" and "天时地利人和" (favorable timing, geographic location, and human factors) and its significance in strategic decision-making. In the decision between only watching the story of "To Borrow Arrows with Thatched Boats" or viewing the entire movie of *Red Cliff II*, the latter was chosen. This way, students can gain a comprehensive understanding of the history of the Three Kingdoms period, the Battle of Red Cliff, and the strategic tactics involved. It will provide them with a better knowledge base for future discussions on the concepts of "天时地利人和" and the strategy of "thinking outside the box" when delving into the story of "To Borrow Arrows with Thatched Boats."

We begin the unit with students sharing their research and learning about the Four Great Classic Novels, historical background, the Battle of Red Cliff, other decisive battles in world history, and the details of the stratagems employed in the movie. The QFT (see section 3 for more details about this technique) is applied to guide students to develop questions of their own interest for this movie unit and to search for the answers and needed target language to express their answers during the learning process. The goal of this lesson is not only to lead students to master the topics mentioned but also to see the power of using their own questions to guide their learning.

While watching the movie, students are expected to take note of various scenes and apply the connection strategy (text-to-text, text-to-self, text-to-world) (refer to chapter 6 for a detailed explanation of this strategy) to establish links relevant to those scenes (refer to appendix 4.5 《草船借箭》 During: Make Connection; Text-to-Text, Text-to-Self, Text-to-World) in their preferred language. This method respects students' prior knowledge and readies them for subsequent discussions and presentations, during which they can openly share their viewpoints about the movie and the connections they've formed. Throughout this process, students get the chance to peer out of the "window" (the film) and perceive the world from a distinct cultural or temporal viewpoint. They also get the opportunity to "look at themselves in the mirror" and contemplate their own experiences, connecting their learning to events unfolding in the broader world. Armed with insights gained through observing, interpreting, analyzing, and evaluating while peering through the "window" and reflecting in the "mirror," students can engage in culturally appropriate communication when they unlatch the "sliding door" and immerse themselves in others' perspectives. Thus, this movie unit of "To Borrow Arrows with Thatched Boats" not only aids in students' language acquisition but also nurtures their intercultural competence development.

3. Methodology Highlight: Question Formulation Technique (QFT)

Question Formulation Technique is a structured method developed by the Right Question Institute (RQI, 2023) to teach and enhance critical thinking, creativity, and problem-solving skills. It is a collaborative and participatory process that empowers individuals to develop better questions and improve their ability to think critically and engage in deeper discussions. QFT brings students' attention to finding the answers to the questions they generate themselves. This methodology is especially useful for teaching classical literature such as 《赤壁之战》 (Chìbì Zhīzhàn, "The Battle of Red Cliff") and "To Borrow Arrows with Thatched Boats," as its rich content may overwhelm students and leave them unclear as to what should be their focus during the learning process.

Enabling students to formulate their own questions and discover answers during the learning process of the Battle of Red Cliff and "To Borrow Arrows with Thatched Boats" encourages critical thinking about the material and emphasizes acquiring both the content and language needed to address those questions. This process prepares students to perform at the end of the unit since the assessments closely tie to the questions they've generated.

In the context of this lesson unit, QFT was found to be most effective when students were equipped with ample background information on the film and its characters. Therefore, the construction of this unit utilizes appropriate pre-teaching materials and activities to help the students gain background knowledge first, then generate meaningful questions during the QFT process before watching the movie *Red Cliff II*. With the questions generated, students can then focus their attention on finding the answers to those questions during the movie-watching process.

4. Curricular Modeling

We offer the following complete set of materials ready for use in the classroom along with accompanying activities. These materials and suggested activities support and are guided by the learning outcomes described for the robust use of backward design principles (McTighe & Wiggins, 2005).

4.1 Learning Objectives and Primary Performance Assessments

Learning objectives are composed of two parts: language performance objectives and intercultural communication competence objectives. All of the learning objectives are written in the "can do" format of "I can . . ." to make learners understand from their perspectives what they can achieve in this unit (ACTFL-NCSSFL, 2017).

Language Performance Objective (Can-Do Statements)

- I can follow the main story of *Red Cliff II* "To Borrow Arrows with Thatched Boats" and some supporting details in the movie and the fictional texts. (*Interpretive*)
- I can tell the story of *Red Cliff II* "To Borrow Arrows with Thatched Boats" and the major strategies applied in writing and speaking through organized paragraphs. (*Presentational* and *Interpersonal*)
- I can apply the lessons learned to relate the three elements of "good timing, geographic location, and human factors" and "thinking outside the box" to my own experience, to the experiences from other texts, and to the world around me. (*Presentational* and *Interpersonal*)

The corresponding ICC development goals are written based on four aspects of ICC known as KASA: knowledge, attitude, skills, and critical intercultural awareness (Byram, 2008, 2021; Byram & Wagner, 2018; inter alia).

Intercultural Communication Competence Objectives

- **Knowledge:** I can describe fully the story of *Red Cliff II and* "To Borrow Arrows with Thatched Boats" *and* explain the strategies applied in the movie.
- **Attitude:** When describing *Red Cliff II and* "To Borrow Arrows with Thatched Boats," I value and appreciate the wisdom exemplified in the stratagems applied during the battles and further develop an appreciation for the resources that I have and show more sympathy to those who do not.
- **Skill:** I can relate the three elements of success – "favorable timing, geographic location, and human factors" – to my own experiences (text-to-self), the ones from other stories, articles, or movies (text-to-text), or experiences in the world around me (text-to-world).
- **Critical Cultural Awareness:** I am aware of the different perspectives and values that different parties of the battles hold. I am also aware of the advantages and disadvantages that both I and others have in terms of "favorable timing, geographic location, and human factors" when it comes to achieving success.

The associated language performance assessments are outlined in the following table, while the interpretive reading assessments and speaking prompts are available in the online supplements for this chapter (refer to the appendices section).

Table 4.1 Main Performance Assessment of "To Borrow Arrows with Thatched Boats"

Communicative Modes	Language Performance Assessment
Interpretive Mode	• Identify the main point and some details in reading selections about the scenes related to the major themes. • Identify the main point and some details that students made in the writing about the movie and text-to-text, text-to-self, text-to-world connections.

Presentational Mode	In writing a well-developed response to the movie *Red Cliff II* that we watched,
	
	• Demonstrate your understanding of the importance of the classic novel *The Romance of the Three Kingdoms*, the significance of this Battle of Red Cliff in Chinese history, and the main strategies applied in the battle.
	• Narrate the story "To Borrow Arrows with Thatched Boats," where Zhūgé Liàng adeptly harnessed the synergy of "favorable timing, geographic location, and human factors" to secure 100,000 arrows. Elaborate on how Zhūgé Liàng strategically employed these three pivotal elements for success in obtaining the arrows.
	• Make connections to reflect on the following two questions:
	  • How have the "favorable timing, geographic location, and human factors," that is, 天时地利人和, played into a notable success in your life?
	  • How have some groups' opportunities been limited by lacking 天时地利人和? (The story shared in the connection can be your own experiences [text-to-self], the ones from other stories, articles, or movies [text-to-text], or experiences in the world around you [text-to-world].)

Interpersonal Mode	Participate in a simulated conversation by responding to a series of six related questions about the film *Red Cliff II*/"To Borrow Arrows with Thatched Boats."

4.2 Learning Materials

Majority of the following classroom-ready materials, along with supplementary resources in an adaptable digital format, are presented in the appendices immediately following the chapter for your convenience.

A. Unit Plan:

- The unit plan provides students with an overview of what will be covered, as well as the assessment methods, major learning vocabulary/structures, and other related resources.

B. Google Slides and one LibGuide

- Introduction to the Battle of Red Cliff.
- Background knowledge building and teamwork Google Slides template.
- LibGuide link (https://libguides.d125.org/redcliff) for students to find the needed information, build background knowledge, and present to classmates using the Google Slides template.

- Applying QFT to generate questions.
- The Battle of Red Cliff portrayed in the film *Red Cliff II*.
- The story of "草船借箭" from the film *Red Cliff II*.
- Highlighting the strategies applied in the film *Red Cliff II*.
- Reviewing the film's main content using the Generating Interaction Between Schemata and Text (GIST) strategy (Schuder et al., 1989).
- The GIST Strategy Google Slides template for teachers to use in any lesson about retelling the main idea of a story, an article, a movie, and more.
- Debriefing on "天时地利人和" and using the connection-making strategy (text-to-text, text-to-self, text-to-world) to relate to students' previous funds of knowledge.
- Debriefing on "thinking outside the box" in the story of "草船借箭" and making connections.
- The Google Slides version of Study Packet for easy presentation to students in class while guiding them to focus on language proficiency with the Study Packet handout.

C. Recommended Video Materials

- Film *Cliff II*, directed by 吴宇森/John Woo
- Animated film 《火烧赤壁》 (www.youtube.com/watch?v=a21Nf0CDo4E)
- *If History Is A Bunch of Meow* 《乱世三国篇》 www.youtube.com/watch?v=MrYH_wNvYjA
- *China's 4 Classic Novels Explained – Learn Chinese Now* www.youtube.com/watch?v=__QKjFXW2Kk
- *Sun Tzu's The Art of War | Overview & Summary* www.youtube.com/watch?v=79-TeEBiKrM (00:00 to 1:15)
- *The 36 Stratagems Explained* www.youtube.com/clip/UgkxTP1gEQMYqk_4PUwVZY6NPz8Qp28tUJG

D. Preview Packet

- The Battle of Red Cliff quick facts (English)
- Introduction of the Battle of Red Cliff and the film *Red Cliff II* (English)
- Main characters relationship chart (Chinese/English)
- Short introduction of the film *Red Cliff II* (Chinese)
- Twenty key vocabulary words (Chinese characters, Pinyin and English meaning)

E. Enrichment Packet

- Various names in Chinese culture, such as 姓，名，字，号
- Whether the story "To Borrow Arrows with Thatched Boats" really happened in history
- Impact of *The Romance of The Three Kingdoms* on Chinese language, literature, and folklore
- The application of the strategies in modern life

F. Worksheets and Study Packet

- Background-building worksheet for notetaking
- Worksheet: "During: Make Connection; Text-to-Text, Text-to-Self, Text-to-World"

- Worksheet: "Post-Reflection after the Movie: Making Connections"
- Study Packet: covering the main ideas/themes in Chinese paragraphs on the left side of the box, and new vocabulary words, Pinyin, and English meanings on the right side

G. Unit-Final Communicative Tasks
- Speaking assessment prompts
- Essay prompts
- Interpretive reading assessment
- Assessment rubrics

4.3. Suggested Lessons and Activities

The sample lessons and activities are geared toward high school students who are in the fourth level of taking Chinese courses as an elective course to meet their high school graduation requirement and/or college admission requirement for world languages. They have a 50-minute Chinese class every day. The majority of the learning takes place in the classroom, including watching the movie; a 10–20-minute homework is assigned for them to review what they have covered on that day. For college students, many activities that do not involve group discussions in stages 2 and 3 can take place outside of class to save classroom instruction time. For high school students, it is still recommended to implement all of them in class due to their maturity and motivation to learn Chinese as an elective course.

Students receive a learning packet containing all the materials in the appendices, along with access to daily instructional Google Slides on the learning management system, Canvas. This enables them to learn or review at their own pace when needed.

> The pace and daily activities can and should be adapted to fit the schedules of your specific class. For college students, moving the noted activities outside of class can reduce classroom instruction time by half; instead of fourteen 50-minute periods, seven 50-minute periods should be sufficient. The following four-stage instruction provides a model for the core stages of the unit that can be adapted to different class schedules.

Stage 1: Pre-Movie Watching. Building Background Knowledge (Periods 1–2, Estimated Time: 45–90 Minutes)

Activity 1: Utilize the Preview Packet for independent study at home prior to commencing the upcoming unit. (High school students may be granted time in class for the purpose of reviewing the Preview Packet.)

Activity 2: Use the Unit Plan to introduce the new unit (topic, learning goals, major performance assessments, learning resources, etc.). (Activities 1 and 2 can be completed in any order.)

"To Borrow Arrows with Thatched Boats" 《草船借箭》

Activity 3: Build background knowledge.

- Use the artwork "To Borrow Arrows with Thatched Boats," designed by 蔡国强 (Cài Guóqiáng) and previously displayed at the National Art Museum of China in Beijing, to capture students' attention.
- Introduce the name of the story "To Borrow Arrows with Thatched Boats" and the novel 《三国演义》 and provide a general introduction to the Four Great Classic Chinese Novels.
- Shift the focus to 《三国演义》 and share the historical background of the Three Kingdoms period, including the Battle of Red Cliff and the three kingdoms and their respective leaders. (In movies, characters may be addressed by various designations, including their given names, artistic names, or style names. Consequently, it is advantageous to furnish students with a concise introduction to the cultural nuances of Chinese names, utilizing the insights outlined in the Enrichment Guide.)
- Organize students into groups for self-study on one of the five topics using the resources available on LibGuide (https://libguides.d125.org/redcliff). Provide them with a given Google Slides template to prepare a presentation about their chosen topic and instruct students to be ready to share it with the class. The five topics are the Four Great Classic Chinese Novels (四大名著), historical background (历史背景), the Battle of Red Cliff (赤壁之战), battles where a minority confronts a majority, known worldwide (世界上以少战多的著名战役), and the stratagems applied in the film.
- Students deliver their presentations, with keywords in Chinese and the rest of the content in English. The activity concludes with students providing a self-report on the background using Formative, and they can refer to the Google Slides presented earlier.

Activity 4: Implement the QFT to engage students and prepare them to find answers to their questions in stage 2.

- Begin by sharing the learning objective: "I can generate questions to guide my learning from the film *Red Cliff II*."
- Present the question focus: "Based on the background knowledge we have learned so far and the movie Red Cliff II that we are going to watch, what questions we will be able to answer at the end of this unit?" To aid students' understanding, present images of "To Borrow Arrows with Thatched Boats," "Four Great Classic Chinese Novels," "Thirty-Six Stratagems," and the film poster for *Red Cliff II*.
- Produce questions: Allow students five to eight minutes to write their own questions, while sharing with them the rules for generating questions:
  - Write as many questions as you can.
  - Do not stop to answer, judge, or discuss.
  - Write down every question that you can think of.
  - Change any statements into questions.
  - Number the questions

- Categorize questions: Have students categorize their questions into closed-ended and open-ended questions. Encourage them to improve their closed-ended questions by changing them into open-ended ones.
- Prioritize questions: Instruct students to select the top three questions they believe are the most important (project the question focus on the projector to assist students in this prioritization process).
- Conduct a voting process for the top six questions: Each student shares their top three questions with their team, and each team votes for the top three to share with the class. The entire class then votes for the top six questions. (Note: The AP Chinese Language and Culture Assessment includes six questions for the interpersonal speaking session.)

The above QFT process was developed by the Right Question Institute. More resources can be found on the RQI website (https://rightquestion.org/what-is-the-qft/) and also in the supplemental materials.

Stage 2: During Movie Watching. Learning and Discussing Major Themes (Periods 3–8, Estimated Time: About 200 Minutes)

Activity 1: Watch the Movie and Take Notes Using the Sheet "During: Make Connection; Text-to-Text, Text-to-Self, Text-to-World."

- Introduce new vocabulary needed for each segment of the film to students.
- Watch the movie and take notes, either about the scenes or the strategies applied. Next to these notes, students can record the connections (text-to-text, text-to-self, text-to-world).
- Allocate the last 5 to 10 minutes of each period for students to:
  - Share their notes (scenes/strategies and connections).
  - Read the Study Packet of the film segment covered, which is written by the instructor and composed of small paragraphs with associated vocabulary and structures. *(Repeat the earlier process until the movie is finished.)*

This process (presenting vocabulary, watching the movie, sharing, and reading the e-book) provides students with meaning-focused input and language-focused input, which will assist them with output later.

Activity 2: Debrief the Story of "To Borrow Arrows with Thatched Boats" and the Strategies Applied

- Provide students with the necessary vocabulary.
- Read the Study Packet with sample text to retell the story of "To Borrow Arrows with Thatched Boats."
- Review the strategies applied and provide input (e-book) on how to describe the implementation of the strategies in the film in Chinese.
- Discuss scenes, stratagems, and strategies related to the questions generated during the QFT.
- Practice new words and reading comprehension using the teacher-provided scene summaries; engage in speaking and writing about "To Borrow Arrows with Thatched Boats" on the Formative Platform.

Activity 3: Debrief the Story of "To Borrow Arrows with Thatched Boats" and Relate It to the Success Factors "天时地利人和."

- Provide students with the necessary vocabulary.
- Introduce the success factors implied in the story of "To Borrow Arrows with Thatched Boats" in Chinese.
- Invite students to the discussion using these two guiding questions: How have "favorable timing, geographic location, and human relations," that is, "天时地利人和," played into a notable success in your life? How have some groups' opportunities been limited by lacking "天时地利人和?"
- Have students summarize the success factors in writing and text-to-text, text-to-self, and text-to-world connections regarding "天时地利人和."

Activity 4: Debrief the Story of "To Borrow Arrows with Thatched Boats" and Relate It to "Thinking Outside the Box" (创新思维 chuàngxīn sīwéi)

- Provide students with the necessary vocabulary.
- Retell the story "To Borrow Arrows with Thatched Boats" by highlighting how Zhūgé Liàng tackled the challenge by "thinking outside the box."
- Present students with a challenging problem and invite them to solve it by "thinking outside the box." (A possible challenge problem can be as follows: The messengers arrived in the Tang Dynasty with the intention of proposing a marriage to a Tang Dynasty princess. Emperor Tàizōng of the Tang Dynasty wanted to test the messengers with a set of questions. He ordered his attendants to take the messengers to the imperial horse stable, where there were 100 mother mares in one stable and 100 young foals in another. He challenged the messengers to accurately pair each foal with its mother mare. The solution can be this: First, starve the young foals for half a day. Then, release all 200 horses together, and the famished foals will immediately seek out their own mothers to nurse.)
- Invite students to think of a scenario in which a problem was solved by "thinking outside the box." Recognize that students may not have personally experienced such situations. Give them the option to share what they have read about or seen in similar cases. This way, students can provide a wider range of different examples.
- Have students share their examples.

Stage 3: Post Movie Watching. Focused Practice to Build Language Fluency (Periods 9–10, Estimated Time: 45–90 Minutes)

Materials: "Post Reflection after the Movie: Making Connections," e-book

Activity 1: Review Key Vocabulary and Scene Summary Using the GIST Strategy

- Students work in pairs to read the Study Packet aloud regarding the major movie scenes and themes, including new words and grammatical patterns.
- Utilize the GIST Strategy to review one scene/theme at a time. Depending on students' proficiency levels, teachers can provide the phrases if students find it

challenging or have students generate their own list of phrases if they are confident. Then follow steps 2, 3, and 4 listed in the following GIST Strategy. The teacher has the flexibility to decide whether to repeat all the steps for each scene/theme or to do step 3 only after completing step 2, especially considering that the movie contains numerous scene/theme summaries.
- Practice speaking with a partner using questions generated during the QFT and questions from the teachers to prepare students for the interpersonal speaking assessment of six questions. Three of the questions come from the teacher, and the other three questions can be chosen by the students from the six questions written by everyone during the QFT.

The GIST activity is an efficient approach to review a story or article, and it involves the following steps:

1) List ten key phrases (at the teacher's discretion, the number of phrases may vary depending on the complexity of the story or article and the students' proficiency level).
2) (Partner exercise) Read the ten phrases aloud to each other and highlight the keywords that both of you have in common.
3) Use the ten key phrases to produce a short summary of the story or article, either spoken or written.
4) (Partner exercise) (If it's a writing exercise, not a speaking exercise) Read the summaries aloud to each other and identify similarities and differences, or help each other correct the grammar.

Activity 2: Practice Making Connections Using the Worksheet "Post Movie Watching Reflection After the Movie: Making Connections."

- Students should locate their notes taken during the movie-watching on the worksheet called "During-Make Connections: Text-to-Text, Text-to-Self, Text-to-World."
- Use the examples provided on the sheet "Post-Reflection after the Movie: Making Connections" to practice summarizing the scene/theme and then making text-to-text, text-to-self, and text-to-world connections. Students can refer to the scene/theme summary in the Study Packet with a focus on improving language accuracy.

Stage 4: End of Unit. Summative Assessment (Periods 11–12, Estimated Time: 45–90 Minutes)

Materials: Presentational writing prompt, questions for interpersonal speaking, reading assessment.

- Write a short response about the movie based on the prompt in the Unit Plan (presentational mode). (Find the prompt in the language performance goal: Presentational Mode, section 4.1 in this chapter.)

- Respond to six questions (Interpersonal speaking).
- Take the reading assessments (part of the writing materials are from students' presentational writing assessment).

In this sample lesson design, students have the opportunity to generate questions based on their research and learning during the background-building activity in the pre-viewing stage. The goal is to spark students' interest in exploring and answering their own questions throughout the unit. As students delve deeper into the discussion of the story "To Borrow Arrows with Thatched Boats" and explore the concept of "favorable timing, geographical factors, and human elements" (天时地利人和), they can make text-to-text, text-to-self, and text-to-world connections to analyze the roles these factors play in achieving success in various aspects. They can also examine how the lack of "天时地利人和" can limit opportunities, both locally and globally, for different groups of people.

By connecting these factors to their own experiences of success and the successes or failures of others, regardless of their ethnic backgrounds, regions, or countries of origin, students practice the skill of analyzing causes and phenomena rather than making hasty judgments. This skill is crucial for their ICC development, fostering a deeper understanding of complex issues and promoting a more thoughtful approach to problem-solving.

Owing to the presence of a substantial number of new vocabulary terms, the performance (whether in written or spoken form) adopts an open-book, open-resource methodology, as it is viewed as an inherent aspect of the learning process. However, it is essential to highlight that copying and pasting directly is not permitted.

4.4. Implementing Question Formulation Technique (QFT)

This QFT activity, developed by the Right Question Institute (RQI, 2023), was mainly used to facilitate discussion and critical thinking, as well as to help guide students in narrowing down their focus before watching the movie. The QFT was applied after students had explored the background knowledge for this movie unit, which includes topics such as the Four Great Classic Chinese Novels, historical background, the Battle of Red Cliff, other battles where a minority confronts a majority in world history, and the stratagems applied in the film. So the students had already acquainted themselves with the major topics covered in the movie. In the QFT activity in class, students are asked to do the following steps: (1) Actively brainstorm and generate questions related to the question focus following a set of rules. These rules include, for example, asking as many questions as possible, refraining from answering or discussing the questions during the process, and striving to ask open-ended questions. (2) Categorize the questions generated. The generated questions are then sorted into open-ended and closed-ended categories. Rewrite the close-ended questions into open-ended questions. (3) Prioritize their questions. Students evaluate and prioritize the questions and choose the most critical ones to share with the class. (4) Choose the top six questions as the ones to explore further as a whole class while watching the movie.

Part of the end-of-the-unit performance assessment is designed to include the questions generated by students. During the movie watching and discussion, students have the opportunity to focus on finding the answers to those questions they are most interested in and acquire the language needed to express the answers in the target language as well. This process of finding the answers to their own questions enables students to master the content more effectively and therefore perform at the end of the unit.

5. Teacher's Reflections

The reflection in this part will be in the format of question and answer.

Q: What is one of the most important factors to help students learn more from the movie?

A: A variety of effective movie teaching approaches have been shared with educators. The one that I experimented with that helped my students to perform at a higher performance level starts with background-knowledge-building in their first language, namely, English in the context of the United States. The movie version played in class has English subtitles, which plays an important role in helping students understand the movie. However, to better comprehend the practice, product, and perspective in the film may require more background knowledge points. Equipped with background knowledge, students will be able to better understand and process the information and therefore have a more productive discussion that helps them not only build up the target language skills but also make more meaningful text-to-text, text-to-self, and text-to-world. Without background-knowledge-building before watching the movie, more questions may very likely be about understanding the product, practice, and perspective shown in the movie. These questions may be asked in students' first language as well.

> Before watching the movie, laying the groundwork with background knowledge is one of the most crucial factors to help students focus their energy on language learning and ICC skills.

Q: How can we deal with the enormous amount of new vocabulary in the film for the intermediate language learner?

A: Based on the topics chosen to delve into for this movie unit, I have written short passages related to the movie's themes and scenes, suitable for intermediate language learners to read. Alongside, I have provided corresponding vocabulary (with Pinyin and English definitions), sentence structures, and additional examples. Therefore, the barrier of encountering new vocabulary is minimized. When students read the text after watching the movie, they can focus more on understanding the meaning (meaning-focused input) and learning the language (language-focused learning), which, in turn, helps them with expressing themselves meaningfully (meaning-focused output) and developing fluency (fluency development) (Nation, 2007). These short paragraphs will be shared in class after watching the corresponding scenes, presented in the form of Google Slides, and uploaded to the Learning Management System for easy reference. Additionally, a hard copy will be provided to each student, ensuring that they have all the movie-related text available in different formats, making it more convenient for their study.

> Present the short paragraphs describing the movie scenes and topics and provide related vocabulary and structures next to the text to help students to focus on the content and acquire the needed language simultaneously.

Q: Can QFT only be used at the beginning of the unit?

A: The QFT approach is used in this sample movie unit after students build up the background knowledge and before watching the movie. The purpose is for students to generate questions of their interest and find answers during the learning process. To make the activity more manageable in this context, since teachers have to prepare learning materials for students to acquire both language and culture skills, it is easier for everyone to focus on the same set of questions. So I had each team share three questions of their choice and the whole class votes for the top six questions as the focus. This practice still allowed students to explore their questions while making the lesson planning from the teacher's end more manageable. In addition to using QFT at the beginning of the unit, it can also be applied at the end of the unit as a review activity before the performance assessment. Students can generate questions that they are able to answer after the movie unit. The review activities of different communication modes can then be built on the questions generated by the students. Once you are familiar with the QFT practice, it can be applied to start the unit/lesson learning or review the unit/lesson. Explore more about QFT on this website: https://rightquestion.org/what-is-the-qft/.

> QFT can be used at the beginning or at the end of the lesson/unit to empower students to learn.

Q: During the discussion, my students do not really have much to share. What is the magic tool to enable students to have rich discussions?

A: The easy-to-apply connection-making strategy (text-to-text, text-to-self, and text-to-world) makes it possible for students to have rich discussions in class. It provides students with the freedom to bring in their previous knowledge about themselves, families, or friends, their learning from other text, and their understanding of the wider world into the discussion. If students only have one option to make either text-to-text, text-to-self, or text-to-world connections, they may not come up with a connection. The three-connection choices make the learning task be more possible. In this unit, when students were asked to make a connection with "天时地利人和" (favorable timing, geographic location, and human factors), they were able to relate to their own experiences, as well as those of their family members or friends. At the same time, they brought in the experience and stories of how opportunities are limited for people in poorer areas/countries or from different time periods. It is those connections that not only empowered the students in the language learning process when "looking outside the window" but also guide them to reflect by "looking at themselves in the mirror" and prepare them to get out of their comfort zone to communicate with others through "the sliding door" in a culturally appropriate approach. This connection-making strategy can be applied at any grade level. Applying it will not only enrich students' discussion but also will allow teachers to learn more about the students from the story or experience shared in their connection.

> To key to motivate students to learn is the connection. One effective connection-making strategy is text-to-text, text-to-self, and text-to-world.

Appendices: Sample Teaching Materials

All materials in the appendices can be read online or downloaded by scanning this QR code. Appendices 4.1 to 4.3 are fully enclosed here, while the remaining appendices are available online.

Appendix 4.1: Preview Packet

《草船借箭》 预习作业 Preview Packet

1. 电影简介 (jiǎnjiè) Movie Introduction

《赤壁II》是由导演吴宇森导演的，在 2009 年上映的一部战争电影。这部电影是根据中国古典小说《三国演义》中著名的赤壁之战改编而成。影片

"To Borrow Arrows with Thatched Boats" 《草船借箭》

以历史战役为背景，讲述了东汉末年三国鼎立的时期，吴、蜀两国联合，成功对抗强大的曹操军队的故事。其中的草船借箭的故事，吴蜀联合，利用了天时地利人和以及一系例的计策，成功的战胜了曹操，成为了中国历史上以少胜多的重要战争之一。

2. 人物 Characters

曹操	cáo cāo	Prime Minister of Han Dynasty
刘备	liú bèi	King of Shu
关羽	guān yǔ	General of Shu
张飞	zhāng fēi	General of Shu
赵云	zhào yún	General of Shu
诸葛亮	zhūgě liàng	Military Advisor General of Shu
孙权	sūn quán	King of Wu
周瑜	zhōu yú	Military Advisor General of Wu
鲁肃	lǔ sù	Diplomat and strategist

	汉朝 hàn cháo	
魏 wèi	蜀 shǔ	吴 wú
曹操（孟德）Prime Minister of Han Dynasty	刘备（玄德）（大哥）Descendant of the founder of Han Dynasty	孙权（仲谋）
神医 华佗 Doctor	关羽（云长）（二哥）General　　张飞（翼德）（三弟）General	周瑜（公瑾）General/strategist　　夫妻　　小乔 Wife (most beautiful women then)
	诸葛亮（孔明）Strategist	鲁肃（子敬）Strategist

3. 生词 zhǔyào cíhuì/main vocabulary

1) 联合　liánhé　to unite, to join
2) 抗　　kàng　　to fight against
3) 势力　shìlì　　force/power
4) 联军　liánjūn　allied force
5) 而且　érqiě　　and
6) 缺　　quē　　to be short of
7) 箭　　jiàn　　arrow
8) 船　　chuán　boat

"To Borrow Arrows with Thatched Boats" 《草船借箭》

9)	艘	sōu	measure word for boats/ships
10)	四周	sìzhōu	around
11)	装满	zhuāngmǎn	to fill and make it full of
12)	草人	cǎorén	scarecrow
13)	雾	wù	fog
14)	靠近	kàojìn	to get close to
15)	放箭	fàngjiàn	to shoot the arrow
16)	阻止	zǔzhǐ	to stop
17)	射到了	shèdàole	to shoot to
18)	计	jì	strategy
19)	借	jiè	to borrow
20)	准备	zhǔnbèi	to prepare
21)	联军	liánjūn	allied force
22)	势力	shìlì	force/power
23)	弱	ruò	weak
24)	赢	yíng	to win
25)	可能性	kěnéng xìng	possibility
26)	连环计	liánhuán jì	The Chain Strategy
27)	使用	shǐyòng	to use
28)	反间计	fǎnjiàn jì	The Spy Discord Strategy
29)	水军	shuǐjūn	navy
30)	将军	jiāngjūn	general
31)	箭	jiàn	arrow
32)	暗中	ànzhōng	secretly
33)	联军	liánjūn	allied force
34)	用计	yòngjì	to use strategies
35)	确信	quèxìn	to assure
36)	把...杀了	bǎ...shā le	to kill ...
37)	除掉	chúdiào	to get rid of
38)	有可能	yǒu kěnéng	to be possible

4. 课文: 《草船借箭》 "Borrowing Arrows from a Straw Boat"

孙权刘备联合抗曹，曹军势力远大于孙刘联军。 而且，孙刘联军还缺十万支箭。 于是周瑜给诸葛亮十天时间准备箭。诸葛亮让鲁肃准备二十艘船，船的四周装满草人。

在一个有大雾的晚上，诸葛亮让船开到曹军附近。 曹军不敢靠近他们的船， 放箭阻击他们。 然后所有的箭都射到了草人上。 诸葛亮用计向曹军"借"到了十万支箭。三天准备好了十万支箭。

孙刘联军的势力比曹军弱得多， 要赢赤壁之战的可能性比较小。所以周瑜诸葛亮使用连环计。周瑜先是使用了反间计， 让曹操觉得水军的两位将军是在暗中帮孙刘联军。 然后诸葛亮又用计草船借箭，这让曹操更加确信两位水军将军是在帮孙刘联军,就把两位将军杀了。

连环计的使用，孙刘联军不但向曹军借了十万支箭，还除掉了对于曹操来说最重要的水军的将军。这让孙刘联军更有可能打赢这场赤壁之战。

5. 练习

1) Use each of the following characters to form two words:

   a) 用：_____ _____
   b) 缺：_____ _____
   c) 抗：_____ _____
   d) 力：_____ _____
   e) 计：_____ _____
   f) 联：_____ _____
   g) 军：_____ _____

2) Read the example using the following vocabulary words, then use it to create new sentences.

   a) 使用
      i) 我每天都使用电脑做功课。
      ii) 现在很多人使用 ChatGPT 来帮他们更好的完成作业或者是工作。
      iii) (Your turn) _____

   b) 借
      i) 我今天又忘了带笔来学校，所以只有又向别人借笔。
      ii) 你知道"有借有还，再借不难"是什么意思吗？
      iii) (Your turn) _____

   c) 有可能
      i) 今天有可能会下雨，把雨伞带上吧。
      ii) 感恩节的时候，东西有可能会便宜一些；要不要等一等再买？
      iii) Your turn) _____

3) Translate the following sentences into English:

   a) 孙权刘备联合抗曹，曹军势力远大于孙刘联军。

   Translate: _____

   b) 孙刘联军的势力比曹军弱得多，要赢赤壁之战的可能性比较小。

   Translate: _____

4) 回答问题 Reading Comprehension:

   a) 《草船借箭》讲的是一个什么故事？你从这个故事中学到了什么？
   b) 《草船借箭》故事中，诸葛亮打破常规思维，在三天内成功的"借到了"十万支箭。你还知道哪一些打破常规思维，最后成功的故事？

88 *"To Borrow Arrows with Thatched Boats"* 《草船借箭》

5) 语法 Grammar/句型 Sentence Structure:

a) The structure "verb + 到了" is used to indicate the completion, attainment of an action, or an achievement of an action. It is similar to using the past tense in English to convey that an action has been accomplished or reached a certain state.

   i) 半年以后，他终于<u>找到了</u>工作。 After half a year, he finally found a job.
   ii) 昨天我终于<u>买到了</u>我最喜欢的新手机。 Yesterday, I finally bought my favorite new phone.
   iii) 十三个小时以后，我们的飞机终于<u>飞到了</u>北京。 After 13 hours, our flight finally reached Beijing.
   iv) (Your turn) _____

b) The structure "verb + 好了" is used to indicate the completion or improvement of an action or state. It can be translated into English as "finished," "ready," "completed," "fixed," or "better now."

   i) 你的手机坏了，我帮你修好了。 Your phone was broken, I fixed it for you.
   ii) 功课做好了，才可以玩。 Finish homework first, then play.
   iii) 等到工作找好了以后，我就请的家人吃一顿大餐。 Once I find a job, I'll treat my family to a big meal.
   iv) (Your turn) _____

c) 向 ... from (孙刘联军不但向曹军借了十万支箭 ...)

   i) 孩子们<u>向</u>老师学习知识。 The children learn knowledge from the teacher.
   ii) 我要<u>向</u>他请教一下，怎么才能学好中文。 I want to consult with him on how to learn Chinese well.
   iii) 他<u>向</u>父母请求帮助来支付学费。 He asked his parents for help to pay the tuition.
   iv) (Your turn) _____

d) A 比 B adj. 得多/多了 A is much more adj. than B. (孙刘联军的势力比曹军弱得多。)

   i) 这本书<u>比</u>那本书<u>有趣得多</u>。 This book is much more interesting than that book.
   ii) 这家餐厅的食物<u>比</u>那家<u>便宜得多</u>。 The food at this restaurant is much cheaper than that one.
   iii) 今年<u>比</u>去年<u>热得多</u>。 This year is much hotter than last year.
   iv) (Your turn) _____

"To Borrow Arrows with Thatched Boats" 《草船借箭》

Appendix 4.2: Enrichment Guide
《草船借箭》 Enrichment Guide

1. Battle of Red Cliff (赤壁 Chìbì) Quick Facts

When and Where	
Date:	Winter of 208 CE
Location:	Near the Yangtze River in South China
Who	
Military coalition of two South China Warlords: • Sūn Quán (ruled the southeast) • Liú Bèi (ruled the southwest) • Zhōu Yú (important general)	The Northern Army: Cáo Cāo (most powerful warlord of all who ruled the north)
Strength	
50,000 troops	300,000 troops
Why	
They were fighting for power and control of South China.	

2. 赤壁之战介绍 Introduction of the Battle of Red Cliff (Chìbì Zhīzhàn)

The Battle of Red Cliff occurred near the present-day city of Wuhan, on the Yangtze River in the year AD 208. It was an engagement between the forces of Northern China, led by war-hungry Cáo Cāo (曹操), and the defenders of Southern Chinese under the rule of Liú Bèi (刘备) and Sūn Quán (孙权).

During this battle, a small fleet of fireships and amphibious troops from Southern China took the enemy by surprise and utterly annihilated Northern China's larger invading force. This decisive battle prevented the ambitions of the northern leader, Cáo Cāo (曹操), from establishing control over the Yangtze River valley and unifying China under a new dynasty.

Cáo Cāo's defeat at the Battle of Red Cliff (赤壁之战 Chìbì Zhīzhàn) marked the beginning of the Three Kingdoms period (AD 168–280) in China, a period often romanticized as one of the most captivating in Chinese history. The Three Kingdoms era is filled with heroes and villains, as well as extraordinary successes and acts of betrayal. All of these elements, and more, have been discussed in China's most renowned historical novel, 《三国演义》 (Sānguó Yǎnyì), known in English as *The Romance of the Three Kingdoms*.

3. "草船借箭" – 历史上真有其事吗？/Did "To Borrow Arrows with Thatched Boats" Really Happen in History?

This story, "To Borrow Arrows with Thatched Boats," has a prototype, but it doesn't align with historical facts. The original inspiration for the story wasn't Zhūgé Liàng, but rather Sūn Quán. In the 18th year of Jian'an, approximately five years after the Battle of Red Cliff, Cáo Cāo led his army in an attack on Eastern Wu, resulting in a month-long standoff at Ruxu. Eventually, Cáo Cāo was left with no option but to retreat. Throughout this campaign, many notable incidents occurred, including one that led to Cáo Cāo's famous remark: "A son born to me should be like Sun Zhongmou" ("生子当如孙仲谋"), when he was impressed by the disciplined and dignified appearance of the Wu army.

After more than a month of this deadlock, the Yangtze River began to experience rising water levels due to the onset of spring. Sūn Quán sent a letter to Cáo Cāo, advising him to leave promptly. Consequently, Cáo Cāo withdrew his troops. According to accounts in the 《魏略》 (Wei Strategy), during this battle, Sūn Quán once took a boat to assess the situation of Cao's army but was spotted by Cao's forces. They showered him with arrows, which stuck on one side of Sūn Quán's boat, causing it to tilt. In response, Sūn Quán ordered the boat to turn around so that the other side would be exposed to the arrows. This led to the arrows filling the other side, ultimately stabilizing the boat and allowing Sūn Quán to escape safely.

In Luó Guànzhōng's novel 《三国演义》, the main character of this story was changed from Sūn Quán to Zhūgé Liàng, and the passive reception of arrows was transformed into an active borrowing of arrows. Additionally, the timeline was adjusted to five years earlier during the Battle of Red Cliff, resulting in the famous "Borrowing Arrows with Thatched Boats" tale.

(Based on www.zhihu.com/question/30910201 & www.163.com/dy/article/F4B5781Q053777HW.html)

4. 关于名字 About the Names

When you watch the film 《赤壁II》, you will encounter this challenging aspect: the abundance of characters, each addressed by various names. For instance, 诸葛亮 (Zhūgé Liàng) is sometimes referred to as 孔明 (Kǒng Míng), and at other times as "卧龙先生" (Wòlóng Xiānshēng). Could it possibly become more intricate?

In traditional Chinese culture, personal names typically comprise several components, each with distinct meanings and purposes:

- 姓 (*xìng*, surname): The surname represents family or blood ties and is the common family name. In Chinese naming conventions, the surname is usually placed at the beginning of the given name. For instance, a person with the surname "Wang" might have the given name Lin as in "Wang Lin."
- 名 (*míng*, given name): The given name is an individual's personal name, distinct from the family name, and usually follows the surname. It serves to identify an individual within the family.
- 字 (*zì*, style name/courtesy name): A style name, also known as a courtesy name, holds significant importance in traditional Chinese culture. It is an alternate

name given by parents to their children, symbolizing parental hopes and aspirations. Style names are typically bestowed by elders or mentors upon a person's coming of age and serve as cultural symbols. In ancient times, people often used style names to address each other instead of their given names.
- 号 (hào, art name/pseudonym): An art name, or pseudonym, is a self-selected alternate name used by ancient Chinese scholars and artists. It is used for signing their works or in social interactions. Art names often reflect personal characteristics, interests, or aspirations and are also known as "雅号" (yǎhào) or "笔名" (bǐmíng).

It's important to note that as modern society has evolved, many individuals now primarily use their surname and given name in daily life, with clan names, style names/courtesy names, and art names gradually falling into disuse. The usage of these elements may also vary among different regions and cultural backgrounds.

5. 对语言、文学和民俗的影响/Impact on Language, Literature, and Folklore

The Three Kingdoms period has captured the Chinese imagination more than any other period in Chinese history. Very early on, storytellers armed with prompt books carried the story of the Three Kingdoms throughout the country. Until recently, they were still doing it. Then, in the 14th century, Luó Guànzhōng wrote his epic novel, *The Romance of the Three Kingdoms*. It wasn't published until 1522. During the Qing Dynasty it was revised in order to make it more historically accurate. This is the novel we know today.

The story of the 赤壁之战, as told in the novel, tells of the intricate plotting that preceded the attack (much of which was not included in the movie). The reader is fascinated by the way these plots are tied together, each one depending on the one before, resulting in the successful surprise attack on Cáo Cāo's forces at 赤壁.

Many poems have been written about 赤壁, the most famous being the Tang poet Du Mu's poem 《赤壁》. The great Song Dynasty poet, 苏轼 (Sū Shì; also known as 苏东坡 Sū Dōngpō), wrote two *fu* (赋) poems, 《前赤壁赋》 and 《后赤壁赋》.

The Chinese language itself has been enriched by many sayings (成语) from the novel. For example:

- "说曹操,曹操到." – "Speak of Cáo Cāo, and Cáo Cāo shall appear."
- When referring to someone as a very bright child, people may use "他/她 是个 小诸葛亮." – "He/she is a little Zhūgé Liàng."
- "疑人不用, 用人不疑." – "Don't employ people you suspect; don't suspect people you employ." (A quote attributed to Cáo Cāo)
- "攻其不备 (出其不意)" – "Attack where the enemy is unprepared; take them by surprise. (From *The Art of War* 《孙子兵法》)
- "天下大事,分久必合,合久必分." – "In all matters under heaven, what is separated will eventually come together, and what is together will eventually separate." (A verse from the epigraph of the novel)

Many of the stratagems used in this novel are also well-known in China. Here are four:

连环计 The Chain Strategy
离间计 The Sowing Discord among the Enemy Strategy
美人计 The Beautiful Woman Strategy
走为上 To Retreat Is the Best Option

6. 计谋在现代生活中的应用/The Application of the Strategies in Modern Lives

The Thirty-Six Stratagems are 36 strategies and tactics included in ancient Chinese military literature, well utilized in *The Romance of the Three Kingdoms*. Although originally designed for warfare, the wisdom and strategic thinking contained within them still hold value in modern life. Here are some applications of the Thirty-Six Stratagems in contemporary living:

- 连环计: In personal career development, the concept of "连环计" can also be applied. For example, by engaging in a series of planned learning and training activities, individuals can gradually enhance their skills and competitiveness, thereby achieving higher career goals.
- 走为上 (To Retreat Is the Best Option): In business negotiations, if you find yourself at a disadvantage or facing difficulties, sometimes choosing to temporarily retreat, reevaluate the situation, and replan is a wise move. In interpersonal relationships, when encountering conflicts or disputes, taking a step back can avoid bigger arguments and maintain harmony in the relationship. In the workplace, if you find that your current job is completely inconsistent with your plans and aspirations, it is indeed worth considering leaving and seeking a different career. This choice can save you time and allow you to focus on developing a field that better suits and aligns with your career goals.
- 抛砖引玉 (literal meaning: "To Throw a Brick to Attract Jade" or giving the enemy something to induce him to lose more valuable things): In innovation and problem-solving, by presenting a preliminary viewpoint, idea, or suggestion, you can guide others to join the discussion and offer better solutions. In marketing, organizing small-scale activities or interactions that spark public interest and participation can attract more attention and engagement.

(Please note that these strategies should be applied with careful consideration and should adhere to ethical and legal principles to avoid negative consequences for others.)

The following YouTube videos explain the 36 tactics and their application in real life.

- The 36 Stratagems Explained https://www.youtube.com/watch?v=75T-4g0V3Is
- The 36 Stratagems Explained by a Psychologist (The Art of War Part 2) (www.youtube.com/watch?v=YCoC-c1VWQM&t=786s)
- Outwit your Competition with these 36 Business Stratagems (https://readingraphics.com/36-business-stratagems/)

Appendix 4.3: Study Packet

《草船借箭》 Study Packet

The Study Packet follows the class film discussion sequence, starting with an introduction to the Four Great Classic Novels. It then delves into the movie, incorporating the story of "To Borrow Arrows with Thatched Boats." The text concludes by examining the interplay between timing, geography, and human factors, emphasizing their relevance to students. Vocabulary explanations accompany the text due to the presence of numerous new words. Key sentence structures, when applicable, are provided after relevant passages.

Instruction: Upon reading the ensuing brief passage aided by the new vocabulary, practice the new sentence structures, and respond to the questions provided at the end.

1. 关于四大名著

中国的四大名著是《红楼梦》、《西游记》、《水浒传》和《三国演义》。《红楼梦》讲的是贾宝玉和林黛玉的爱情故事和几大家族的故事。《西游记》讲的是孙悟空保护唐僧去取经的冒险故事。《水浒传》讲的是梁山好汉的英勇事迹。《三国演义》讲的是三国时期的战争和智谋斗争。这些书不仅有趣，还反映了古代中国的历史和文化。《赤壁之战》还有《草船借箭》的故事就来自于四大名著中的《三国演义》。

1)	名著	míngzhù	classic works
2)	《红楼梦》	hónglóumèng	*Dream of the Red Chamber*
3)	《水浒传》	shuǐhǔzhuà	*Outlaws of the Marsh*
4)	《西游记》	xīyóujì	*Journey to the West*
5)	《三国演义》	sānguó yǎnyì	*The Romance of The Three Kingdoms*
6)	爱情	àiqíng	love
7)	故事	gùshì	story
8)	家族	jiāzú	family
9)	保护	bǎohù	to protect
10)	取经	qǔjīng	to obtain the scriptures
11)	冒险	màoxiǎn	adventure
12)	梁山好汉	Liángshān Hǎohàn	heroes of the marsh
13)	英勇事迹	yīngyǒng shìjì	heroic deeds
14)	战争	zhànzhēng	war

"To Borrow Arrows with Thatched Boats" 《草船借箭》

15)	智谋斗争	zhìmóu dòuzhēng	tactical battle
16)	反映	fǎnyìng	to reflect

2. 赤壁之战前后三方势力强弱变化

曹操是汉朝的丞相，拥有最高的权利。他带着军队去南方攻打刘备和孙权，想要控制南方的土地。孙刘没有曹操的势力强大，所以孙刘成为盟友，一起抗曹。赤壁之战以前，曹操（魏）的势力最强大。赤壁之战后，魏变弱，蜀吴势力加强，形成了三分天下的格局。

1)	汉朝	háncháo	Han Dynasty
2)	丞相	chéngxiàng	prime minister
3)	拥有	yōngyǒu	to own
4)	权力	quánlì	power
5)	军队	jūnduì	army
6)	势力	shìlì	power
7)	形成	xíngchéng	to form
8)	变	biàn	to change
9)	三分天下	ān fēn tiānxià	to divide the world into three kingdoms
10)	强大	qiángdà	strong
11)	格局	géjú	pattern
12)	加强	jiāqiáng	to strengthen
13)	攻打	gōngdǎ	to attack
14)	控制	kòngzhì	to control
15)	土地	tǔdì	land
16)	盟友	méngyǒu	ally
17)	抗曹	kàngcáo	to fight with Cao

3. 成功三要素: 天时地人和 Favorable Timing, Geographic Location, and Human Factors

天时 timing and climate conditions 有利的气候，泛指时间上的各种有利条件，包括天气、时机、机遇等	时机　shíjī　timing 机遇　jīyù　opportunity 有利　yǒulì　favorable 气候　qìhòu　climate 泛指　fànzhǐ　generally refer to 条件　tiáojiàn　condition
地利 advantageous terrain and location 有利地形，泛指空间上的各种有利条件，包括地形、地势、地利位置等	地利位置　dìlì wèizhì　geographical location 地形/势　dìxíng/shì　terrian 空间　kōngjiān　space
人和 popular support and numerical superiority.得到人们拥护，帮助，上下同心，泛指人的优势	上下同心　shàngxià tóngxīn　teamwork; work together; band together; unite 得到　dédào　to get 拥护　yōnghù　support 优势　yōushì　advantages

4. 天时

"天时"指的是在时间上的优势,包括有利的天气,时间等等。 在赤壁之战中,风向本来是对曹军有利。但是在冬天的时候,风向偶尔会改变。孙刘联军利用了改变后的风向,火烧赤壁,赢了曹军。

在草船借箭时,诸葛亮也是很好的利用了"天时"。他熟悉当地的气候,知道三天之后会有大雾,所以带了20艘草船,靠近曹军刚好箭能够射到的地方。曹军因为雾大,害怕有埋伏,就只是放箭,不敢靠近。大部分的箭都射到了草船上,这样诸葛亮就得到了曹军的十万支箭。

1)	指的是	zhǐ de shì	refer to
2)	优势	yōushì	advantage
3)	包括	bāokuò	include
4)	有利	yǒulì	favorable
5)	天气	tiānqì	weather
6)	风向	fēngxiàng	wind direction
7)	本来	běnlái	originally
8)	改变	gǎibiàn	to change
9)	火烧	huǒshā	to burn
10)	利用	lìyòng	use
11)	熟悉	shúxī	familiar
12)	当地	dāngdì	local
13)	气候	qìhòu	climate
14)	大雾	dàwù	heavy fog
15)	草船	cǎochuán	thatched boats
16)	靠近	kàojìn	to get close
17)	害怕	hàipà	fear

句型 Structures

1) 对...有利 be beneficial for (...风向本来是对曹军有利。)

   a) 多喝水对身体有利。 Drinking more water is beneficial for the body.
   b) 这项政策对经济发展有利。 This policy is beneficial for economic development.
   c) 锻炼对心理健康有利。 Exercise is beneficial for mental health.
   d) 学习外语对找工作有利。 Learning a foreign language is advantageous for finding a job.
   e) (Your turn) _____

2) 大部分的... (大部分的箭都射到了草船上...)

   a) 大部分的学生都参加了学校组织的校园活动。 The majority of students participated in the campus activities organized by the school.
   b) 大部分的人都认为健康饮食和锻炼是保持健康的关键。 The majority of people believe that a healthy diet and exercise are essential for maintaining good health.

c) 这个城市<u>大部分</u>的居民都喜欢在周末去公园放松休闲。 Most residents of this city enjoy relaxing and leisure activities in the park during weekends.
d) (Your turn) _____

5. 地利

地利是指有利地形，泛指空间上的各种有利条件，包括地形、地势等。曹操南下攻打孙刘，不熟悉当地的地形，士兵们到了新的地方水土不服，很多人得了伤寒，生病去世了。曹军没有"地利"的优势。

孙刘联军一直住在南方，对当地的地形更加熟悉，所以孙刘联军有"地利"的优势。

诸葛亮草船借箭的时候，也有"地利"的优势。 因为长江水面宽，他们的船可以在离曹军箭能射到的地方一字排开，这样曹军射箭的时候，箭就能射到草船上。 没有"地利"的优势，诸葛亮也不能得到曹军的箭。

1)	地利	dìlì	geographical advantage
2)	有利	yǒulì	favorable
3)	地形/势	dìxíng/shì	terrain
4)	空间	kōngjiān	space
5)	条件	tiáojiàn	condition
6)	攻打	gōngdǎ	attack
7)	熟悉	shúxī	familiar
8)	士兵	shìbīng	soldier
9)	水土不服	shuǐtǔ bùfú	not acclimatized
10)	风寒	fēnghán	typhoid fever
11)	地利	dìlì	geographical advantage
12)	有利	yǒulì	favorable
13)	地形/势	dìxíng/shì	terrain
14)	空间	kōngjiān	space
15)	条件	tiáojiàn	condition
16)	箭	jiàn	arrow
17)	优势	yōushì	advantage
18)	长江	chángjiāng	Yangtze River
19)	水面	shuǐmiàn	water surface
20)	宽	kuān	width

句型 Structures

1) 对...很熟悉 （对当地的地形更加熟悉...）

   a) 我<u>对</u>这个城市<u>很熟悉</u>，因为我在这里生活了很多年。 I am very familiar with this city as I have been living here for many years.
   b) 她<u>对</u>这门课程<u>很熟悉</u>，因为她以前学习过类似的内容。 She is very familiar with this course because she studied similar content before.

c) 我们的团队对这个项目很熟悉，我们之前已经完成了类似的工作。
Our team is very familiar with this project as we have completed similar tasks before.

d) (Your turn) _____

6. 人和

人和是指得到人们拥护，上下同心，泛指人的优势。曹操有很多人拥护他，所以他可以带兵南下攻打孙刘联军。 孙刘联军也有很多人拥护他们抵抗曹军。

孙刘用"反间计"让曹操和他的水军将军"人不和"于是曹操杀了水军将军，少了必要的"人和"的优势。

1) 拥护 yōnghù support
2) 上下同心 shàng xià tóng xīn work together
3) 泛指 fànzhǐ generally refer to
4) 优势 yōushì advantage
5) 带兵 dài bīng lead troops
6) 抵抗 dǐkàng resistance
7) 反间计 fǎnjiàn jì The Sowing Discord Among the Enemy Strategy
8) 水军 shuǐjūn navy
9) 将军 jiāngjūn the general

7. 口语题目练习 Speaking Practice Questions

1) 关于整部电影

   a) 中国的四大名著是哪四大？讲的是什么？ 赤壁来自于哪一本名著？
   b) 赤壁之战为什么很重要/很有名？
   c) 周瑜说："我们都输了"。这句话是什么意思？
   d) 赤壁之战/草船借箭是快两千年前发生的故事，你能从中看到哪一些跟我们现在生活相关的地方？

2) 关于计策

   a) 在赤壁之战中，孙权刘备以及曹操用了哪几个计策？你觉得哪一个计策最有用？
   b) 在赤壁之战中,他们是如何使用不同的计策的？

3) 关于"天时地利人和"

   a) "天时地利人和"是什么意思？
   b) 在《赤壁》中，你觉得"天时地利人和"哪一个优势对赤壁的结尾影响最大？
   c) 交战双方是怎么用成功三要素来打仗的？
   d) "天时地利人和"，你觉得哪一个最重要？为什么？
   e) 你觉得你现在的生活和学习有"天时地利人和"吗？为什么有/没有？

4) 关于《草船借箭》的故事
   a) 《草船借箭》讲的是一个什么故事？你从这个故事中学到了什么？
   c) 《草船借箭》故事中，诸葛亮打破常规思维，在三天内成功的"借到了"十万支箭。你还知道哪一些打破常规思维，最后成功的故事？

References

ACTFL-NCSSFL. (2017). NCSSFL-ACTFL can-do statements. Retrieved May 5th, 2024, from https://www.actfl.org/resources/ncssfl-actfl-can-do-statements

Byram, M. (2008). *From foreign language education to education for intercultural citizenship: Essays and reflections*. Clevedon: Multilingual Matters.

Byram, M. (2021). *Teaching and assessing intercultural communicative competence* (2nd ed.). Clevedon: Multilingual Matters.

Byram, M., & Wagner, M. (2018). Making a difference: Language education for intercultural and international dialogue. *Foreign Language Annals, 51*(1), 140–151.

McTighe, G., & Wiggins, J. (2005). *Understanding by design* (2nd ed.). Alexandria, VA: Assn. for Supervision & Curriculum Development ASCD.

Nation, P. (2007). The four strands. *Innovation in Language Learning and Teaching, 1*(1), 2–13.

Right Question Institute (RQI). (2023) *What is the QFT?* Retrieved from https://rightquestion.org/what-is-the-qft/

Schuder, T., Clewell, S., & Jackson, N. (1989). Getting the gist of expository text. In K. D. Muth (Ed.), *Children's comprehension of text*. Newark, DE: International Reading Association.

5 "Cháng'é Ascending to the Moon" 《嫦娥奔月》 (Cháng'é Bēnyuè)

Teaching Ancient Chinese Mythology through Social Semiotics

- **Language Proficiency Level:** Advanced low; can be adapted for advanced-mid and advanced-high;
- **ICC Developmental Goals:** Compare practices and products of the Chinese moon aesthetics in traditional, modern, and global contexts; recognize differences in products and practices and relate them to context and perspective;
- **High School/AP Theme:** Families and communities – family relationship; moon aesthetics – perspectives of nature in Chinese culture; contemporary life – holidays and celebrations;
- **Suggested College Course:** Chinese Communication and Composition; Advanced Chinese Language and Culture; Advanced Chinese Language and Culture through Stories;
- **Suggested Instructional Time:** Three lessons, about one instructional hour each, followed by a performance-based task.

1. Introduction

《嫦娥奔月》 (Cháng'é Bēnyuè, 'Cháng'é Ascending to the Moon') is a well-known story in Chinese mythology, along with other stories such as 《盘古开天劈地》 (Pángǔ Kāitiān Pīdì, 'Pángǔ Splitting Up the Sky and Earth'), 《女娲造人》 (Nǚwā Zàorén, 'Nǚwā Creating Humans'), 《女娲补天》 (Nǚwā Bǔtiān, 'Nǚwā Repairing the Broken Sky'), 《后羿射日》 (Hòuyì Shèrì, 'Hòuyì Shooting Down the Suns'), and 《大禹治水》 (Dàyǔ Zhìshuǐ, 'Dàyǔ Taming the Flood'). The story about Cháng'é, who is a moon goddess, arguably is the origin of a full range of Chinese aesthetic practices centered on the moon as a symbol for the fragility and resilience of life as well as a symbol for family in unity. The story of Cháng'é lends itself well to exploring the traditions of 中秋节 (Zhōngqiū jié, the Mid-Autumn Festival). The animated film 《飞奔到月球》 (Fēibēn Dào Yuèqiú, *Over the Moon*) produced by Netflix (Keane, 2020) provides a modern context to connect traditional Chinese moon aesthetics with regards to life as a cycle, with contemporary life conditions, especially, the state of depression caused by

DOI: 10.4324/9781003377276-5

irreversible losses in life. This unit demonstrates how teachers can connect traditional cultural mythology with contemporary life conditions and explore Chinese aesthetics within the context of a globalized Chinese culture.

The current unit situates the story of Cháng'é in the broader context of Chinese mythology as this story is connected with the story of 《后羿射日》 (Hòuyì Shèrì, 'Hòuyì Shooting Down the Suns') where Cháng'é and Hòuyì are a married couple in the immortal world condemned to live on earth as mortals. Through teamwork, critical discussion, and creative tasks, students will develop a cross-cultural perspective on Chinese mythology relevant to both heritage and non-heritage Chinese language learners who seek a global understanding of the connections between history, language, and culture.

2. Contextualizing the Topic

Every culture has its ancient mythology that reveals the imagination of the culture's ancestors on the origin of the universe and the beginning of civilization. "Cháng'é Ascending to the Moon" is one such story that reflects the Chinese ancestors' ruminations about the moon. A skeletal version of the story goes as follows:

> *Cháng'é was married to Hòuyì, a famous archer. They lived as immortals in a heavenly realm ruled by the emperor of heaven, Tiandi. Tiandi had ten sons in training to become sun gods. Each day, one of the sons would take a turn in the sky to give light and warmth to the people on earth. However, the ten sun gods grew bored of the routine and decided to appear in the sky together. This caused extreme heat that scorched the earth, destroying crops and trees and killing people and animals. Tiandi called upon Hòuyì for help and gave him a special bow and arrows. Hòuyì was meant to scare the sun gods, but he ended up shooting down nine of them, leaving only one. Though the people on earth were saved, Tiandi was furious about losing his nine sons. As punishment, Hòuyì and Cháng'é were stripped of their immortality and had to live as mortals on earth. Hòuyì struggled to make a living by teaching archery and hunting. Hòuyì couldn't bear to see Cháng'é living in poverty and growing old, so he sought help from Mother Queen of the West. She gave him two doses of an elixir that could grant immortality only on earth. However, Cháng'é consumed both doses, and as a result, she transformed back into a heavenly being. Her body floated up, and she flew to the moon, where she resides to this day.*

This skeletal story leaves much space for details, and it is in the details that the story conveys its moral overtone. Some versions of the story depict Cháng'é as a loving, loyal wife who swallowed both portions of the elixir when she tried to guard it against Péng Méng, a greedy, calculating apprentice of Hòuyì who wanted the elixir for himself. Other versions depict her as a selfish woman who wanted the life of an immortal all for herself. In the various versions, the reason for Cháng'é's choosing the moon as a permanent home also differs. Some stories depict Cháng'é as feeling too ashamed to return to the heavenly realm and choosing to live alone on the moon. Other stories imagined that the strength of the elixir waned off before Cháng'é could reach heaven, or that Cháng'é chose the moon because it was the celestial object closest to earth where she could see her husband from afar. These different versions notwithstanding, a constant element among the variations is that the moon is a lonesome place and Cháng'é was condemned to living in perpetual loneliness while her husband lived and died as a mortal being on earth.

While the origin of the story of Cháng'é came from a later text, the story of Hòuyì, along with most other ancient Chinese mythology, was originally recorded in the legendary text 《山海经》 (Shānhǎijīng, *The Guideways through Mountains and Seas*; ca. 4th century BCE; the English translation of the title is based on Strassberg, 2002), which was attributed to the travel logs of 大禹 (Dàyǔ, or Yǔ the Great Engineer), as he spent years traveling through central China leading a monumental-scale engineering project focused on flood control (袁珂, 1983).

Cháng'é's story, like the multitudes of stories about the moon across cultures, is imagined to account for the shadowy shapes on the moon visible to the human eyes on a bright night. The gentle, calming energy of the moon, in contrast to the powerful sun, correlates to the imagination of Cháng'é with features of femininity reflecting the traditional role of women in Chinese society. The story of Cháng'é initially appeared in a Daoist text titled 《淮南子》 (Huáinánzi), written by 刘安 (Liú Ān; ca. 139 BCE). Although the original appearance of the story was recorded in just a few lines, the symbol of Cháng'é ascending to the moon has inspired a large volume of classical poetry and verses which in turn have created rich aesthetics centering on the moon. Moon aesthetics is arguably one of the most prevalent aesthetic practices in Chinese culture preserved in the rituals of the Mid-Autumn Festival (i.e., Moon Festival) and the sentiments evoked by the sight of a full moon that are shared among members of Chinese communities.

The lessons illustrated in this chapter comprise a one-week unit in a college-level Chinese language course titled "Chinese Culture through Classic Stories." The course is an advanced-level, 15-week elective course for students pursuing a Chinese minor, typically taken in a student's fourth year of study. The curriculum is designed to accommodate a mixed-levels class where students may come from a range of Chinese heritage and non-heritage backgrounds as well as students whose Chinese L1 background was interrupted upon arriving in the United States during their pre-teenage years.

The course is structured around thematic units aimed at exposing students to Chinese classic stories by sampling selective stories retold for language learners. Because the course is mixed levels, to account for both Chinese-as-a-foreign language learners and students from a Chinese heritage background with prior familiarity with the stories, the methodology is collaborative during class and self-paced at home, allowing for the most flexibility in individualized learning, to reserve class time for a "meeting of the minds" where the discussions benefit from different learner backgrounds.

A close study of the "Cháng'é Ascending to the Moon" story is based on the class's input text, written for language learners accompanied by authentic children's cartoons that tell the same plot in two contrasting versions. The contrasting versions are chosen to raise students' awareness that myths are cultural products. The moral values sustaining the internal logic of the story are subject to the dominant assumptions about gender roles in that time and the social context in which the story was transmitted. Throughout this unit we situate the plot of the story within an understanding of the symbolism of the moon in Chinese culture that is shared with or different from other cultures.

Toward the end of the unit, the activities connect the traditional story of Cháng'é with contemporary globalized Chinese culture based on a discussion of Netflix's *Over the Moon*, an animated musical movie about a young girl named 菲菲 (Fēifēi) in her quest to fly to the moon, find Cháng'é, and learn the secret of true love. The story is set in an imaginary town modeled after 乌镇 (Wūzhèn), a historical scenic town in eastern China. The connection between the classic Cháng'é story and *Over the Moon* is obvious: Cháng'é is one of the main characters in the film who helps Fēifēi to cope with the loss of her mother to cancer and her father marrying again. Fēifēi, in turn, helps Cháng'é to cope with the loss of her husband. At the end of the film, both Fēifēi and Cháng'é overcome their depressive states and are able to hope and love again.

Another reason for incorporating Netflix's retelling of the Cháng'é story is to utilize the rich symbolisms in the film that directly pay tribute to the original story while building on a globalized Chinese culture. Students are guided to notice the symbols from the traditional story utilized in the animated film. The film also has scenes recognizable as stages of grief. In addition, the surprising appearance of Cháng'é as a flashy superstar on the moon is so dramatically different from the traditional image of Cháng'é that the contrast encourages students to reflect on classic cultural stories as symbolic and malleable.

The particular lesson unit we outline here takes inspiration from social semiotics (see section 3). Social semiotics is an approach that examines signs as being socially constructed. For example, to understand the meaning of the moon (the sign) as a significant symbol in Chinese culture, we need to understand the sociocultural and literary contexts from which the sign emerged and how its meanings get fixed over time. This approach, in the context of classic fables, suggests that we do not focus on the story itself but focus on how the story gave rise to and constitutes components of Chinese people's metaphors and sentiments about the moon aesthetically and philosophically. This approach can overcome the "fatigue" of teaching a well-known traditional story by facilitating students to use the story as a source for their imaginations.

3. Methodology Highlight: Social Semiotics

Signs are everywhere around us: language as spoken, written down, and signed; still and moving images; sounds and music; gestures; colors; street signs; tattoos on bodies; and so on. We are surrounded by forms that signal meaning to us. Semiotics is the study of signs and how signs become vehicles of meaning. Social semiotics is a specific theoretical framework for signs that sees meaning as socially constructed (Bezemer & Kress, 2016; Jewit & Kress, 2003; Lemke, 1993; Van Leeuwen,

2005). Departing from the traditional view in semiotics that focuses on signs as autonomous systems of meaning, social semiotics focuses on the social environment where signs are created, fixed, consumed, altered, and re-invented. Gunther Kress and Theo Van Leeuwen are pioneers in applying the principles of social semiotics to the classroom setting where students are guided to approach meaning through personalized, individualized lenses capable of connecting the existing signs to new space, time, and audience. By understanding signs as social practice, students are no longer consumers of cultural products; they can deconstruct comprising elements of cultural symbols and apply these elements in new contexts.

In this chapter, we demonstrate that the crucial approach to traditional cultural stories, as guided by social semiotics, is to equip students with the tools from semiotics to notice, interpret, and even create new meanings for signs. This methodology is especially useful for teaching "fatigued" stories where it may appear at first glance that nothing new can be learned. This methodology is also useful for teaching a mixed-level class where students may differ in their language proficiency, but where the focus is on cognitive skills such as noticing, observing, categorizing, inferencing, and creating based on signs that are not only text-based but primarily visual and aural. Students can communicate in the target language with personally meaningful contents that are refreshing and new to one another.

In the context of this lesson unit, social semiotics was found to be most effective when students were given step-by-step guidance and were able to build on initial intuitive reactions to signs. Therefore, the construction of this unit utilizes scaffolded pre-teaching materials, in-class activities, and collaborative performative assessment to help the students to develop their own skills but to do so collaboratively.

Details on implementing this approach are discussed in section 5.

4. Curricular Modeling

We begin the unit by introducing the story of Cháng'é as part of the suite of ancient Chinese myths where we introduce the classic text 《山海经》 (Shānhǎijīng). We introduce the book's cultural status and use a subtitled "crash course" style animation clip to help students develop an introductory understanding of the main mythical figures of ancient Chinese times. This survey of classic Chinese mythology serves as the prerequisite cultural context for the focused attention on 《后羿射日》 (Hòuyì Shèrì) and 《嫦娥奔月》 (Cháng'é Bēnyuè) as two parts of one story. After students have gotten familiar with the story through the input text, students watch two children's cartoons that portray two different versions of the story – the contrast helps to raise awareness of traditional gender roles prescribed to Cháng'é as well as to strengthen vocabulary and sentence patterns that are repeated in the authentic input. The last hour of the unit focuses on the film 《飞奔到月球》 (Fēibēn Dào Yuèqiú, *Over the Moon*) to raise students' awareness of common as well as changed cultural elements and to build intercultural perspectives.

By focusing on different versions of the story of Cháng'é both traditionally told in Chinese culture and told for a global contemporary audience, the unit aims to help students develop intercultural communicative skills where students use the story as a form to express what the moon symbolizes in traditional Chinese culture and connect traditional Chinese aesthetics with a conscious reflection of how the moon aesthetics can help people in different cultures to be resilient against obstacles and aversive changes in life.

4.1 Learning Outcomes

The following learning outcomes are two-fold, integrated by situating language skills development into ICC skills development and vice versa. In addition to the sample course context used for illustration, "Chinese Culture through Classic Stories," we also offer sample learning outcomes related to the macro language functions for the four language skills and integrated spoken and written communication. You can adapt the two sets of learning outcomes for your course context. The important, common consideration is how these unit-specific learning outcomes, course-specific learning outcomes, language performance descriptor, and ICC developing goals relate to one another and are exemplified in the class activities. The learning outcomes provide the most important compass for backward design and assessment (McTighe & Wiggins, 2005).

Learning Outcomes as Part of the "Chinese Culture through Classic Stories" Course

The overall class goal is to provide you with (1) an explicit knowledge about Chinese myths and fables that have shaped the Chinese culture and (2) skills for advanced communication in Chinese. Overall, you will develop:

- better understanding of Chinese myths and fables
- skills in discussing myths and fables related to their cultural meaning and relating them to your own understanding of cultural differences
- the ability to tell stories and comment on them in standard Mandarin Chinese in oral and written modes
- better knowledge of idioms, including their historical meaning and current usage
- fluency, accuracy, and comprehensibility in overall spoken and written communication in Mandarin Chinese
- confidence, knowledge, and skills for navigating intercultural communication

---

The corresponding language performance goals of this specific unit are written in the "can do" format of "I can . . ." to make learners understand from their perspectives what they can achieve in this unit (ACTFL-NCSSFL, 2017).

Language Performance Objective (Can-Do Statements)

- I can follow the main story of "Cháng'é Ascending to the Moon" and "Hòuyì Shoots Down the Suns" and some supporting details across major time frames in fictional texts. (*Interpretive*)
- I can describe the basic facts about Shānhǎijīng. (*Presentational*)
- I can describe the customs of the Mid-Autumn Festival. (*Presentational*)
- I can explain the moon aesthetics in Chinese culture and apply them to discuss experiences dealing with challenges in family life. (*Presentational, Interpersonal*)

The corresponding ICC development goals are written based on four aspects of ICC: knowledge, attitude, skills, and critical cultural awareness (Byram, 2008, 2021; Byram & Wagner, 2018; inter alia).

Intercultural Communicative Competence Developmental Goals

- **Knowledge:** I can describe fully the story of "Cháng'é Ascending to the Moon" and "Hòuyì Shooting Down the Suns." I can describe the impact of Shānhǎijīng as the source of ancient Chinese mythology. I can describe the moon's symbolism in Chinese culture for a sense of unity and the cycle of life.
- **Attitude:** When describing "Cháng'é Ascending to the Moon," I can withhold judgment on Cháng'é's behavior but see her as a product of prescribed female gender roles in traditional patriarchal society. I can see the value of resilience in cultivating a balanced attitude when dealing with loss and aversive changes in life.
- **Skill:** I can explain the ways the moon is perceived in Chinese culture as a symbol for unity and a symbol for the cycle of life. I can recognize a range of concrete symbols in Chinese moon iconography.
- **Critical Cultural Awareness:** I am aware that the traditional fables are varied according to changing social contexts. I'm aware of the connection of the "Cháng'é Ascending to the Moon" story with the Mid-Autumn Festival. I am aware that literary practices have shaped Chinese moon aesthetics. I have become more aware of my own ideological practices and values about challenges in life as similar to or different from those of others and have consequently broadened my own perspective.

4.2. Materials

A. PowerPoint Lecture Slides and Student Handouts

- Introduction to ancient mythology
- Introduction to Shānhǎijīng
- Activating students' background knowledge
- Connecting Chinese culture with universal themes of ancient mythology
- Reinforcing language and ICC goals throughout collaborative activities and guided discussion

B. Video Materials

- A "crash course" style video with bilingual captions for a survey of mythical figures in ancient Chinese mythology
- Film *Over the Moon*
- Two children's cartoons from YouTube

C. Preview Packet

- The full text of 《后羿射日, 嫦娥奔月》 with vocabulary list, comprehension questions, and selected grammar patterns
- Online supplement: New words in two sets, one with Pinyin and one without Pinyin, hosted on Quizlet.com
- Online supplement: Self-paced quiz to assess initial story comprehension

D. Enrichment Packet

- Introduction to Shānhǎijīng in more detail and relevant vocabulary
- Introduction to the literary origin of the Cháng'é and variations of the story
- Introduction to Chinese moon iconography and relevant vocabulary
- Sampling classic poetry that gives rise to aesthetics about the moon

E. Study Packet

- Revisiting the story text told in the preview packet, accompanied by learning materials focused on specific language proficiency outcomes and the ICC learning outcomes of the unit
- Online supplement: Self-paced quiz to assess cultural knowledge and language skills.
- Unit-final communicative tasks

4.3. Suggested Learning Activities

This sample unit is divided into three lessons, approximately one hour each. The activities are geared toward advanced-low college students who are serious about Chinese learning. As a college-level class, contact hours are limited and much of the learning is expected to take place outside of class. The lessons use flipped instruction principles so that students can efficiently complete preparatory learning activities outside of class at their own pace, aided by media and language learning technology. The activities in class build on the assumption that students have completed the homework assignments on time and are ready to perform, discuss, and collaborate in class.

The timeline demonstrated in this sample unit proceeds with the first instructional hour on Monday, followed by homework on Tuesday (with the preview packet), the second instructional hour on Wednesday, followed by assigning the study packet that students work through to the weekend, giving flexible time for self-paced focused study and fluency-building. The third instructional hour occurs on Friday after students have watched the film *Over the Moon* on their own to focus the class time on exploring intercultural perspectives.

Lesson 1: Schema Activation; Introduction to Ancient Mythology

> Objectives: activate students' prior knowledge; raise awareness of current language proficiency for performing a narrative; develop a survey knowledge of ancient Chinese mythology.

The first instructional hour assumes no prior preparation and aims to activate schemata about the moon's symbolism and pique students' interest in the unit by situating the familiar stories about Hòuyì and Cháng'é in the less commonly known book, Shānhǎijīng. Because "Cháng'é Ascending to the Moon" is a very well-known story connected to one of the most celebrated Chinese festivals, the Mid-Autumn Festival, students from heritage and non-heritage backgrounds likely have some prior familiarity with the story. It is thus necessary to "reintroduce" the story as but one of a suite of ancient mythology, thus encouraging students to relate the unique story in the Chinese culture to common themes found in ancient mythology across culture.

Activity 1 (Estimated Time: 15 Minutes)

Materials: PowerPoint lecture slides; student handouts

- Start the lesson with iconic images from ancient Chinese mythology. Students work in groups to name the stories they can recognize from the images.
- Students self-assess how familiar they are with the stories and how confident they are in telling these stories in Chinese.

Activity 2 (Estimated Time: 25 Minutes)

Materials: PowerPoint lecture slides; a crash course video clip on Chinese mythology; Student Listening Handout

- Utilize the "crash course" style video of Chinese mythology to familiarize students with the suite of ancient Chinese mythology.

- Students complete a listening comprehension handout while they watch the video.
- Students work in groups to share notes from their listening comprehension handout. Each group nominate one person to speak a recap for one of the mythical figures.

Activity 3 (Estimated Time: 10 Minutes)

Materials: PowerPoint lecture slides

- Teacher lecture on 《山海经》 based on the PowerPoint lecture slides. Make explicit connection between the mythical figures that students just discussed in activity 2.
- Teacher announces homework and asks students to prepare one slide before the next class based on what they find interesting from reading the Enrichment Guide.

Homework after Lesson 1

- Assign the preview packet, which contains the story, new vocabulary, and exercises for initial story comprehension. Instruct students to study the story in the preview packet, become familiar with the plot, watch the two children's cartoons as assigned in the preview packet and be ready to share their views in next session.
- Assign the enrichment packet. Explain the function of the enrichment packet (i.e., to generate interest and provide additional context). Remind students they will each prepare a slide and present in Chinese on one of the cultural topics they find interesting from reading the enrichment guide.
- Before the next class, in the course Learning Management System (LMS), students complete an online self-paced quiz with comprehension questions, vocabulary exercise, and cultural knowledge tasks based on the preview packet and the enrichment packet.

Lesson 2: Story Plot Clarification; Student Presentations

> Objectives: review vocabulary and cultural knowledge about ancient Chinese mythology; clarify story plot; practice speaking while personalizing and diversifying perspectives on moon symbolism and ancient mythology.

After completing the preview packet, students should come to lesson 2 already familiar with the story plot and related vocabulary. Also, each student should have contributed one slide to the class lecture slide deck and be ready to give a short, informal presentation in Chinese. To help students continue absorbing the new cultural themes and terminology, the first half of the second hour is devoted mainly to review, clarify, and assess knowledge from lesson 1 as well as the preview packet and the enrichment packet. Once the story plot is sorted out, the remaining time is designated for the mini presentation by each student. This design relies on the maturity and self-study skills of the students. Lesson 2 is a pivotal lesson where the teacher facilitates students' comprehension of the story's plot while starting to focus on intercultural perspectives.

Activity 1: Review Mythology and Related New Words (Estimated Time: 5 Minutes)

Materials: PowerPoint lecture slides; the "Spot the Errors" activity in the Slides deck

- In groups, students work on recalling the ancient myths and use the "Spot the Errors" exercise to enjoy reviewing new words related to the ancient myths.
- Teacher solicits answers from students and clarify as needed.

Activity 2: Story Plot Clarification; Story Personalization (Estimated Time: 15 Minutes)

Materials: Student Role-and-Answer Handout

- Students work in groups and play a roll-and-answer dice game to clarify the plot of the Cháng'é story. Teacher walks around and clarify the plot for groups as needed.
- Regroup for whole-class discussion. Teacher briefly recaps the open-ended question from the preview packet homework regarding why the two cartoon stories present Cháng'é's behaviors differently.
- Project the unit-final speaking task on the lecture slide. Ask students to work in groups to share preliminary ideas in preparation for part 2 of the speaking task.

Activity 3: Student-led Cultural Presentation (Estimated Time: 30 Minutes)

Materials: PowerPoint lecture slides deck with students' slides added

- Students take turns delivering their short presentation on the cultural symbols they prepared as homework.
- Each student presenter asks their audience a question; each next student is charged with asking a question in return.

Homework after Lesson 2

- Instruct students to use the study packet to reinforce vocabulary, reading fluency, grammar skill, and critical cultural understanding.
- Students watch the film *Over the Moon* on their own.
- Students start preparing for the unit-final speaking and writing tasks.

110 *Cháng'é Ascending to the Moon* 《嫦娥奔月》

Lesson 3: Film Discussion; Moon Iconography and ICC Skills

> <u>Objectives:</u> compare and contrast cultural elements in story adaptation; critically understand Chinese moon iconography; develop intercultural communicative skills.

This lesson helps students to use language actively for exploring intercultural perspectives. Students should have watched *Over the Moon* on their own and planned some preliminary ideas for their unit final task. The activities start from simple schema activation to recognition of cultural symbols and conclude with a creative discussion on adaptations of mythological stories.

Activity 1: Warm Up (Estimated Time: 5 Minutes)

Materials: "I have never ever . . ." section of the PowerPoint lecture slides

- Uses the "I have never ever . . ." slide deck to activate students' recall of the plot of *Over the Moon* and orient students' attention to the story adaptation and symbolisms used in the film. The activity is a simple poll. Students raise their hands if they "have never ever" done the activity described on the slides. Teacher or a student volunteer can tally the poll results which yield a class profile in relation to the various cultural activities that comprise the "ambience" of the film.
- Ask students how they like the film. Do a quick poll of students' reaction to the film on a scale of one to seven (one being 不喜欢 and seven being 非常喜欢).

Activity 2: Plot Discussion (Estimated Time: 10 Minutes)

Materials: PowerPoint lecture slides

- Show the unit-final writing task on the lecture slide.
- Students share their reactions to the film by focusing on any of the three prompts.
- This activity should transition smoothy from activity 1 because it gives students a chance to discuss among themselves why their rating of the film was as such.

Activity 3: Moon Iconography; Story Adaptation (Estimated Time: 20 Minutes)

Materials: PowerPoint lecture slides; storyboard and moon iconography handout

- Using the lecture slides, teacher presents selective elements from the film adapted from the original moon goddess story – including how the

characters were changed, and how the settings were changed. The images on the slide draw from images from archeological findings, traditional Chinese paintings and images in *Over the Moon* designed for a contemporary global audience.
- Model what a storyboard looks like by using *Over the Moon* as an example. Most of the elements are self-explanatory. Stages of grief and the state of depression, symbolized by the transformed Moon Palace in the film, needs to be explicitly pointed out.
- Students work in groups to create their own storyboard.
- Students present their storyboard. Encourage different members to speak for their group.

Homework for Lesson 3

- Instruct students to complete the self-paced quiz for the study packet.
- Students complete the speaking and writing tasks for the unit.

4.4. Implementing Social Semiotics

Throughout the lessons, the focus is on cultural symbols and cultural stories as socially constructed. The informal presentation on cultural symbols (lesson 2, activity 3) serves as an activity template that can be used for any topic where students explore meaning construction and help each other to see meaning as socially constructed.

[Sample instruction for lesson 2, activity 3]

Research something you find interesting from reading the Enrichment Guide. You can delve deeper into the book 《山海经》, explore in detail another version of the Cháng'é story, or study a poem in full about the moon sampled in the Enrichment Guide. You could discuss another aspect of the moon's symbolism for you personally or a similar but different moon symbolism in your own culture. You could also talk about how your family celebrate 中秋节. You will add a slide to the class slide deck that includes:

1) a brief description in Chinese,
2) an image; and
3) a question for your classmates.

Please do this by midnight of the end of the day before our next class and be ready to present your slide for two minutes during class followed by one minute for questions. It is an informal, small presentation focusing on ideas.

This low-stakes activity leverages the diverse language and cultural backgrounds of students to see the same cultural symbol (the moon) from different angles. In our experience, students from heritage backgrounds, with more connection to Chinese culture outside of the class, may talk about the poems they could recite since childhood about the moon; students who completed elementary education in China were more familiar with 《山海经》 and often chose to present mythical creatures from the book. Students from non-heritage backgrounds tended to compare moon symbolism in Chinese culture to their own L1 culture, such as by contrasting the mythology of a wolf-man changing shape at the full moon or seeing the moon as made of cheese. These mini-presentations practice advanced language skills such as narrating and comparison and contrast. The short length and the mandate for a Q&A format helped students in different proficiency levels to engage with the contents while enjoying the diversity of the topics. The question component also gets students to engage in the interactive mode versus the presentational mode of language use. For example, a student presented on the nine-tailed fox 九尾狐 (Jiǔwěihú) and asked whether peers knew other stories based on the nine-tailed fox, which began a conversation about a similar mythical creature in Korean drama, Japanese anime, and video games. Without being technical on social semiotics, this peer-presentation activity gets students to focus on symbols and their social meaning while building their advanced Chinese skills.

Students enjoyed this activity because of its flexibility, allowing them to incorporate their own interests while connecting with instructed material and to see peers' different views without needing extensive vocabulary preparation and heavy cognitive processing. However, this activity is predicated on the class size being small so each student has up to two minutes of speaking time with one minute for questions. If the class is larger, students would need to be paired up, or more contact hours for this unit would need to be planned into the syllabus. The key to this activity is giving students solo time at the front of the classroom like a peer teacher. An important part of this activity is to require interaction: the presenter is instructed to ask their classmates a question, and the next presenter in line is charged with asking the presenter a question. There is no mandate on the types of questions to ask; the suspense is what keeps students interested, and it forefronts the goal of seeing meaning as varied and subject to sociocultural context.

All three activities in lesson 3 also intentionally utilize the social semiotics framework. These activities foreground the notion that cultural symbols are created in cultural contexts and change over time. These activities benefit from group work as different students notice and focus on different aspects of the film's adaptation which help broaden everyone's perspectives on elements of mythology and iconography as established and continuing to evolve. The storyboard activity encourages students to decide which new elements and setting reflecting their own life experiences and/or new social trends.

4.5. Assessment and Student Sample Work

Assessments of language proficiency goals and ICC goals are conducted outside of class at students' own pace in the rehearsed condition. This choice differs from some of the other chapters in this book where proficiency and performance assessment is done in class. This choice of self-paced assessment outside of class is geared toward a multi-level class. When students come from a mixture of heritage, non-heritage backgrounds, having the same assessment in a spontaneous, timed manner could be unrealistic and create a high-anxiety condition for non-heritage learners.

Formative Assessments

Formative assessments include impromptu speaking tasks in class, the slides students contribute to the class slide deck, the informal mini presentation and Q&As in class, the storyboard activity, and the self-paced quiz questions in the preview and the study packet. These assessments are completed by students at their own pace where the feedback helps students to gauge how well they are learning.

Summative Assessments

The unit-final tasks are spoken and written, assessed based on a product-oriented set of rubrics. Students are guided to reflect on their experience with cultural practices related to the Mid-Autumn Festival, about the moon story while articulating their intercultural reflections. The speaking task both asks students to read the story text aloud, which assesses students' overall pronunciation and intonation, and gives students options to reflect on the (inter)cultural theme of this unit. The writing task is connected to the film *Over the Moon* encouraging students to describe and elaborate on specific cultural elements from a critical or intercultural perspective. This unit-final writing task provides a multilayered context to revisit the Cháng'é and Hòuyì stories in relation to their modern rendition in *Over the Moon* for a global audience. The three prompts motivate students to write a response based on what they resonate with the most. Each prompt focuses on some interpretation of the film in connection with the original Cháng'é and Hòuyì stories and the utilization of cultural symbols for storytelling in the contemporary context for a global audience (for details of the prompts, see appendix 5.3).

As demonstrated in the student sample below that responded to the first prompt, for the language learning goals, the final task gives students opportunities to incorporate advanced language skills such as describing details, narrating over different time frames, inferencing, synthesizing, and making connections. As for the ICC goals, students demonstrated increased awareness related to knowledge, attitude, skill, and critical awareness.

主题：尽管失去了亲人，但幸福很重要☺
菲菲的母亲年轻时就去世了。菲菲非常难过，很想念她的妈妈。四年后，她的父亲正在考虑再次结婚。但是菲菲尚未处理妈妈的去世，不愿意欢迎一个新的妈妈和一个讨厌的弟弟。

我认为菲菲认同月亮女神，他们俩都在等待亲人回来。菲菲希望她的父亲也能等待并记住她的妈妈。菲菲认为，如果她的父亲如果像嫦娥的后羿一样，那么他不会再婚。我认为这部电影可以帮助孩子们理解现实生活。没有我们的爱人可能很难生活，但是保持悲伤并不健康。嫦娥告诉菲菲，她的母亲将永远和她在一起。菲菲不应该像她自己一样伤心。

在电影的结尾，嫦娥让自己开心起来，因为她不能活在过去。她有很多朋友，这些朋友非常爱她，希望她幸福。菲菲回到地球之前，她让自己的兔子呆在月球上，这是菲菲变得更加成熟的一个例子，因为菲菲的兔子爱上了月亮上嫦娥的兔子，她不想让兔子过得不快乐。同样，她也允许父亲再婚。虽然他的新妻子不能代替妈妈，但是菲菲知道她的母亲将永远和她在一起，她需要过上幸福的生活。

[Theme: Despite Losing Loved Ones, Happiness Is Important J

Feifei's mother passed away when she was young. Feifei was very sad and missed her mother dearly. Four years later, her father was considering getting married again. However, Feifei had not yet dealt with her mother's death and was reluctant to welcome a new stepmother and a disliked stepbrother.

I believe Feifei identifies with the moon goddess, as both of them are waiting for their loved ones to return. Feifei hopes her father can also wait and remember her mother. Feifei thinks that if her father were like Hòuyì, Cháng'é's husband, he would not remarry. I think this film can help children understand real-life situations. It can be challenging to live without our loved ones, but holding onto grief is not healthy. Cháng'é tells Feifei that her mother will always be with her. Feifei shouldn't be as sad as she is.

At the end of the movie, Cháng'é encourages herself to be happy because she cannot live in the past. She has many friends who love her dearly and want her to be happy. Before returning to Earth, Feifei leaves her rabbit on the moon. This is an example of Feifei maturing, as her rabbit has fallen in love with Cháng'é's rabbit on the moon, and she doesn't want the rabbit to be unhappy. Similarly, she allows her father to remarry. Although his new wife cannot replace her mother, Feifei knows her mother will always be with her, and she needs to live a happy life.]

5. Teacher's Reflections

One of the pioneers of social semiotics, J.L. Lemke argues, "Most of the creative capacity of our society is vested in the capability of individuals to connect networks not usually connected" (1993, p. 20). In this unit, we demonstrate that through classic stories, we have the opportunity to engage with stories not told for one community only but for the same community in different times and across cultural boundaries.

This unit is primarily designed for a mixed-levels college classroom, as seen in the many activities that are based on group work; this allows students to benefit from one another's views and perspectives. Explicit language practice inside the classroom is rare. Students in a mixed-levels course tend to not benefit from explicit language practice in the classroom or assessment using the same prompts because of their different proficiency levels and cultural familiarity. Thus, the activities are designed to have a variety of self-paced language practice opportunities, performed in class under rehearsed conditions, and final assessment provides multiple options where students can engage based on the depth of their cultural knowledge as well as their personal interest. Adaptations can be made if you have a relatively homogeneous group of all heritage or all non-heritage students. For example, you can adapt the pace of the lessons based on several other chapters where more explicit language practice and explicit in-class language assessment are incorporated and the class uses the same prompts and language-proficiency benchmarks (e.g., chapter 2). This sample unit makes use of flipped instruction principles where knowledge-building and language preparation occur as homework outside of class. It works best when students take great care in preparing for each instructional hour. This is suited for a college-level setting, as students tend to be motivated and resourceful learners. For high school students, the activities set for homework are adaptable for face-to-face learning with more contact hours.

There are numerous cartoon clips on YouTube that tell the "Cháng'é Ascending to the Moon" story. The current unit selected two short children's cartoons for these reasons: (1) the language is clear with standard Mandarin suited for advanced-low students; (2) there are subtitles; (3) the two versions differ in their depiction of Cháng'é (in one story, she is loving and loyal and in another version, although not explicitly said, Cháng'é's actions appear to be selfish and greedy; the contrasting plots allow students to reflect on perspectives in storytelling); (4) the cartoons themselves are drawn with simple images such that students are not overloaded with visual cues and can focus on listening to the story; (5) the story focuses on Cháng'é and the moon festival customs, without other complicating characters peripheral to the learning outcomes of this unit; thus, the choice of the cartoons controls the complexity of the input to allow time to focus on the language and ICC goals of the unit.

The Cháng'é story has been featured in numerous classic poems and told to children in storybooks and cartoons. However, the Cháng'é story has not been adapted for the big screen, as far as we know, probably because it is a simple and well-known story lacking allure for a general audience. Netflix's *Over the Moon* is a fresh take on the Cháng'é story and the moon aesthetics set in China but appeals to a wider audience, particularly Chinese Americans. The parallel between Cháng'é's traditional story and *Over the Moon* is unique; the new story does not focus on Cháng'é but on a young girl who flies to the moon on her firecracker-fueled, magnet suspension, train-inspired spacecraft, accompanied by her new half-brother who is a table tennis enthusiast and her pet rabbit. Although students are to watch the film on their own, the teacher can play several one-minute scenes in class to highlight the theme of the cycle of life. Cháng'é's depressive state, visualized in Pavilion of the Broken Heart (断肠阁 Duàncháng gé) on the moon, provides a powerful image of the mental state of depression and makes her recovery, with the help of her companions and Feifei, even more touching and empowering. Playing some of the scenes in class could spark conversations and solidify the ICC goals of the class, as well as make sure that students notice and understand some of the powerful images.

Over the Moon is one of Netflix's attempts to "nativize" its contents such that the film was produced with a multicultural and multilingual team. The dialogue and the song lyrics are not dubbed but written differently in English and Chinese, well-suited for the linguistic complexity and cultural expectations of the respective target audiences. Audiences who watch the Chinese version of the film enjoy the Chinese dialogue without the often "tilted" translated versions used in traditional films. The songs featured on the film are gems, varying in style from pop to hip-hop to ballads.

In addition, as our model expounds, the sequencing works on a macro-micro-macro principle, where background and contexts are front-loaded for students first, before the focus shifts to the input text for the story, then shifts again to grammar and language-focusing work to return to macro levels of expression and discussion that analyzes cultural values and intercultural inquiries. These four strands of activities and the sequencing ensure that the classroom activities are varied and purposeful and give students the language support they need as well as opportunities to develop fluent communication in the target skills.

Appendices: Sample Teaching Materials

Additional materials, including the PowerPoint lecture slides, sample quiz, Quizlet vocabulary sets, and handouts for in-class activities, can be requested online by scanning this QR code.

Appendix 5.1: Preview Packet

《后羿射日、嫦娥奔月》 预习作业（Preview Packet）

1. 课文 Lesson Text

《后羿射日、嫦娥奔月》

很久很久以前，天上住着一对<u>相亲相爱</u>的**夫妻**，**丈夫**叫**后羿**，是一名**神箭手**，**妻子**叫**嫦娥**，<u>操持家务</u>，<u>温柔能干</u>。

后羿、嫦娥和天上**众多**神仙一样，都归**天帝**管，天帝的妻子是太阳女神，生了十个太阳儿子。太阳兄弟们住在大海里一棵巨大的**扶桑树**里，每天轮着去天空上班，晚上又回到大海里。小太阳们慢慢长大，开始觉得这样**周而复始**的工作**无趣**极了。一天,兄弟们说,"**咱们兄弟十个一起去上班吧,一起说说笑笑**,比一个人有趣多了!"

于是,天上同时出现了十个太阳,**河流**一下子就被晒干了,农田、树木**瞬间就**被烤焦了,地上的小动物都被热死了,**凶猛**的大蛇也热得从地底爬出来,可怕极了。老百姓们**苦苦哀求**太阳兄弟,"求求你们,回家吧!我们**实在**热得受不了了!"兄弟们却觉得更有趣了,**哈哈大笑**起来。

消息传到了天帝那里。天帝请**神箭手**后羿去人间**教训教训**他的太阳儿子们,并给了后羿一张红色的**弓**,十支**镶着红色羽毛**的白色的箭。

后羿来到人间,看到老百姓们的可怕**遭遇**,就**警告**太阳兄弟,说:"你们这些**顽劣**的孩子,马上回家,要不然,别怪我的箭不长眼睛!"

太阳兄弟们**自诩**是天帝的儿子,根本就不把后羿放在眼里。他们不但不**听警告**,还**变本加厉**,跳起舞来,大地瞬间变成了火海。

后羿没时间多想,他**拉弓射箭**,"嗖!嗖!嗖!"九个太阳都掉下来,落在地上变成了金色的**乌鸦**。后羿还准备射出第十支箭,被老百姓们拉住了,说,"给我们留一个太阳吧,没有太阳也不行啊!"

天空**恢复**正常以后,后羿准备回天上,没想到天帝传下**命令**来,说,"后羿,既然你救了人间的老百姓,人间不能没有你,你就作为**凡人留在人间**吧。"

后羿这才明白,自己把天帝的九个孩子射死了,**得罪**了天帝。嫦娥也随着丈夫来到人间,成了凡人。为了**谋生**,后羿打猎,教人射箭,嫦娥**省吃俭用**,把日子过得**井井有条**。

后羿看见心爱的嫦娥一天天像凡人一样地老去,心里非常难过。他听说昆仑山的西王母有**长生不老药**,就翻过**燃烧**的**火焰山**,游过连羽毛都浮不起来的**弱水河**,来到昆仑山,向西王母求**长生不老药**。西王母说,"你来得**真巧**。一万年才能做好一颗**长生不老药**,我刚刚做好了两颗,我因为救百姓而得罪了天帝,变成了凡人,我就把这两颗药送给你,吃一颗可以**长生不老**,吃两颗可以**重新变成神仙**。"

后羿仔细地把药收好,游过弱水河,翻过火焰山,回到家,把西王母的话告诉了妻子。两人打算一起吃长生不老药,一人一颗。

没想到,**夫妻**间的对话被后羿的一个**心术不正**的弟子蓬蒙听见了。第二天,后羿带着弟子们出去打猎了,蓬蒙**假装**生病不能去。等后羿他们走远了以后,蓬蒙**闯进**嫦娥的家,逼嫦娥交出**长生不老药**。嫦娥情急之下,把两颗药**藏在**嘴里,不小心**吞**了下去,她的身体越来越轻,**不由自主地飘**起来,从窗户**飘**出去,越飘越高,越飘越远。

"怎么办?怎么办?"嫦娥**舍不得**离开后羿,就朝着月亮的方向飞去。"月亮是离地球最近的地方,让我留在月亮上吧!"

嫦娥飞到月亮上,看见月亮上只有一棵桂花树,树下有一只小白兔。嫦娥把兔子抱在怀里,望着地球的方向,眼泪一串串地掉下来。

后羿回到家,**伤心欲绝**,**夜晚**,他抬头看天,发现月亮和平常不一样,月亮洁白明亮的**表面**出现了一个**熟悉的身影**。后羿在院子里摆出桌子,放上嫦娥平时最爱的点心和水果,抬头看着月亮,轻轻地呼唤妻子的名字。

后来,每年的八月十五日这一天,是月亮最圆最亮的时候,老百姓也跟后羿一起纪念嫦娥,吃月饼,看月亮,庆祝合家团圆,这一天就变成了中秋节。

"Cháng'é Ascending to the Moon" 《嫦娥奔月》

Language Coding Key

Bold: new vocabulary
<u>Underlined</u>: formal register, four-character fixed expressions
Italic: grammatical indicators

2. 故事里的人物和地名 Characters and Places from the Story Text

1) 嫦娥　　　　Cháng'é　　　　　　　Cháng'é the moon goddess
2) 后羿　　　　Hòuyì　　　　　　　　Hòuyì the Legendary Archer
3) 天帝　　　　Tiāndì　　　　　　　　Emperor of Heaven
4) 太阳女神　　tàiyáng nǚshén　　　　the sun goddess
5) 扶桑树　　　fúsāng shù　　　　　　hibiscus tree
6) 西王母　　　Xīwángmǔ　　　　　　Queen Mother of the West
7) 长生不老药　chángshēng bùlǎo yào　elixir for immortality
8) 火焰山　　　Huǒyàn shān　　　　　Flame Mountain
9) 弱水河　　　Ruòshuǐ hé　　　　　　Ruoshui River
10) 昆仑山　　　Kūnlún shān　　　　　Kunlun Mountain
11) 蓬蒙　　　　Péng Méng　　　　　　Péng Méng, Hòuyì's apprentice
12) 地球　　　　dìqiú　　　　　　　　Earth
13) 月亮　　　　yuèliàng　　　　　　　Moon
14) 桂花树　　　guìhuā shù　　　　　　osmanthus tree
15) 小白兔　　　xiǎo bái tù　　　　　　little white rabbit

3. New Words from the Lesson Text 故事里的生词

16) 相亲相爱　　xiāngqīn xiāng'ài　　　love each other
17) 夫妻　　　　fūqī　　　　　　　　　husband and wife
18) 神箭手　　　shénjiànshǒu　　　　　legendary archer
19) 丈夫　　　　zhàngfū　　　　　　　husband
20) 妻子　　　　qīzi　　　　　　　　　wife
21) 温柔能干　　wēnróu nénggàn　　　　gentle and capable
22) 操持家务　　cāochí jiāwù　　　　　manage housework
23) 众多　　　　zhòngduō　　　　　　　numerous
24) 周而复始　　zhōu'érfùshǐ　　　　　repeatedly
25) 无趣　　　　wúqù　　　　　　　　　boring
26) 说说笑笑　　shuōshuō xiàoxiào　　　talk and laugh
27) 咱们　　　　zánmen　　　　　　　　we (including the addressee, colloquial)
28) 河流　　　　héliú　　　　　　　　　rivers
29) 晒干　　　　shài gān　　　　　　　dried up
30) 瞬间　　　　shùnjiān　　　　　　　momentarily
31) 烤焦　　　　kǎo jiāo　　　　　　　burnt up
32) 凶猛　　　　xiōngměng　　　　　　ferocious
33) 地底　　　　dìdǐ　　　　　　　　　underground

34)	爬	pá	crawl
35)	苦苦哀求	kǔkǔ āiqiú	beg
36)	实在	shízài	really
37)	哈哈大笑	hāhā dà xiào	laugh out loud
38)	消息	xiāoxī	news
39)	羽毛	yǔmáo	feather
40)	一张弓	yī zhānggōng	a bow
41)	一支箭	yī zhī jiàn	an arrow
42)	教训	jiàoxùn	teach a lesson
43)	叮嘱	dīngzhǔ	ask; pay attention to
44)	可怕遭遇	kěpà zāoyù	terrible experience
45)	警告	jǐnggào	warn
46)	顽劣	wánliè	naughty and awful
47)	别怪	bié guài	don't blame
48)	自诩	zìxǔ regard	oneself as
49)	变本加厉	biànběnjiālì	be worse
50)	拉弓射箭	lāgōng shèjiàn	draw bow and archery
51)	嗖	sōu	whoosh
52)	乌鸦	wūyā	crow
53)	准备	zhǔnbèi	prepare
54)	恢复	huīfù	recover
55)	命令	mìnglìng	order
56)	凡人	fánrén	mortal
57)	人间	rénjiān	human world
58)	得罪	dézuì	offend
59)	谋生	móushēng	make a living
60)	省吃俭用	shěng chī jiǎn yòng	live frugally
61)	内疚	nèijiù	feeling guilty
62)	长生不老	chángshēng bùlǎo	live forever
63)	燃烧	ránshāo	burn, in fire
64)	重新	chóngxīn	again
65)	心术不正	xīnshù bùzhèng	bad character, evil-spirited
66)	假装	jiǎzhuāng	pretend
67)	闯进	chuǎng jìn	break into
68)	情急之下	qíngjí zhī xià	in desperation
69)	藏	cáng	hide
70)	吞下去	tūn xiàqù	swallow
71)	身体	shēntǐ	Body
72)	不由自主	bùyóuzìzhǔ	involuntarily
73)	飘	piāo	fly
74)	舍不得	shěbudé	unwilling to
75)	朝着	cháozhe	toward
76)	伤心欲绝	shāngxīn yù jué	heartbroken
77)	夜晚	yèwǎn	night

78)	洁白明亮	jiébái míngliàng	white and bright
79)	表面	biǎomiàn	surface
80)	熟悉的身影	shúxīde shēnyǐng	familiar figure

4. 生词练习

a) Match the fixed expressions on the left to their colloquial paraphrase on the right.

心术不正	自己不能控制自己
伤心欲绝	不乱买贵的东西吃，不随便花钱
长生不老	反反复复，结束了又开始
相亲相爱	太着急了，没有时间准备
周而复始	永远活着，不会变老
变本加厉	脾气很好，做事情也做得很好
省吃俭用	非常伤心，想死的感觉。
不由自主	品格不好，会做坏事
情急之下	互相爱着，很亲的感觉
温柔能干	比原来更坏了，更糟糕了。

b) Match the verb (action) on the left with a suitable object on the right based on the story text.

射	弓
拉	箭
吞	名字
呼唤	药
翻过	焦
烤	火焰山
游过	家务
操持	弱水河

5. 课文理解 Text Comprehension

a) Answer the following questions in full sentences based on the story you read. Try your best to incorporate new words and fixed expressions.

1) 后羿是谁？嫦娥是谁？
2) 天上为什么出现了十个太阳？人间变成了什么样子？
3) 后羿怎么得罪了天帝，被留在了人间？
4) 后羿为什么需要长生不老药，他去哪儿、从谁那里得到了长生不老药？
5) 为什么嫦娥自己吞下了长生不老药？然后发生了什么？
6) 为什么嫦娥飘去了月亮上？月亮上有什么？
7) 后羿回家知道嫦娥不见了，他开心还是不开心？ 他看到了什么，然后做了什么？

b) Watch the two kids' cartoons telling the same story with different details. 这两个视频都是讲《后羿射日、嫦娥奔月》的故事，有什么不一样？你觉得为什么会不一样？Be ready to share your answers in class.

https://youtu.be/ahcQYuPIgtg (Watch the first 9 minutes)
https://youtu.be/NjL9n4RRINQ

6. Cultural Enrichments 文化延展

Read the Enrichment Guide. Complement the Preview Packet quiz online.

Appendix 5.2: Enrichment Guide

《后羿射日、嫦娥奔月》Enrichment Guide

1. 中国的上古神话和《山海经》Ancient Chinese Mythology and Shānhǎijīng

Much of what we know of ancient Chinese mythology (上古神话 shànggǔ shénhuà) was first recorded 《山海经》 (Shānhǎijīng, *The Guideways through Mountains and Seas*), such as Pángǔ splitting up the earth and sky (盘古开天辟地 Pángǔ kāitiānpìdì), Nǚwā repairing the broken sky with colorful stones (女娲补天 Nǚwā bǔtiān), Nǚwā creating humans and giving their power to procreate (女娲造人 Nǚwā zàorén), Yǔ the Great Engineer constructing flood-control systems (大禹治水 Dàyǔ zhìshuǐ), the tribal leader Kuāfù chasing the sun and succumbing to thirst (夸父追日 Kuāfù zhuī rì), as well as ancient wars (黄帝蚩尤之战 Huángdì Chīyóu zhī zhàn) and the origin of the Chinese (written) language (仓颉造字 Cāngjié zàozì).

Keywords

1)	《山海经》	Shānhǎijīng	The Guideways through Mountains and Seas
2)	上古神话	shànggǔ shénhuà	ancient mythology
3)	盘古开天辟地	Pángǔ kāitiānpìdì Pángǔ	Splitting up the Sky and the Earth
4)	仓颉造字	Cāngjié zàozì Cāngjié	Creating Chinese Characters
5)	女娲补天	Nǚwā bǔtiān Nǚwa	Mending the Sky
6)	女娲造人	Nǚwā zàorén Nǚwa	Creating Humans
7)	大禹治水	Dàyǔ zhìshuǐ Dàyǔ	Controlling the Great Flood
8)	黄帝	Huángdì	The Yellow Emperor
9)	蚩尤	Chīyóu Chīyóu,	a powerful tribal leader

2. 《山海经》是一本有趣的古书

Written around the 4th century BCE (公元前四世纪 Gōngyuán qián sì shìjì), Shānhǎijīng did not have a known authorship, but its origin was often attributed to the travelling logs of the mythological figure Yu the Great Engineer (大禹) during his leadership of a ten-year flood-control project that took him across various regions of China. Shānhǎijīng describes the geography and culture of China in the pre-Qin period (先秦时期 xiānqín shíqí). The book combines the realistic and the fantastical. The rich details and vivid imaginations in the book offer insights into China's rich landscapes (地貌 dìmào), minerals (矿物 kuàngwù), plants (植物 zhíwù), animals (动物 dòngwù), and ancient mythology (上古神话 shànggǔ shénhuà).

This encyclopedic-style book describes over 500 mountains (500多座山), more than 300 rivers (300条河), 277 animals (277种动物), and over 50 mythical figures (50多位神话人物). The descriptions vary from the mundane to the fantastical, featuring creatures like the nine-tailed fox (九尾狐), a fish with nine bodies (九身鱼), and the guardian beast at Kunlun Mountain with nine human heads (有九张人脸的昆仑兽).

The mythical figures are equally extraordinary; for instance, the Queen Mother of the West (西王母) possesses a human body, tiger's teeth, and a cheetah's tail (人身, 虎牙, 豹尾). Scholars such as Yuán Kē (袁珂) and Lǔ Xùn (鲁迅) suggest that Shānhǎijīng is best interpreted as a witchcraft book (巫书) used during the pre-Qin era to legitimize witchcraft in the name of Yu the Great Engineer (大禹). This interpretation also elucidates why the book intricately blends mundane and fantastical details and why it takes particular interest in recording the medicinal uses of various plants and animals.

Shānhǎijīng is now recognized as an encyclopedia (神话地理志 or 博物志). Shānhǎijīng is gaining popularity among today's younger generations. The ancient, fantastical world depicted in the book has inspired numerous creative endeavors, influencing product branding, costume design, and fantastical characters in various forms of art, movies, television, and video games.

Keywords

1)	公元前	gōngyuán qián	BCE
2)	公元	gōngyuán	CE
3)	先秦时期	xiān Qín shíqí pre-Qin	period
4)	动物	dòngwù	animal
5)	植物	zhíwù	plant
6)	地貌	dìmào	landscape, geological features
7)	矿物	kuàngwù	mineral
8)	西王母	Xīwángmǔ	Queen Mother of the West
9)	昆仑兽	Kūnlún shòu	the guardian beast of Kunlun Mountain
10)	九身鱼	jiǔshēn yú	nine-bodied fish
11)	九尾狐	jiǔwěi hú	nine-tailed fox
12)	虎牙	hǔyá	tiger teeth
13)	豹尾	bàowěi	cheetah tail
14)	袁珂	Yuán Kē Yuán Kē,	scholar on Chinese mythology

15)	鲁迅	Lǔ Xùn Lǔ Xùn,	writer, essayist, and scholar
16)	神话人物	shénhuà rénwù	mythical figures
17)	巫书	wūshū	witchcraft book
18)	神话地理志	shénhuà dìlǐ zhì	mythological geographic accounts
19)	博物志	bówù zhì	records of natural history

3. 关于嫦娥的多种说法 Various Versions of the Tale of Cháng'é

Cháng'é and Hòuyì were a married couple in Chinese mythology, but their stories did not originate from the same period. Hòuyì's story first appeared in Shānhǎijīng where Hòuyì is a famed archer who shot down nine suns which saved the people on earth. In the same text, the moon goddess was not associated with 后羿 (Hòuyì). Her name was 常曦 (Chángxī), and she was portrayed as the wife of the Emperor of Heaven. The Emperor of Heaven had two wives – the sun goddess, who gave birth to ten suns, and the moon goddess, who gave birth to twelve moon daughters. Shānhǎijīng depicted the moon goddess bathing her twelve daughters in the heavenly river. This imagery reveals that, from the inception of Chinese philosophical thinking about the natural world, the moon is connected with water and femininity, both representing the yin side of the yin-yang balance of energy in ancient Chinese cosmology.

The contemporary story of the moon goddess, where she is Hòuyì's wife and secretly consumes the elixir of immortality, resulting in her ascending to the moon, was initially recorded in 《淮南子》 (Huáinánzi), a collection of essays compiled by the Western Han scholar 刘安 (Liú Ān) in the 2nd century BCE. Essay Six of Huáinánzi describes the following where the name attributed to the moon goddess was 姮娥 (Héng'é):

> …羿请不死药于西王母，姮娥窃以奔月，怅然有丧，无以续之。
>
> "(Hòu)yì requested the elixir of immortality from the Queen Mother of the West, and Héng'é stole it to ascend to the moon. (Hòuyì) felt deep loss and sorrow and there was no way the loss could be recovered from."

This version of the story depicts the moon goddess in poor moral character. Scholarly annotations of Huáinánzi further perpetuated this gender-based stigma. According to the annotation of Huáinánzi by Gāo Yòu (高诱) in the Eastern Han (25–220 CE) period:

> …姮娥，羿妻；羿请不死药于西王母，未及服食之，姮娥盗食之，得仙，奔入月中为月精也。
>
> "Héng'é was (Hòu)yì's wife; Yì sought the elixir of immortality from the Queen Mother of the West. Before he could consume it, Héng'é stole it and ate it, attained immortality, and flew into the moon where she became the Spirit of the Moon."

The questionable moral character ascribed to the moon goddess reflects a common rhetoric in traditional patriarchal society where women are often depicted as emotional and a source of trouble (红颜祸水 hóngyán huò huǐ, "a beautiful woman is a source of calamity"). Numerous annotations and folktales expanded on the story of the moon goddess in Huáinánzi. For instance, one version suggests that she consumed the elixir out of anger toward her husband, who was involved in an extramarital affair. In an alternate narrative, Hòuyì transforms into a tyrannical ruler on Earth, and Cháng'é consumes the elixir to prevent the cruel Hòuyì from achieving immortality.

Keywords

1) 月亮　　　yuè liàng　　　　　　the Moon
2) 嫦娥　　　Cháng'é Cháng'é　　　(name of the moon goddess)
3) 姮娥　　　Héng'é Héng'é　　　　(another name of a moon goddess)
4) 常曦　　　Chángxī Chángxī　　　(yet another name of a moon goddess)
5) 《淮南子》 Huáinánzi Huáinánzi　(a collection of essays)
6) 刘安　　　Liú Ān Liú Ān　　　　(Western Han scholar, compiler of Huáinánzi)
7) 红颜祸水　hóngyán huò huǐ　　　A beautiful woman is a source of calamity
8) 西汉　　　Xīhàn　　　　　　　　the Western Hàn Dynasty

4. 嫦娥奔月的意象 Iconography of Cháng'é Ascending to the Moon

Besides Cháng'é, who resides on the moon, various folktales and literary sources have introduced additional characters on the moon. These include an osmanthus tree, a man who chops at the tree, a rabbit running or pounding with a mortar and pestle, a toad, and a palace where Cháng'é lives. Archaeological findings provide evidence for the popularity and evolution of moon iconography over time. A Tang Dynasty bronze mirror is adorned with depictions of Cháng'é, an osmanthus tree, a toad, and a rabbit with a mortar and pestle. The well-known T-shaped silk banner discovered in one of the tombs at Mawangdui (马王堆) in Changsha, China, features an image of a massive toad and a dancing rabbit on the moon. In this scene, Cháng'é is depicted flying toward the moon while riding on a half-bird, half-dragon creature. The cultural meanings of the various components of Chinese moon iconography are outlined here:

- 吴刚伐桂 (Wú Gāng fá guì, 'Wú Gāng Chopping at the Osmanthus Tree')

Huáinánzi mentioned the presence of an osmanthus tree on the moon, arguably to explain the shadows on the moon's surface visible from Earth. Later texts from the Tang Dynasty introduced the mythical tale of Wú Gāng. Wú Gāng, a devout Daoist, pursued the goal of achieving immortality. His arrogance offended the Emperor of Heaven, resulting in his punishment of endlessly chopping at the osmanthus tree on the moon. The osmanthus tree possessed self-healing power, regenerating each time Wú Gāng chopped at it.

- 蟾蜍 (chánchú, 'toad')

In Gāo Yòu's annotation of Huáinánzi, it is mentioned that Cháng'é flew to the moon, where she instantly transformed into 月精 (yuè jīng, 'spirit of the moon'). Subsequent literary texts expanded on this narrative, describing the moon spirit taking the form of a toad – an unflattering image likely associated with a sense of "punishment" for Cháng'é, who had stolen the elixir. However, scholars like 闻一多 (Wén Yīduō, 1899–1946) have suggested that the archaic pronunciation of the Chinese words for "rabbit" and "toad" were similar. Plausibly, the idea of a toad might have resulted from a phonetic error, with "rabbit" being mistakenly interpreted as "toad."

- 广寒宫 (Guǎnghángōng, 'Moon. Place'), 月宫 (Yuègōng, 'Moon Palace'), 蟾宫 (Chángōng, 'Toad Palace')

The palace where Cháng'é resides has several names. Guǎnghángōng evokes the image of the palace as 广 (guǎng, 'spacious') and 寒 (hán, 'cold'). Various ancient paintings depict the Moon Palace with traditional architecture featuring carved wooden beams and pillars and ornate roofs with upturned eaves. In these depictions, Cháng'é is often shown wearing a sorrowful expression, adorned in elaborate celestial attire, typically in white or other pale colors.

- 月桂 (yuè guì, 'moon osmanthus' or 'the osmanthus tree on the moon')/蟾宫折桂 (Chán gōng zhé guì 'to obtain a branch of the osmanthus tree in the Toad Palace.')

The osmanthus tree (桂花树, guìhuā shù) blooms fragrantly in autumn, coinciding with the period of the Mid-Autumn Festival. Dried flowers from this tree are commonly used as ingredients in pastries and desserts offered during the festival, as well as added to teas. Since the mention in Huáinánzi that a magical osmanthus tree grows on the moon, subsequent literary texts have gradually associated the osmanthus tree on the moon with the highest achievement for scholars in the imperial examination. The expression 蟾宫折桂 (Chángōng zhé guì, "obtaining a branch of the osmanthus tree at the Toad Palace") serves as a metaphor for that scholarly achievement.

- 玉兔捣药 (Yùtù dǎo yào, 'Jade Rabbit pounding with a mortar and pestle')

In Chinese moon culture, the jade rabbit iconography features a white rabbit (or hare) diligently pounding with a mortar and pestle. The substance being pounded is believed to be the elixir for immortality, which Cháng'é wishes to create for her husband, or simply the ingredients for making mooncakes. The rabbit is described ornamentally as "jade," both because jade is white and symbolizes a cool and calming substance. The jade rabbit has evolved into a symbol of loyalty and companionship. Artworks depicting the jade rabbit pounding with a mortar and pestle can be found in various decorations during the Mid-Autumn Festival.

Keywords

1) 桂树　　　guì shù　　　osmanthus tree
2) 吴刚伐桂　Wú Gāng fá guì　Wú Gāng chopping at the osmanthus tree

3)	蟾蜍	chánchú	toad
4)	月宫	Yuègōng	Moon Palace
5)	广寒宫	Guǎnghángōng	Guǎnghán Palace (another name of the Moon Place)
6)	蟾宫	Chángōng	Toad Palace (another name of the Moon Palace)
7)	月桂	yuè guì	Moon osmanthus (osmanthus tree on the Moon)
8)	蟾宫折桂	Chángōng zhé guì	obtaining a branch of the osmanthus tree at the Toad Palace
9)	玉兔捣药	Yùtù dǎo yào	Jade Rabbit pounding with a mortar and pestle

5. 中秋节的习俗 Customs of the Mid-Autumn Festival

The moon goddess story gave rise to the traditions of the Mid-Autumn Festival (中秋节 zhōngqiūjié). On August 15 of the lunar calendar, Chinese families celebrate (庆祝 qìngzhù) the Mid-Autumn Festival. This usually falls in September or early October in the solar calendar.

- Family Reunion Dinner (吃团圆饭 chī tuányuán fàn)

The foods featured at the Mid-Autumn Festival, besides the moon cakes, sample typical autumn harvests based on the agricultural traditions of different regions; for example, crabs are a common delicacy on the Mid-Autumn Festival table in eastern coastal parts of China, and taro roots are featured on the festive tables in southern regions of China. Lotus roots, pomegranates, water chestnuts, and osmanthus flower wine are also unique autumn delicacies with auspicious meanings.

- Mooncakes (月饼 yuèbǐng)

Mooncakes are round pastries filled with sweet or savory fillings like lotus seed paste, red bean paste, nuts, or salted egg yolk, or minced meats and ham. These round pastries often have intricate designs on top, featuring traditional patterns and Chinese characters indicating the ingredients inside the pastry. Gifting mooncakes is very common during the Mid-Autumn Festival.

- Appreciating the Full Moon (赏月 shǎngyuè).

The full moon during the Mid-Autumn Festival is considered the brightest and roundest of the year. Families often go outside to admire the moon and indulge in activities like carrying lanterns, reciting poems, or enjoying moonlit walks. It is also a tradition to appreciate the moon by flowing water such as the ocean, the lake, or the river, to appreciate the reflection of the moon. The full, bright moon rising above water and the glimmering reflection of moon light is a metaphor for family in unity as well as a metaphor for appreciating life's good fortune despite the unavoidable ups and downs as the waxing and waning of the moon.

Keywords

1)	中秋节	Zhōngqiū Jié	Mid-Autumn Festival
2)	庆祝	qìngzhù zhōngqiū	celebrate
3)	农历八月十五	nónglì bāyuè shíwǔ	15th day of the eighth month in the lunar calendar
4)	阳历	yánglì	solar calendar
5)	吃团圆饭	Chī tuányuán fàn	eating a reunion dinner
6)	螃蟹	pángxiè	crabs
7)	芋头	yùtou	taro roots
8)	莲藕	liánǒu	lotus roots
9)	石榴	shíliú	pomegranates
10)	桂花酒	guìhuā jiǔ	osmanthus flower wine
11)	月饼	yuèbǐng	mooncakes
12)	甜的	tián de	sweet
13)	咸的	xián de	salty
14)	五仁的	wǔrén de	five-nut (a type of filling in mooncakes)
15)	肉的	ròu de	meat-filled
16)	火腿的	huǒtuǐ de	ham-filled
17)	莲蓉的	liánróng de	lotus seed paste-filled
18)	蛋黄	dànhuáng	salted egg yolk
19)	传统图案	chuántǒng Tú'àn	traditional patterns
20)	赏月	shǎng yuè	admiring the moon
21)	倒影	dàoyǐng	reflections

6. 嫦娥奔月的神话和中国的探月工程 The Moon Goddess Mythology and China's Lunar Exploration Program

Mythical figures are often incorporated into branding and product naming. The China National Space Administration (CNSA, 中国国家航天局, Zhōngguó Guójiā Hángtiān Jú) named its moon probes "嫦娥" (serially named 嫦娥一号, or Chang'e 1; 嫦娥二号, or Chang'e 2; etc.) and the moon rovers "玉兔" (also serially named 玉兔一号, or Yutu 1; 玉兔二号, or Yutu 2; etc.). The mythology-derived names contribute to the cultural pride associated with these scientific advancements.

Keywords

1)	探月工程	Tàn Yuè Gōngchéng	Lunar Exploration Program
2)	月球探测器	Yuèqiú tàncèqì	Lunar probe
3)	中国国家航天局	Zhōngguó Guójiā Hángtiān Jú	China National Space Administration (CNSA)
4)	嫦娥一号	Cháng'é Yī Hào	Chang'e 1 (the first lunar probe)
5)	嫦娥二号	Cháng'é Èr Hào	Chang'e 2 (the second lunar probe)

6) 玉兔一号　　　Yùtù Yī Hào　　　Yutu 1 (the first moon rover)
7) 玉兔二号　　　Yùtù Èr Hào　　　Yutu 2 (the second moon rover)
8) 月球车　　　　Yuèqiú Chē　　　moon rover

7. 《嫦娥奔月》神话对中文的影响 The Impact of the Moon Goddess Mythology on the Chinese Language

The moon holds significant symbolism in Chinese culture. Its monthly transformation, shifting from the crescent moon to the full moon, serves as a metaphor for the cycle of life where change is the only constant. The tale of Cháng'é, forever separated from her husband, imbues the full moon with symbolism representing family unity and romantic partnership. Numerous poems and essays in Chinese classic literature have contributed to the full moon rising above the sea becoming a symbol of friendship and universal benevolence that transcends time and space. The following is a collection of some of the most celebrated verses in Chinese classical poetry (古诗 gǔshī) about the full moon, intricately woven with Chinese Moon mythology.

作者	中文	翻译
苏轼 Sū Shì (Northern Song Dynasty, 1037–1101)	人有悲欢离合，月有阴晴圆缺，此事古难全。 Rén yǒu bēi huān lí hé, yuè yǒu yīn qíng yuán quē, cǐ shì gǔ nán quán.	People experience sorrow and joy, separation and reunion; the moon has its cloudy and clear times, and it keeps waxing and waning. Life is never perfect since ancient times.
	明月几时有，把酒问青天，不知天上宫阙，今夕是何年。 Míng yuè jǐ shí yǒu, bǎ jiǔ wèn qīng tiān, bù zhī tiān shàng gōng què, jīn xī shì hé nián.	When will there be a bright moon? I raise my wine glass and ask the sky: What year is it tonight in the celestial palace?
李白 Lǐ Bái (Tang Dynasty, 701–762)	床前明月光，疑是地上霜，举头望明月，低头思故乡。 Chuáng qián míng yuè guāng, yí shì dì shàng shuāng, jǔ tóu wàng míng yuè, dī tóu sī gù xiāng.	Bright moonlight before my bed, I thought it was frost on the ground. I lift my head to gaze at the bright moon, I look downward and think of my hometown.
	露从今夜白，月是故乡明。 Lù cóng jīn yè bái, yuè shì gù xiāng míng.	The dew is white from this night on, and the moon is the brightest in my hometown.

(continued)

"Cháng'é Ascending to the Moon" 《嫦娥奔月》   129

(continued)

作者	中文	翻译
	今人不见古时月，今月曾经照古人。古人今人若流水，共看明月皆如此。 Jīn rén bù jiàn gǔ shí yuè, jīn yuè céng jīng zhào gǔ rén. Gǔ rén jīn rén ruò liú shuǐ, gòng kàn míng yuè jiē rú cǐ.	People today do not see the moon of ancient times; the present moon has shone on the people of the past. Whether ancient or modern, people are like flowing water; they all gaze at the bright moon in the same way.
李商隐 Lǐ Shāngyǐn (Tang Dynasty, 813–858)	嫦娥应悔偷灵药，碧海青天夜夜心。 Cháng'é yīng huǐ tōu líng yào, bì hǎi qīng tiān yè yè xīn.	Chang'e should regret stealing the elixir; her heart is troubled night after night above the blue sea and under the azure sky.
张九龄 Zhāng Jiǔlíng (Tang Dynasty, 678–740)	海上生明月，天涯共此时。 Hǎi shàng shēng míng yuè, tiān yá gòng cǐ shí.	The bright moon rises over the sea; on distant ends of the earth, we share this moment.
张若虚 Zhāng Ruòxū (Tang Dynasty, 660–720)	春江潮水连海平，海上明月共潮生 Chūn jiāng cháo shuǐ lián hǎi píng, hǎi shàng míng yuè gòng cháo shēng.	The spring river tide merges with the level of the sea; the bright moon over the sea rises with the tide.
李清照 Lǐ Qīngzhào (Song Dynasty, 1084–1155)	云中谁寄锦书来？雁字回时，月满西楼。 Yún zhōng shéi jì jǐn shū lái? Yàn zì huí shí, yuè mǎn xī lóu.	Who sends a brocade letter from the clouds? When the wild geese return with their message, the moon is full over the west tower.

Appendix 5.3: Study Packet

《后羿射日、嫦娥奔月》 Study Packet

Read the story again and complete the activities.

1. Grammar

A. 被字句 bèizìjù is a passive construction in Chinese. Instead of the typical "who does what to whom" active sentence construction, the passive sentence construction starts with the "to whom" part of a situation, that is, it starts with the person or entity that an action has been done to. Then the do-er of the action is introduced into the sentence construction by the particle 被 bèi.

Recipient of the Action + 被 + **Do-er of the Action** + the Action w/Result

"Cháng'é Ascending to the Moon" 《嫦娥奔月》

a) <u>夫妻间的对话被心术不正的蓬蒙听见了</u>。

Translate: _____

b) <u>后羿被老百姓们拉住了</u>。

Translate: _____

Your sentences
c) _____
d) _____

The do-er can be omitted too, focusing on the consequence of the situation.

e) 天上同时出现了十个太阳，<u>河流一下子就被</u>(...)<u>晒干了</u>，农田、树木瞬间就被 (...) 烤焦了，地上的小动物都被 (...) 热死了。

Translate: _____

Your sentences
f) _____
g) _____

B. 把字句 bǎzìjù is an active sentence construction in Chinese that puts focus on the goal of an action. Instead of the typical "who does what to whom" active sentence construction, the particle 把 brings the recipient of the action early in the sentence. The effect is to make the reader focus on what happened to the object marked by 把.

<u>Do-er of the Action</u> + 把+ **Recipient of the Action** + <u>the Action w/Goal</u>

a) <u>嫦娥情急之下把</u>**两颗长生不老药**<u>藏在嘴里</u>.

Translate: _____

b) <u>太阳兄弟自诩是天帝的儿子，根本就不把</u>**后羿**<u>看在眼里</u>。

Translate: _____

c) <u>后羿拉开弓</u>，"嗖嗖嗖"一下子射了九支箭，把**九个太阳**<u>射了下来</u>。

Translate: _____

d) 因为后羿救了老百姓，<u>西王母把</u>**两颗长生不死药**<u>送给了后羿</u>。

Translate: _____

Your sentences
e) _____
f) _____

2. 复述故事

Answer the following questions in full sentences based on the story you read and incorporate the new words.

1) 后羿是谁？嫦娥是谁？(神仙，神箭手，操持家务，温柔能干，丈夫，妻子)
2) 天上为什么出现了十个太阳？人间变成什么样？（轮着，周而复始，无趣，一起，瞬间/都…被…了）
3) 后羿因为什么得罪了天帝，被留在了人间？（警告，变本加厉，把…射死，老百姓，救）
4) 后羿为什么想要长生不老药，从哪儿、怎么得到了长生不老药？（凡人，西王母，火焰山，弱水河，昆仑山）
5) 为什么嫦娥吞下了长生不老药？然后发生了什么？（蓬蒙，心术不正，闯进，逼，情急之下，把…藏在…，不小心，吞，不由自主）
6) 为什么嫦娥飘到了月亮上？月亮上有什么？（舍不得，离…最近，桂花树，小白兔）
7) 后羿回家发现嫦娥不见了，做了什么？（伤心欲绝，看月亮，发现，摆出，放上，呼唤，最圆最亮，纪念，合家团圆中秋节）

3. Speaking

Submit a recording on our class Padlet wall for this unit. Pay attention to your pace, word groups, tones, and pronunciation. Be as fluent, accurate and natural as you can for part 1. Be thorough and detailed, and incorporate class materials for part 2. *You are also required to listen to two peers' posts and leave a spoken or written comment for each of the two posts.*

Part 1: Record the lesson text.
Part 2: 说说你的想法：

- Option A: 你庆祝中秋节吗？说一说上一次印象比较深的一次，是怎么庆祝中秋节的（谁，做了什么，吃了什么，发生了什么，什么感觉）。
- Option B: 说一说月亮在中国文化里的寓意有哪一些，你自己最喜欢哪一个寓意，为什么呢？具体说一个跟这个寓意有关的经历。
- Option C: 在别的文化里，有关于月亮的神话故事吗？把这个故事跟嫦娥奔月比一比，有什么一样和不一样的地方？

4. Writing

Throughout this unit, we have studied two stories related to the sun and the moon (《后羿射日、嫦娥奔月》) as a part of ancient Chinese mythology. We've also watched a modern adaptation of the Cháng'é story created by Netflix for the global audience. Stories continue to be told and retold, and cultural notions of the moon continue to evolve. Your task is to write a reflection on the film by choosing one of the prompts below. Your post needs to be a minimum length of 400 Chinese characters and include an image. The post should be ready for final assessment, which means it should be proofread and error-free and it should reflect your best efforts to convey your thoughts clearly and oroughly and to demonstrate explicit connections to the topic.

1) 电影里嫦娥和后羿的故事的主题.

Pinpoint one theme based on the Cháng'é and Hòuyì stories utilized in the film. Describe relevant elements in the story, how it relates to the original Cháng'é and Hòuyì stories, and how you thought of this connection. Be specific in your answer.

2) 电影里的文化元素以及文化比较

Comment on several scenes in the film that depict Chinese culture while specifically paying tribute to the original Cháng'é and Hòuyì stories. Describe the scenes, explain how they are both depictions of Chinese culture and connected to the original Cháng'é and Hòuyì stories. Compare these cultural elements to practices in another culture you are familiar with.

3) 电影里喜欢的一幕和不太喜欢的一幕

Comment on one scene from the film that you really liked and one scene you don't quite like. Describe the two scenes, then explain your reasons for liking them or having some reservations about them. Connect your discussion to the film's adaptation of the original Cháng'é and Hòuyì stories.

Appendix 5.4: Storyboard Activity

A shorter, informal version of this activity is demonstrated in lesson 3 – activity 3 (section 4.3). The template below is based on using this activity as a unit-final project including a formal presentation and grading rubrics.

故事新编 Storyboard Activity Template

课堂讨论

如果把《嫦娥奔月》的故事改成一个现代的故事，你觉得什么元素是不能变的，什么元素特别适合现在的社会？Circle the ones that you think should remain the same; put a check mark to the ones that are good for modern adaptation. Be ready to share.

和月亮有关的：捣药的兔子，蟾蜍，月宫 ，桂花树，很冷，空空的，没有别人
嫦娥：美丽温柔，操持家务，神仙，和后羿相亲相爱，月亮女神，奔月，住在月宫里，孤独，思念后羿，吃了长生不死药
后羿：神箭手，从神仙变成凡人，和嫦娥相亲相爱，会死

"Cháng'é Ascending to the Moon"《嫦娥奔月》

月亮的文化寓意: 周而复始, 悲欢离合, 阴晴圆缺, 中秋节, 月饼, 家人团圆
别的:

讨论故事的改编

下面是《飞奔到月球》的故事板。跟同学们一起说一说你的想法: 哪些改编是你觉得最有创意的? 哪些是你意料中的, 哪些你觉得脑洞大开? 哪些你最喜欢? 哪些不很喜欢, 但是觉得很合适?

苏州/中国的水乡小镇/21世纪 (爱豆文化, 磁悬浮列车, 抑郁症)

Setting: time / place / social environment

菲菲: 她是一个中学生。从小就非常喜欢嫦娥的故事, 是和妈妈在一起的美好回忆

Main new character: who and their characteristics

妈妈因病去世了, 爸爸开始新的爱情, 菲菲很伤心, 觉得爸爸把妈妈忘了

Crisis / conflicts the main character is confronted with

菲菲造了火箭, 去了月球, 请嫦娥帮她找回爸爸和妈妈的真爱, 菲菲帮嫦娥走出了抑郁, 嫦娥帮菲菲接受新生活

Development: what happened; how the conflicts get resolved? What happened? What happened in the end?

菲菲带着对妈妈的回忆开始了新生活

Coda: Is there happily ever after?

嫦娥: 变成了月宫的爱豆, 因为见不到后羿得了抑郁症; 她的眼泪是月宫的能源

后羿: 还是一个凡人, 不能见到永生的嫦娥。

奔月: 变成了火箭奔月

玉兔: 变成了两只-宠物兔子和药剂师兔子

Connection to Chinese mythology: what elements from the classic story are incorporated in your new story?

策划新故事

Imagine you are leading the creative team of a media production company. With your group, brainstorm a new story with the 《嫦娥奔月》 story motif. Use the given storyboard to structure what you need to include. Be ready to present your ideas.

Your task is to create your unique storyboard. Put on Padlet or use the traditional PowerPoint slides and be ready to present your story. In your presentation, include these elements:

Part 1: Self-introduction (who you are); use several bullet points to give a bio sketch of you as the story creator.
Part 2: Comment on the work process while keeping your story sketch a secret yet.
How did the idea start (what inspired your new story)?
What is the most enjoyable (or the easiest) part of creating the story?
What is the most challenging part of creating the story?
Part 3: Present the sketch of your new story. Walk us through your story sketch; highlight cool elements. You must showcase how the story is both an adaptation (so the original motif is recognizable) and a novel approach.
Part 4: Questions and answers. Prepare one questions to ask the audience; then answer at least two questions from the audience; each next group is charged with asking questions.
Total time: 10 to 15 minutes.

Grading Rubric

Content (30 points): Addressed task fully. Personalized and related to class instructed materials accurately. Story original and interesting. Demonstrated depth of knowledge and critical thinking on the topic.
Visual (20 points): The audio-visual aspects of the project complement the topic very well. Demonstrated polished product for an engaging presentation.
Language (30 points): Greeted and thanked audience. Fluent, prepared, did not read from a script or do so only minimally with the help with speaker notes while carrying out a spontaneous, interactive manner. Used Mandarin consistently without needing to break into English. Used grammar and words that are suitable for a casual academic setting (think it like a serious conversation with some content-specific words). Good control of pace and flow.
Interaction (20 points): Engaged always. Spontaneous interaction. Demonstrated good time control. Always focused. Interacted with the audience well. Good orientation to the audience's background knowledge. Asked questions to audience and answered questions professionally with thorough information.

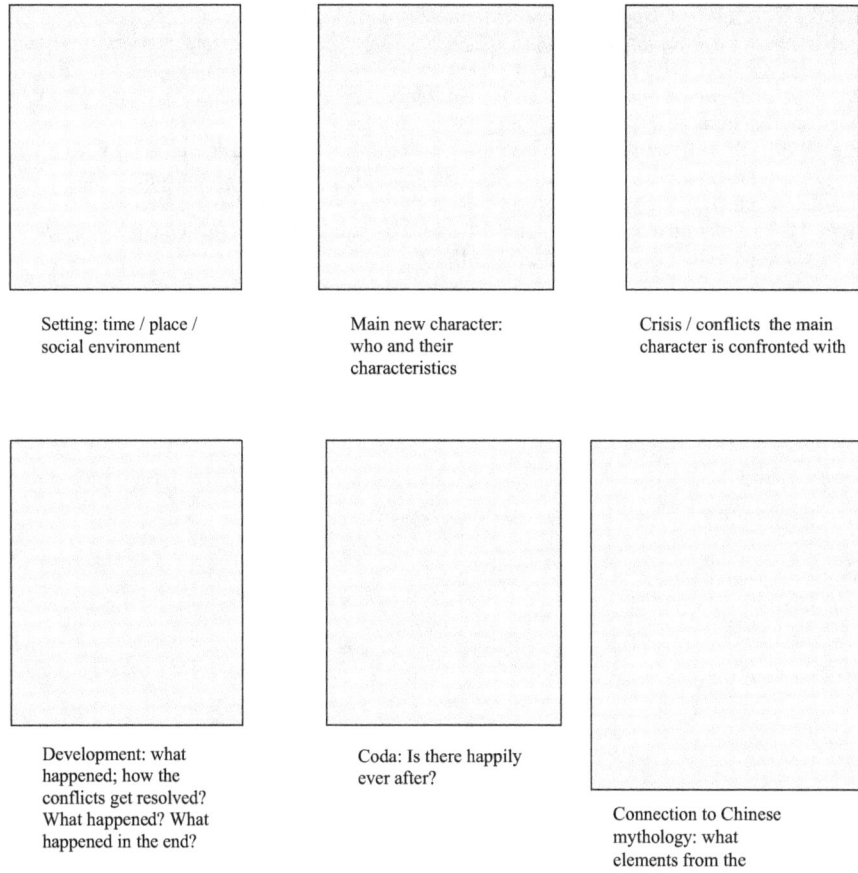

Setting: time / place / social environment

Main new character: who and their characteristics

Crisis / conflicts the main character is confronted with

Development: what happened; how the conflicts get resolved? What happened? What happened in the end?

Coda: Is there happily ever after?

Connection to Chinese mythology: what elements from the classic story are incorporated in your new story?

References

ACTFL-NCSSFL. (2017). *NCSSFL-ACTFL can-do statements*. Retrieved June 1, 2022, from www.actfl.org/resources/ncssfl-actfl-can-do-statements

Bezemer, J. J., & Kress, G. R. (2016). *Multimodality, learning and communication : A social semiotic frame*. Abingdon, UK: Routledge.

Byram, M. (2008). *From foreign language education to education for intercultural citizenship: Essays and reflections*. Clevedon: Multilingual Matters.

Byram, M. (2021). *Teaching and assessing intercultural communicative competence* (2nd ed.). Clevedon: Multilingual Matters.

Byram, M., & Wagner, M. (2018). Making a difference: Language education for intercultural and international dialogue. *Foreign Language Annals, 51*(1), 140–151.

Jewitt, C., & Kress, G. R. (2003). *Multimodal literacy*. New York, NY: Peter Lang.

Keane, G. (Director). (2020). *Over the Moon* (飞奔到月球) [Film]. Netflix and Pearl Studio.

Lemke, J. L. (1993). Cognition, context and learning: A social semiotic perspective. In D. Kirshner (Ed.), *Situated cognition theory: Social, neurological, and semiotic perspectives*. Mahwah, NJ: Erlbaum.

McTighe, G., & Wiggins, J. (2005). *Understanding by design* (2nd ed.). Alexandria, VA: Assn. for Supervision & Curriculum Development ASCD.

Strassberg, R. (Ed. and Trans.) (2002). *A Chinese bestiary: Strange creatures from the guideways through mountains and seas*. Berkeley: University of California Press.

Van Leeuwen, T. (2005). *Introducing social semiotics*. New York: Routledge.

袁珂 《中国神话传说》上海: 商务印书馆./Yuan Ke. (1983). *An introduction to Chinese mythology*. Shanghai: The Commercial Press.

6 Nézhā 《哪吒》

Teaching the Mythology of Nézhā through the *Text-to-Text, Text-to-Self, and Text-to-World* Connection-Making Strategy

- **Language Proficiency Level:** Intermediate mid to high;
- **ICC Development Goals:** Willingness to question the presupposition in one's social group;
- **High School/AP Theme:** Personal and public identity – self-image and the role of the individual in society; global challenges – diversity issues; families and communities – relationships and friendship; perspectives of ethnicity;
- **Suggested High School Course:** Chinese Level 4 or AP Chinese;
- **Suggested College Course:** Chinese Communication and Composition; Chinese Culture through Classic Course;
- **Suggested Instructional Time:** Fourteen 50-minute lessons (assessment time included).

1. Introduction

The story of 哪吒 (Nézhā) stands as one of the most beloved Chinese myths within Generation Z students in both the United States and around the world. This can be largely attributed to the popularity of various animated film adaptations produced in China (a 1997 film, a 2019 rendition, and a 2021 rendition). The 2019 version was chosen as an innovative vehicle for introducing students to the Nézhā myth, as it delves into a range of topics apparent in the movie, including contemplating the determinants of one's destiny, pondering the potential for altering one's fate, and investigating prevalent biases and prejudices within communities and societies. Students are also prompted to question whether these biases can be transformed and how they personally respond to bias in their surroundings. Moreover, the movie encourages discussions about one's support network, the dynamics of mutual assistance within it, and the evolution of life goals across different eras and generations.

The utilization of the text-to-text, text-to-self, and text-to-world approach empowers students to forge connections between timeless literary works and their individual experiences or existing knowledge. This process significantly contributes to the refinement of their intercultural communicative competence (ICC), enhancing their ability to navigate and engage with diverse cultural contexts.

2. Contextualizing the Topic

Chinese program in our high school has been developing its own thematic units for all levels for more than ten years, except for AP Chinese Language and Culture. This exception grants instructors' greater autonomy to incorporate the most up-to-date materials. Feedback from students universally indicates that this evolving curriculum fosters heightened engagement and a sense of accomplishment in their learning journey. Consequently, the enrollment in our Chinese language program has consistently witnessed an upward trajectory. The unit of lessons featured in this chapter is a component of the high school Chinese world language course titled *Chinese Four Accelerated.* This course also functions as a one-year dual-credit offering. Over 90% of the students enrolled are heritage speakers who possess prior Chinese language exposure before entering high school. Placement within various levels is determined through the ACTFL Assessment of Performance toward Proficiency in Languages® (AAPPL) test results. Following *Chinese Four Accelerated,* students can progress to more advanced Chinese courses, including *AP Chinese Language and Culture, Chinese Literature, Media, and Culture. Chinese Four Accelerated* encompasses a range of thematic units, including current and historical figures, customs and traditions, environmental protection, teenagers' lives, and the Chinese movies.

Utilizing movies as a pedagogical tool is among the most captivating methods to facilitate language and cultural learning. The Chinese Movies curriculum units provide students with an avenue to delve into various facets of Chinese culture and history. Through the film *Ne Zha*, students explore Chinese mythology; *Red Cliff II* delves into a segment of ancient Chinese history, while *To Live* presents a glimpse into modern history. The selection of *Ne Zha* as a focal point for this unit was guided by two primary factors. First, the movie achieved exceptional popularity upon its release, securing the distinction of being the third-highest-grossing film in China and the highest-grossing animated film originating from outside the United States. Additionally, *Ne Zha* offers an abundance of themes and quotes that prompt robust discussions and enable students to establish meaningful connections. Five central themes have been singled out for exploration in this movie unit: fate, bias/prejudice, the circle of support, parental roles, and life goals. Equally essential topics, including identity transformation, belonging, and the evolving role of women, warrant substantial classroom time for both high school and college students. Depending on instructional objectives and the maturity levels of the students, each of these topics can serve as a fertile ground for engaging discussions that enrich the learning experience.

The movie *Ne Zha* has produced many classic quotes, providing students with material for discussing the aforementioned central themes. Consequently, students can not only take note of the scenes but also record the quotes that resonate with them. This practice extends further as they establish connections that emerge from these interactions. Such an approach underscores the value of students' pre-existing knowledge and fosters a deeper engagement with the learning process. In the summative performance, students are afforded the opportunity to share their reflections on the movie while concurrently drawing connections to insights gained from other texts, their personal experiences and occurrences within their immediate or broader world. Throughout this process, students engage in a multifaceted exploration: they gaze out of the metaphorical "window" to observe the world through a different cultural and temporal lens; they introspectively "look at themselves in the mirror" and contemplate their individual experiences; and by interrelating their learning with events unfolding in their immediate or larger context, they nurture their ICC skills encompassing observation, interpretation, analysis, and evaluation. These skills, in turn, equip them to engage more effectively with others as they metaphorically open the "sliding door" (Bishop, 1990) to venture into the world and communicate across cultural boundaries. In essence, this *Ne Zha* movie unit functions as more than a language and cultural learning tool; it acts as a catalyst for students' ICC development, fostering their ability to navigate and interact within a culturally diverse landscape.

3. Methodology Highlight: *Text-to-Text, Text-to-Self, and Text-to-World* Connection-Making Strategy

Insights from expert reading specialists shed light on how world language teachers can more effectively guide students in their language learning using the four strands principle (Nation, 2007) and honing the skills required for ICC development. One of the ICC skills recommended by Byram (1997) is "interpreting and relating." The connection-making strategy of text-to-text, text-to-self, and text-to-world serves the purpose of "relating" perfectly. Keene and Zimmerman (1997) concluded that students comprehend better when they establish different types of connections: text-to-text, text-to-self, and text-to-world. The strategy of forming text-to-self connections involves forging deeply personal links between a piece of text and the reader's own experiences or life. Reading becomes more engaging and relatable when a text-to-self connection is established. For instance, a reader might express, "Nézhā's mom playing 毽子 (jiànzi), similar to shuttlecock, with him brings back sweet memories of my mom playing Pingpong with me when I was little."

Moreover, experienced readers often find themselves making connections to other texts they have read, whether these are works by the same author, stories from a similar genre, or texts on the same topic. These connections, termed text-to-text connections, offer valuable insights as readers relate the encountered information to familiar texts. For instance, stating, "Nézhā's fate is reminiscent of the one I encountered in the book *To Kill a Mockingbird*," exemplifies a text-to-text connection. Lastly, text-to-world connections encompass the broader associations readers bring to their reading experience. Our understanding of the world extends beyond personal experiences and is often shaped by information gathered from sources like television, movies, social media, magazines, and newspapers. Teachers frequently encourage text-to-world connections, particularly when imparting lessons in science, social studies, and language.

An example of a text-to-world connection would be when a reader reflects, "Nézhā's experience of isolation reminds me of some students' encounters with being singled out at school due to their appearance or their identity as minorities."

In the framework of this lesson, the connection-making strategy encompassing text-to-text, text-to-self, and text-to-world connections emerged as remarkably effective. This effectiveness stems from the fact that all five themes (fate, bias/prejudice, the circle of support, parental roles, and life goals) presented in the movie *Ne Zha* remain pertinent to students' lives in contemporary society. As a result, the activities conducted before, during, and after movie viewing are intricately aligned with the principles of the connection-making strategy.

4. Curricular Modeling

The following complete set of materials are ready for use in the classroom along with accompanying activities. These materials and suggested activities support and are guided by the learning outcomes described for the robust use of backward design principles (McTighe & Wiggins, 2005).

4.1 Learning Objectives and Primary Performance Assessments

Learning objectives are composed of two parts: language performance objectives and intercultural communication competence objectives. All of the learning objectives are written in the "can do" format of "I can . . ." to make learners understand from their perspectives what they can achieve in this unit (ACTFL-NCSSFL, 2017).

Language Performance Objective (Can-Do Statements)

关于神话故事 About Mythology

1) 我会描述中国和希腊神话故事中最主要的神话人物。I can describe the major mythological figures in Chinese and Greek mythology.
2) 我会描述神话故事中人神仙的能力区别以及地位如何转变。I can describe the difference between human beings' and immortals' powers and the status change between human beings and immortals in Chinese mythologies.

关于命运 About Fate

3) 我会表达我对命运这个话题的看法，比如说：命运由谁定？你能改变自己的命运吗？一生中有哪一些命运转变的机会？I can demonstrate my point of view about fate. I can discuss questions such as: Who decides one's fate? Can you change your fate? What are the major turning points of one's fate?

关于成见 *About Bias & Prejudice*

4) 我会表达我对于成见这个话题的看法，比如说：-人心中的成见可以改变吗？你对别人对你的成见的反应是什么？I can demonstrate my point of view on bias and prejudice by responding to questions such as: Can one's bias be changed? How would you respond to the bias toward you?

关于支持家人/朋友 *About Supporting Families and Friends*

5) 我会描述我的支持圈里有谁以及我们是如何相互支持的。I can list the individuals within my support circle and describe how we reciprocally aid one another.
6) 我会描述父母为了孩子的成功，付出的努力和做出的牺牲。I can describe the efforts and sacrifices that parents make for their children in order to help them succeed.

关于父母和孩子的关系/角色 *About Parent and Children's Relationship/Role*

7) 我会描述父母亲在家庭中的角色以及父母亲对孩子个性/人格形成的影响。I will describe the role of parents in the family and their influence on the formation of the child's personality.

关于人生奋斗目标 *About Life Goal*

8) 我会描述我和我的父母的奋斗目标，还有哪吒，敖丙的奋斗目标以及人生的奋斗目标是什么以及是如何在不同的时间阶段和不同的世代之间演变的。I will describe the goals of my parents and myself, as well as those of Nézhā and Áobǐng, and explore the goals in life and how they evolve across different time periods and generations.

The corresponding ICC development goals are written based on four aspects of ICC known as KASA: knowledge, attitude, skills, and critical intercultural awareness (Byram, 2008, 2021; Byram & Wagner, 2018; inter alia).

Intercultural Communicative Competence Developmental Goals

- **Knowledge**: I can describe fully the story of *Ne Zha*, list several key quotes, and explain the perspectives and values illustrated in the story.

> - **Attitudes:** When describing the plot of *Ne Zha,* I can withhold judgment about different figures' treatment of Nézhā in the episodes and keep an open mind about the differing perspectives and values that motivate various practices in the story.
> - **Skill:** I can relate Nézhā's experience of being labeled as an evil child, being always supported by parents, being misunderstood by villagers, and striving to change his own fate to the ones that I have encountered in my life, to the ones that I have read from other texts, and/or to the ones that are happening in my own world and the wider world. I can also further analyze the different perspectives and values that led to Nézhā's unique experience to help me think through similar issues that I encounter and offer solutions.
> - **Critical Intercultural Awareness:** I am aware that across different cultures and time periods, people's practices, perspectives, and values remain similar though difference exists.

The associated language performance assessments are outlined below, while the interpretive reading assessments and speaking prompts are available in the online supplements for this chapter.

4.2 Learning Materials

Learning materials for this *Ne Zha* movie unit are mainly in five categories: Google Slides, and video materials, a preview packet, an enrichment guide, and a study

Table 6.1 Primary Performance Assessment of the *Ne Zha* Unit

Communicative Modes	Language Performance Assessment
Interpretive Mode	• I can identify the main point and some details in reading selections about the scenes related to the major themes in the movie *Ne Zha*. • I can identify the main point and some details that students made in the writing about the movie and text-to-text, text-to-self, and text-to-world connections.
Presentational Mode	I can write a well-developed response to the movie *Ne Zha* using the following prompt: You've just finished watching the film *Ne Zha* and you're bursting with excitement to share your thoughts about it on your blog. In your writing, demonstrate your understanding of the main idea(s) of the movie/movie scenes. In this explanation, make connections to the characters and story with your own experiences (self), with other stories, articles, or movies that you know (text), and with the events that happen in the world around you (world).
Interpersonal Mode	I can participate in a simulated conversation by responding to a series of six related questions on the movie of *Ne Zha*.

packet (worksheet). The classroom-ready materials are presented in full in the appendices immediately after the chapter. The same materials and additional supplemental resources, in a flexible digital format, can be downloaded (refer to the appendices section).

A. Unit Plan:
   - The unit plan provides students with an overview of what will be covered, as well as the assessment methods, major learning vocabulary/structures, and other related resources.

B. Google Slides
   - Introduction of the well-known stories and characters in Chinese mythology, as well as the characters in Greek mythology.
   - Introduction to the differences between humans, gods, immortals, and supernatural beings.
   - Introduction of the major characters and their relationship to each other.
   - A comprehensive Chinese recap of each key plot point is paired with movie watching, exploring themes such as fate, prejudice, social status, self-identity, life goals, family bonds, friendship, etc. Additionally, insights are provided to connect with students' existing knowledge frameworks.
   - In-depth Chinese character profiles for each individual, accompanied by a vocabulary glossary.
   - Discussion of the classic quotes and make connections (text-to-text, text-to-self, and text-to-world).
   - Explanation and practice of key sentence structures.

C. Video Materials:
   - 《盘古开天劈地》 *Pángǔ Opens the Heavens and Splits the Earth*
   - 《女娲补天》 *Nǚwā Mends the Sky*
   - The 2019 version of the movie 《哪吒之魔童降世》 *Ne Zha*
   - 1979 《哪吒闹海》 *Prince Nézhā's Triumph Against Dragon King*

D. Preview Packet
   - The main characters and the character relationship chart.
   - The main plot of the movie 《哪吒之魔丸降世》 with vocabulary list, and comprehension questions.
   - Self-paced quiz to assess initial story comprehension.
   - Discussion questions related to the major unit themes.

E. Enrichment Guide
   - The background of Nézhā and the origin of his name.
   - Similarities between two popular Chinese mythological figures: Nézhā and Sūn Wùkōng.
   - The plot of the 1979 version of the animated movie 1979 《哪吒闹海》 *Prince Nézhā's Triumph Against Dragon King.*

144 *Nézhā* 《哪吒》

- The comparison between the 1979 and 2019 editions of the film.
- Ancient Chinese views on fate.

F. Worksheet and Study Packet

- Worksheet: "During: Make Connection; Text-to-Text, Text-to-Self, Text-to-World."
- Worksheet: "Post-Reflection after the Movie: Making Connections."
- Important quotes related to the same five themes discussed in the pre-movie activity.
- Study packet covering the main movie quotes, accompanied by English translations, vocabulary, and a set of exercises to further explore the meaning of the quotes.

G. Unit-Final Communicative Tasks

- Speaking assessment prompts.
- Essay prompts.
- Interpretive reading assessment.
- Assessment rubrics.

4.3 *Suggested Lessons and Activities*

The sample lessons and activities are designed for high school students who are in their fourth level of Chinese courses, which they have chosen as an elective course to fulfill either their high school graduation requirement or college admission requirement. They have a 50-minute Chinese class every day. Most of the learning occurs in the classroom, including watching a movie, and they are assigned a 10–20-minute homework task to review the day's material. The activities described in stage 2, which are detailed in the following, can be rearranged so that students can complete them outside of class, allowing for more in-person instruction time for activities that require it.

> *Notes on language choice for film viewing:* Our focus is on students' understanding of the story and the quotes in the film. It is important that the film comes with English subtitles. Later, students are guided to closely watch selected clips that highlight the selected topics/themes for this movie unit. For these selected clips that facilitate text-to-self, text-to-text, and text-to-world discussion, we provide the quotes in Chinese, with Pinyin and English meanings.

Students are provided with a learning packet encompassing all the materials listed in section 4.2. They also have access to all the daily instruction slides on the learning management system on Canvas, which enables students to retrieve all the resources to learn/review at their own pace when needed.

Nézhā 《哪吒》 145

> The pace and daily activities can and should be adjusted to align with the schedules of your particular class. For college students, moving activities from stage 2 out of the classroom can reduce instructional time by half. Instead of requiring fourteen 50-minute periods, seven 50-minute periods should be adequate. The five-stage activities outlined further here offer a framework for the fundamental phases of the unit, which can be customized to accommodate various class schedules.

The following five stages are the primary phases encompassing this movie unit. The lessons are meticulously crafted following the tenets of backward design and the four strands principles as outlined by Paul Nation (2007). Drawing from research in second language acquisition, Nation posits that a comprehensive language curriculum should allocate equitable attention to four distinct activity types: meaning-focused input, meaning-focused output, language-focused learning, and fluency development. These four strands of activities ensure a diverse and purpose-driven classroom experience, providing students not only with essential language support but also with opportunities to engage in meaningful communication, thereby enhancing their fluency in the targeted language.

Stage 1: Pre-Movie Watching. Building Background Knowledge (Periods 1–2, Estimated Time: 45–90 Minutes)

- Utilize the Unit Plan to introduce the new unit, incorporating information about the topic, learning objectives, major performance assessments, and learning resources.
- Employ the Preview Packet to gather information about the main character, Nézhā, and the main content of the movie.
- Introduce the five major themes of the movie (fate, bias/prejudice, the circle of support, parental roles, and life goals) and encourage students to share their thoughts and perspectives on these themes before viewing the film.

Stage 2: During Movie Watching. Learning and Discussing Five Major Themes (Periods 3–8, Estimated Time: About 200 Minutes)

- Prepare students with the necessary vocabulary for each scene using Quizlet and the vocabulary listed in the Study Packet.
- Watch the movie one scene at a time while taking notes, using the worksheet named "During: Make Connection; Text-to-Text, Text-to-Self, Text-to-World" to make connections.
- Facilitate a discussion about the five themes mentioned earlier in relation to the movie clips watched during that period. Encourage students to share the connections they have made in terms of text-to-text, text-to-self, and text-to-world.

146 *Nézhā* 《哪吒》

- Practice new vocabulary, enhance reading comprehension by using plot summaries in shared with students in the google slides for scenes watched during that period, and develop speaking and writing skills using a Formative platform (links in the online supplements for this chapter).
- Repeat the process until students finish watching the film.

Stage 3: Post Movie Watching. Further Learning and Discussion of Five Major Themes and Develop ICC Skills (Periods 9–10, About 45–90 Minutes)

- Prepare students with the necessary vocabulary for the movie quotes using Quizlet and the vocabulary listed in the Study Packet.
- Watch the movie trailer to capture students' attention regarding the key quotes.
- In pairs, students review/role-play the quotes in the Study Packet to understand their meanings.
- Initiate discussions about the important quotes related to the six themes, encouraging text-to-text, text-to-self, and text-to-world connections.

Stage 4: Post Movie Watching. Focused Practice to Build Language Fluency (Period 11, Estimated Time: 45 Minutes)

- Practice new vocabulary and grammatical patterns using Quizlet and the vocabulary listed in the Preview Packet and in the Study Packet (input).
- Focus on using the words in context by reading the introduction about the movie, the characters, and the major plot points written by the instructor (input).
- Engage in speaking practice with a partner using a set of questions related to the movie scenes and the six themes (output)

Stage 5: End of Unit. Summative Assessment (Periods 12–14, Estimated Time: 45–90 Minutes)

- Using the example provided in the worksheet "Post-Reflection after the Movie: Making Connections," students refer to their own notes on the worksheet "During: Make Connection; Text-to-Text, Text-to-Self, Text-to-World," which they worked on while watching the movie, and summarize the themes of their choice and deliberate on the connection.
- Using the ideas generated, write a response to the prompt listed in "Presentational Mode" in table 6.1.
- Interpersonal speaking assessments will be in the format of AP Chinese language and cultural test style, consisting of six questions. (Presentational writing assessment and interpersonal assessment can take place in the order of your preference.)

- Taking reading assessments about the major movie scenes, themes, and quotes. The excerpt from students' presentational writing can also be part of the reading assessments, especially the connections that they have made. If this aligns with your preference, have students take the reading assessment last.

For college students, all the activities in stage 2 and vocabulary preparation can take place outside of class to save classroom instruction time. For high school students, it is recommended to implement all the stages in class due to their maturity and motivation to learn Chinese as a selective course.

As students engage in discussions both during and following the movie, the connection-making strategy involving text-to-text, text-to-self, and text-to-world connections offers them a pathway to "gaze beyond the window, reflect within the mirror" and equips them for "passing through the sliding door" (Bishop, 1990) to engage in meaningful communication with others. The initial "text" pertains to the film *Ne Zha*, serving as a "window" through which students can explore the perspectives of others. When establishing text-to-self connections, they are enabled to relate their own experiences, as well as those of their family members and friends, to the events depicted in the movie *Ne Zha*. By forging text-to-text connections, they leverage their familiarity with books, videos, and other media to enhance understanding. Moreover, in making text-to-world connections, they gain the ability to share occurrences taking place around them – locally, nationally, and even globally – often among individuals from diverse backgrounds. Their descriptions of these connections frequently reveal particular attitudes, which can be analyzed to trace the development of their ICC with respect to the attitudinal component.

Owing to the presence of a substantial number of new vocabulary and terms, the performance (whether in written or spoken form) adopts an open-book, open-resource methodology, as it is viewed as an inherent aspect of the learning process. However, it's essential to highlight that copying and pasting directly is not permitted.

4.4 Implementing Text-to-Text, Text-to-Self, and Text-to-World Connection-Making Strategy

Keene and Zimmerman (1997) concluded that students achieve a deeper comprehension when they establish diverse types of connections: text-to-self, text-to-text, and text-to-world. This connection-making strategy aids students in cultivating the practice of forging these connections as they engage with reading or viewing material. By assigning a purpose to their reading or viewing, students enhance their comprehension and capacity to derive meaning from the content.

As detailed in section 4.3, which outlines the primary teaching and learning stages of the film *Ne Zha* unit, stages 2, 3, and 5 involve a progression from taking notes on the five key themes while watching the movie in the language of their choice (stage 2), to group sharing and discussions regarding scenes and significant quotes during and after the movie, primarily conducted in the target language (stage 3), and finally culminating in speaking, writing, and interpretive reading assessments (stage 5). Throughout all these stages, the connection-making strategy serves as a guiding framework, facilitating the learning process.

For a practical illustration of how to implement the connection-making strategy within this unit, reference can be made to the files "During: Make Connection; Text-to-Text, Text-to-Self, Text-to-World" and "Post-Reflection after the Movie: Making Connections."

5. Teacher's Reflections

Our high school's Chinese program embarked on the journey of crafting our unique curriculum units for all levels approximately a decade ago, with the exception of *AP Chinese Language and Culture*. This exception grants teacher's greater autonomy to incorporate the most current and authentic materials, amplifying the program's flexibility. As a result, the students' interest in learning Chinese has shown a consistent upswing since the adoption of this innovative approach.

Despite the escalating enthusiasm among students for learning Chinese, the substantial volume of new vocabulary required for successful completion of the movie unit poses a persistent challenge. To address this, an effective strategy involves equipping students with the necessary vocabulary and corresponding text aligned with each "digestible" topic. These topics encompass essential aspects like the movie's general introduction, character profiles and their dynamics, individual scenes, and more. By providing students access to vocabulary resources – potentially through platforms like Quizlet and/or within the Study Packet – and allowing them time to study these linguistic components prior to watching the movie, subsequently immersing themselves in context during the viewing, students are offered enhanced language input through both visual and auditory channels. Following each day's instruction, students are encouraged to reinforce their learning through diverse modes such as read-aloud exercises, typing, reading, and listening activities, facilitated by platforms like Formative. This comprehensive approach, incorporating both meaning-focused and language-focused learning, establishes a stronger foundation for students and bolsters their ability to perform effectively in subsequent assessments.

Additionally, adopting a forward-looking teaching approach and applying the connection-making strategy empowers students to attain levels of performance that might have eluded students in previous years. The Preview Packet proves indispensable in building students' background knowledge, removing comprehension barriers posed by the language and content during movie viewing. Resource such as the worksheets "During: Make Connection; Text-to-Text,

Text-to-Self, Text-to-World," "Post-Reflection after the Movie: Making Connections," "Important Quotes," and "Study Packet" within the Study Packet aid in maintaining students' focus on the content and language pertinent to their forthcoming performance. Moreover, the writing samples provided in the file "Post-Reflection after the Movie: Making Connections" offer students a clear benchmark for their final writing task. This writing assessment, designed as an open book evaluation, aligns with the philosophy that assessment is an integral part of the learning process. In facing the challenge of articulating their distinct ideas in Chinese, students find support through vocabulary lists, personal notes, samples, the Study Packet, and Google Slides. These resources make the assessment more manageable, and even learners who face considerable challenges are able to express their learning and establish meaningful connections, with minimal grammatical errors (note that copy and paste is prohibited during the writing assessment).

Among the three movies covered in the Chinese 4 Accelerated class (*Ne Zha, Red Cliff II, To Live*), *Ne Zha* consistently emerges as the students' favorite. If you haven't yet introduced this movie in your teaching, I encourage you to give it a try using the available resources – worksheets, vocabulary lists, Study Packet, Google Slides, Formative exercises, and assessments across all three modes. Your students might very well develop a fondness for the movie, much like their affection for the character Nézhā.

Appendices: Sample Teaching Materials

All materials in the appendices can be read online or downloaded by scanning the following QR code. Appendices 6.1 to 6.3 are fully enclosed here, while the remaining appendices are available online.

Appendix 6.1: Preview Packet

电影《哪吒》 预习作业 Preview Packet

Nézhā zhī mó tóng jiàngshì
哪吒之魔童降世
The Devil Child Nezha Came into the World

Nézhā 《哪吒》

1. 人物 Characters

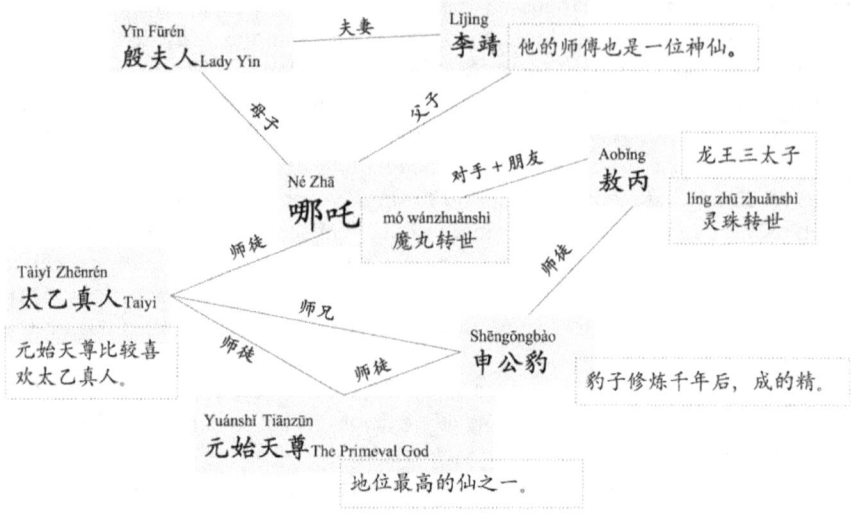

1) 元始天尊 Yuánshǐ Tiānzūn – Primeval God:

   Role: A powerful god whom Taiyi and Shen want to impress to become the 12th Golden Immortal.
   Actions: Split the Chaos Pearl, creating the demon orb and spirit pearl.

2) 太乙真人 Tàiyǐ Zhēnrén – Taiyi:

   Description: A funny immortal speaking a southern dialect. Though seeming foolish, he's well-trained in spells.
   Role: Competing for the 12th Golden Immortal position.

3) 申公豹 Shēn Gōngbào – Shen Gongbao:

   Description: Taiyi's rival who believes bias keeps him from becoming the 12th Golden Immortal due to his demon spirit.
   Perspective: Feels the world, including Yuanshi, is biased against him.

4) 李靖 Lǐ Jìng – Lord Li:

   Description: Nǎzhā's father and protector of Chentang Pass. Struggles to keep Nǎzhā safe despite challenges.
   Role: Central figure safeguarding his son and the pass.

5) 殷夫人 Yīn Fūrén – Lady Yin:

   Description: Nǎzhā's mother and lady of Chentang Pass. A soldier who loves and cheers up Nǎzhā.
   Interaction: Plays Jianzi with Nǎzhā to support him when isolated by villagers.

6) 敖丙 Áo Bǐng – Ao Bing:

   Description: The dragon king's son, empowered by the spirit pearl, tasked with improving the clan's life.
   Relationship: Develops a complex relationship with Nǎzhā, going from enemies to friends and back.

2. 课文 Lesson Text

很久以前，天地灵气形成混元珠，分为灵珠和魔丸。灵珠会转世为英雄；魔丸会转世成为恶魔，但只能活三年。元始天尊让太乙真人把灵珠送给李靖夫妇，让灵珠转世到他们马上要出生的孩子身上。但是灵珠被调了包，魔丸转世成为了哪吒。因为是魔丸转世，村民都害怕他，都叫他"妖怪"，也都不让自己的孩子和他玩。所以哪吒没有朋友。太乙真人于是收哪吒为徒，教他法术；父母和太乙真人都让哪吒以为自己是灵珠转世，所以哪吒天天练习法术，想以后帮助老百姓降妖除魔，让老百姓改变对他的看法。

而灵珠被申公豹偷走，送给了龙王。灵珠投胎到了龙王的三儿子敖丙身上。龙王希望敖丙有了灵珠的力量，能够改变龙族的命运，所以从小就让他每天练功，敖丙也没有时间交朋友。这样，哪吒和敖丙两个人都没朋友。每天的工作就是练习法术，准备帮助百姓斩妖除魔。在一次帮助老百姓除妖时，哪吒见到了敖丙，他俩成了对方唯一的朋友。也是在那一次帮助村民除妖时，村民误以为认哪吒伤人，哪吒觉得很委屈。

在哪吒三岁生日那一天，哪吒得知自己是魔丸，不是灵珠，而且那一天也是他生命的最后一天。哪吒非常生气，想要大开杀戒。最终，在父母，太乙真人和朋友敖丙的帮助下，哪吒活了下来。同时，哪吒也消除了老百姓面临的灭顶之灾。老百姓最终真诚地感谢哪吒救了他们，知道哪吒不是妖怪，而是一心想帮助他们的人。

3. 生词 New Vocabulary

1)	很久以前	hěn jiǔ yǐqián	long ago
2)	天地灵气	tiāndì língqì	heavenly and earthly spiritual energy
3)	混元珠	hùnyuán zhū	primordial pearl
4)	魔丸	mówán	demon orb, reincarnates someone into a demon
5)	灵珠	língzhū	spirit pearl, reincarnates someone into a hero
6)	转世	zhuǎnshì	reincarnate
7)	灵珠转世	língzhūzhuǎnshì	Spirit pearl was reincarnated into a human.
8)	魔丸转世	mówán zhuǎnshì	Demon orb was reincarnated into a human.
9)	英雄	yīngxióng	hero
10)	恶魔	èmó	demon
11)	元始天尊	yuánshǐ tiānzūn	Primeval God
12)	太乙真人	tàiyǐ zhēnrén	a Taoist immortal
13)	李靖夫妇	lǐ jìng fūfù	Mr. and Mrs. Li Jing
14)	调了包	diào le bāo	switched
15)	申公豹	shēn gōng bào	Shen Gongbao (a character in Chinese mythology)

16)	龙王	lóngwáng	dragon king
17)	敖丙	áo bǐng	Ao Bing (the character's name)
18)	法术	fǎshù	magical arts
19)	降妖除魔	xiáng yāo chú mó	subdue demons and eliminate evil
20)	生气	shēngqì	angry
21)	大开杀戒	dà kāi shā jiè	unleash the killing aura
22)	消除	xiāochú	eliminate
23)	灭顶之灾	miè dǐng zhī zāi	catastrophe
24)	感谢	gǎnxiè	thank
25)	知道	zhīdào	know
26)	一心想	yīxīn xiǎng	wholeheartedly want

4. 课文理解 Text Comprehension

Answer the following questions in full sentences based on the story you read. Try your best to incorporate new words and fixed expressions.

1) 灵珠魔丸最后转世成为了谁？
2) 哪吒生下来以后，村民怎么对待他的？为什么？
3) 太乙真人为什么决定收哪吒为徒？他教哪吒什么？
4) 魔丸转世的哪吒和灵珠转世的敖丙，他们有朋友吗？是谁？
5) 哪吒三岁生日那一天发生了什么？
6) 老百姓最终对哪吒的看法变了吗？为什么他们的看法变了？

5. 讨论话题 Discussion Topics

1) 关于命运 About Fate:

   a) 命运由谁定？Who determines fate?
   b) 你能改变自己的命运吗？Can you change your own fate?
   c) 一生中有哪一些命运转变的机会？What are some opportunities for fate to change during a lifetime?

2) 关于成见 About Bias:

   a) 人心中的成见可以改变吗？Can bias in people's hearts be changed?
   b) 你对成见的反应？How do you react to bias?

3) 关于支持家人/朋友 About Supporting Family/Friends:

   a) 谁在你的支持圈？Who are the individuals within your support circle?
   b) 你们是如何相互支持的？How do you reciprocally aid one another?
   c) 父母为了孩子的成功，付出的哪一些努力，做出的哪一些牺牲？What efforts do parents exert and what sacrifices do they make for their children's success?

4) 关于父母和孩子的关系 About Parent-Child Relationship:

   a) 父母亲在家庭中的角色是什么？What is the role of parents in the family?

b) 父母亲对孩子个性/人格形成的影响？How do parents influence the development of a child's personality?
c) 父母亲与孩子的关系是什么？What is the relationship between parents and children?

5) 关于人生的人生目标 About Life Goals:
a) 你的父母的/你的人生目标是什么？？What are your parents'/your life goals?
b) 哪吒，敖丙的人生目标是什么/What are Nǎzhā and Aobing's life goals?

Appendix 6.2: Enrichment Guide

《哪吒》 Enrichment Guide

1. 关于哪吒 About Nézhā

哪吒 (Nézhā) is a character from Chinese mythology who acts as a guardian for young people. According to the myth, Nézhā showed incredible powers and intelligence right from birth, following an unusually long pregnancy of three years and six months. Notably, Nézhā had great physical strength and the ability to speak. Originally, Nézhā's name came from the Hindu deity Nalakuvara, which was translated into Chinese as 那罗鸠婆罗 (Nàluójiūpóluó). Over time, his name went through changes and eventually became the simplified form Nézhā, later Romanized as 哪吒.

(Visit the website https://mythopedia.com/topics/nezha to learn more about the etymology of Nézhā's name, his attributes, his family, and his mythology.)

2. 哪吒和孙悟空 Nézhā and Sūnwùkōng

Nézhā is a unique and rebellious character in Chinese culture, similar to the Monkey King, Sūn Wùkōng. Both of them are fearless, challenging authority in both heaven and earth. They make an intriguing pair in Chinese mythology, with similarities and distinct qualities. What's interesting is that neither of them is entirely human; they are a mix of demon and deity. Surprisingly, when people talk about these two, there's a strong sense of familiarity, as if they are not just fictional characters but familiar friends from real life.

（Based on 《李陀、毛尖：从新旧哪吒电影说起》）

3. 1979年的动画片 《哪吒闹海》 主要剧情 The Plot of 1979 Version of the Animation Movie Ne Zha Conquers the Dragon King

The movie is based on a Chinese myth called 《封神演义》 "Investiture of the Gods," focusing on the warrior god Nézhā. It starts with Lady Yin, General Lǐ Jìng's wife, giving birth to a special fleshball after an unusual three-and-a-half-year pregnancy. This fleshball turns into a lotus flower, and Nézhā comes out fully formed, able to walk and talk. He becomes a disciple of the immortal Tàiyǐ Zhēnrén.

In the story, the Sea Dragon Kings, tired of peace, turn evil and cause trouble in China by creating storms and a severe drought. Despite people asking for rain, the East Sea Dragon King, Áo guǎng, ignores them and orders a creature named Yèchā to find children for him to eat. Nézhā's friend is captured, and in a fight, Nézhā hurts Yèchā. This makes Áo guǎng angry, and he sends his son Ǎo Bǐng to deal with Nézhā, but Nézhā ends up killing Ǎo Bǐng, making Áo guǎng even more furious.

Nézhā and Áo guǎng have many fights, causing storms, floods, and disasters. Seeing the destruction, Nézhā decides to use his father's sword, returns his flesh and bones to his parents, seeks help from his master, and sadly ends his own life. With his master's guidance, Nézhā is reborn from a lotus blossom with new powers. He breaks into Áo guǎng's palace and defeats the Dragon Kings, bringing peace back.

1979 年版本的《哪吒闹海》在YouTube 上可以免费看： www.youtube.com/watch?v=UqbkYVv5yBs&t=1725s

4. 1979 and 2019 《哪吒》电影的对比

Both the 1979 and 2019 versions of Nézhā tell the story of the legendary character from Chinese mythology. They both highlight Nézhā's amazing powers and his role as a protector against supernatural threats.

Both movies include Chinese cultural elements like traditional clothing, settings, and mythical creatures.

However, there are differences:

Storytelling Style: The 1979 version tells the original legend in a straightforward way. On the other hand, the 2019 version takes a more modern approach, adding new elements and exploring characters more deeply.

Cultural Impact: The 1979 version is a classic in China and loved by many generations. In comparison, the 2019 version achieved huge success globally, setting records at the box office and introducing Nézhā to a broader international audience.

To explore more topics about Nézhā, feel free to copy and paste the following prompts (or create your own prompts) in ChatGPT or other AI platforms:

1) "What are the two similarities and differences between the parent and child relationship in 1979 Ne Zha and the 2019 rendition?"
2) "What are the two similarities and differences between one's destiny or fate in 1979 Ne Zha and the 2019 rendition?"
3) "What are the two similarities and differences between the role of Woman in 1979 Ne Zha a and the 2019 rendition?"

看看李陀毛尖的《从新旧哪吒电影说起》https://mp.weixin.qq.com/s/CFqU-u23bd02RmWK_q7Q1TQ 作为引子，看看你还能找到哪一些相同点和不同点？(It is all in Chinese and might be challenging for us to get all the ideas.)

5. 中国古代的命运观

The idea "我命由我不由天" from Daoism means "I control my destiny, not God." Another saying, "成事在天，谋事在人," translates to "God decides the outcome, but it's our job to plan and work for success." These reflect the ancient Chinese view on fate.

The movie *Ne Zha: Birth of the Demon Child* not only broke records but also popularized the idea "My destiny is determined by myself, not by heaven." At the end, there's a line, "Don't accept the fate is Nézhā's fate," adding to the idea of controlling one's destiny. It shows a belief in fate but also a desire to defy it and change one's destiny. *Ne Zha* is like a "new story" about challenging predetermined fate, similar to the ancient Greek play *Oedipus Rex*. The struggle between "fate" and "self" represents the core of ancient Chinese views on destiny. (Reference: "我命由我不由天"：电影《哪吒》与中国古代命运观-中华读书报-光明网) https://epaper.gmw.cn/zhdsb/html/2019-08/28/nw.D110000zhdsb_20190828_1-09.htm)

Research the following prompts and answer the questions to the best of your ability. Please include links to web pages you use to get the information.

1) What were the ancient Chinese beliefs about destiny or fate?
2) What are the modern Chinese beliefs about destiny or fate?
3) In Chinese and Western mythology, what are the main similarities and differences in beliefs about destiny?
4) Who is the most representative figure in Chinese and Western mythology who struggles against fate? Are there any related stories?

Appendix 6.3: Study Packet
《哪吒》电影金句

Movie Quotes

1. 和朋友一起读一读下面的电影金句，看看谁读得最生动。Read the following famous movie quotes with a friend and see who can read them most vividly.

A. <u>关于命运</u>

1) 哪吒："我命由我不由天。" I am the master of my own fate.
2) 哪吒："是魔是仙，只有我自己说了算。" Whether I'm a demon or an immortal only I get to decide.
3) 哪吒："若命运不公，就和它斗到。" If fate is unfair, then fight against it.
4) 哪吒："生而为魔，那又如何。" I was born to be a demon, so who cares?

5) 哪吒: "去你个鸟命。" Forget your fate.
6) 哪吒: "我会让所有人刮目相看，走着瞧！" I will impress everyone. Just wait and see.
7) 哪吒: "你到底是不是灵珠？我一个魔丸都比你活得像个人样。" Are you the spirit pearl? I am the demon orb that lives more like a human compared to you.
8) 太乙真人: "如果你问我，人能否改变自己的命运，我也不晓得，但是不认命，就是哪吒的命。"（在电影最后）If you ask me whether a person can change their own fate, I don't know either. But refusing to accept fate is Nézhā's destiny. (At the end of the movie)
9) 申公豹: "一生中能改变命运的机会，可不多呀！" The opportunity to change your destiny only comes once in a lifetime
10) 敖丙: "我是妖族。出生那一刻，命就定了！" I am from the demon family. My fate is decided at birth.
11) 敖丙: "别挣扎了，这是命中注定的。" Stop struggling. It is destined.

B. <u>关于成见</u>

12) 哪吒: "别人的看法都是狗屁，你是谁只有你自己说了才算，这是爹教我的道理。" My dad taught me that other people's opinions don't matter, who you are is determined by you.
13) 哪吒: "我是小妖怪，逍遥又自在，杀人不眨眼，吃人不放盐！一口七八个，肚子要撑破。" I am a little monster, carefree and free-spirited. I kill without hesitation, and devour without adding salt! I can eat seven or eight in one gulp; my stomach is about to burst.
14) 申公豹: "人心中的成见是一座大山，任你怎么努力都休想搬动。" Bias in people's hearts is like a mountain, no matter how hard you try, you can never move it.
15) 老百姓: "妖怪，滚回家去。" Monster, go back home.
16) 老百姓: "把他关起来，关到死为止。" Lock him up, keep him imprisoned until death.
17) 老百姓: "狗改不了吃屎。" A leopard can't change its spots.
18) 哪吒: "白白搭上一条命，你傻不傻？" You're sacrificing your life for nothing, are you stupid?

C. <u>关于支持家人和朋友</u>

19) 哪吒: "你是我唯一的朋友。" You are my only friend.
20) 敖丙: "你也是我唯一的朋友。" You are also my only friend.
21) 哪吒: "白白搭上一条命，你傻不傻？" You're sacrificing your life for nothing, are you stupid?

D. <u>关于父母和孩子的关系</u>

22) 李靖: "别在意别人的看法。你是谁，只有你自己说了才算！"（生日宴上，父亲对哪吒说的话。）Don't care about what others think. Who you are is only defined by yourself! (Spoken by the father to Nézhā at the birthday banquet)

23) 李靖："爹一直对你很严，知道你心里有气，但是也没有办法。"（生日宴上，父亲对哪吒说的话。）I have always been strict with you, and I know you are upset about it, but I have no other choice. (Spoken by the father to Nézhā at the birthday banquet)

24) 殷夫人："你们看哪吒玩儿得多开心啊。好久没看他这么高兴了。" You all look so happy playing, especially Nézhā. It's been a while since I've seen him this happy.

25) 殷夫人："回来娘给你做好吃的。" When you come back, Mom will make delicious food for you.

26) 哪吒："我自己的命我自己扛，不连累别人！" I will be responsible for my own fate without burdening others. (生日宴上，哪吒知道父亲给他的生日礼物是换命符。At the birthday banquet, Nézhā found out that the birthday gift his father gave him was a life-exchange talisman.)

E. **关于人生目标**

27) 哪吒："我会让所有人刮目相看，走着瞧！" I will let people see that I've changed, wait and see.

28) 哪吒："替天行道是使命，斩妖除魔我最厉害。"（在海边）Carrying out justice is my mission; I'm the best at slaying demons and monsters. (At the seaside)

F. **关于归属感/被接受**

29) 殷夫人："其实你心里是想被别人接受的，对不对？只是因为别人的偏见让你受了委屈。" Deep down, you actually want to be accepted by others, right? It's just that others' prejudices have caused you harm.

30) 哪吒："陈塘关所有的人都会来给我庆生。"（哪吒邀请敖丙来参加他的生日宴。）Everyone from Chéntáng Pass will come to celebrate my birthday. (Nézhā inviting Ǎo Bǐng to attend his birthday banquet)

Related vocabulary Quizlet links: https://quizlet.com/686716952/%E5%93%AA%E5%90%92_10-%E9%87%91%E5%8F%A5-classic-quotes-flash-cards/?new=&setIdOrUsername=686716952

关于金句的生词 Vocabulary for the Classic Quotes

1) 金句 — jīnjù — important quotes (in a story, movie, etc.), classic quotes
2) 命（运）— mìng (yùn) — fate
3) 命 — mìng — fate, life
4) 我自己说了算 — wǒ zìjǐ shuō le suàn — I have the final say
5) 若命运不公 — ruò mìngyùn bù gōng — if fate is unfair
6) 我就和它斗到底 — wǒ jiù hé tā dòu dàodǐ — I will fight with it (the unfair fate) till the end
7) 如何 — rúhé — how
8) 所有人 — suǒyǒu rén — all of the people

9)	刮目相看	guāmùxiāngkàn	to view someone from a new (mostly) positive perspective
10)	走着瞧	zǒuzhe qiáo	wait and see
11)	到底	dàodǐ	in the end
12)	活得像个人样	huó dé xiàng gè rén yàng	to live like a decent person/a real man
13)	能否	néng fǒu	whether or not
14)	改变	gǎibiàn	to change
15)	不晓得	bù xiǎo de	do not know
16)	认命	rènmìng	to accept one's fate (without fighting)
17)	一生中	yīshēng zhōng	in (one's) life
18)	机会	jīhuì	opportunity
19)	妖族	yāozú	the demon clan
20)	出生	chūshēng	birth
21)	挣扎	zhēngzhá	to fight against
22)	别人	biérén	others
23)	看法	kànfǎ	views, opinions
24)	爹	diē	dad
25)	娘	niáng	mom
26)	成见	chéngjiàn	bias
27)	一座山	zuò dà shān	one huge mountain
28)	任你怎么 + verb	rèn nǐ zěnme + verb	no matter how you + verb
29)	努力	nǔlì	to work hard
30)	休想搬动它	xiūxiǎng bāndòng tā	never want/can move it a bit
31)	滚回去	gúnhuíqù	go back (rude way)
32)	关起来	guānqǐlái	lock . . . up
33)	关到死为止	guān dào sǐ wéizhǐ	lock . . . up till death
34)	狗改不了吃屎	gǒu gǎi bùliǎo chī shǐ	literally means "Dogs can't stop eating shit"; similar to "A leopard can't change its spots" or "Old habits die hard"
35)	唯一	wéiyī	the only
36)	傻	shǎ	stupid
37)	白白搭上一条命	bái bái dā shàng yītiáo mìng	sacrifice one's life for nothing
38)	在意	zàiyì	to care about
39)	严	yán	be strict
40)	有气	yǒuqì	be mad
41)	连累	liánlèi	to have someone innocent suffer
42)	替天行道	tì tiān xíngdào	to get rid of bad guys
43)	斩妖除魔	zhǎn yāo chú mó	slay demons
44)	厉害	lìhài	awesome
45)	人生目标	rénshēng mùbiāo	life goal
46)	归属感	guīshǔ gǎn	sense of belonging

47)	被接受	bèi jiēshòu	been accepted
48)	偏见	piānjiàn	prejudice, bias
49)	受委屈	shòu wěiqu	to be treated unfairly

2. 再读一下上面的金句，选三个你最喜欢的金句，请写下来，并分享给你的朋友：为什么你选了这三句？他/她们是在什么情况下说的？ Read these memorable quotes, choose three that you like the most, write them down, and share them with your friends. Why did you choose these three quotes? In what situations were they said?

1) _____
2) _____
3) _____

3. 读下面的金句，看看是谁说的。Read the quotes and identify the speaker.

1) _____:"我命由我不由天。"
2) _____:"是魔是仙，只有我自己说了算。"
1) _____: "如果你问我，人能否改变自己的命运，我也不晓得，但是不认命，就是哪吒的命。"
2) _____:"人心中的成见是一座大山，任你怎么努力都休想搬动。"
3) _____: "别在意别人的看法。你是谁，只有你自己说了才算！"
4) _____:"你也是我唯一的朋友。"

4. 看看你看电影时做的笔记，看看哪一个金句能让你想起发生在你/你的家人/朋友身上的事情，或者是你在别的读物/视频/电影里看到的内容，或者是发生在你身边的的事情。Take a look at these quotes and the notes that you have taken while watching the movie. What connections (text-to-text, text-to-self, text-to-world) can you make with the quote?

1) 哪一个金句？_____
_____
2) 你能想到和这个金句的联系是：_____
_____
_____
_____
_____
_____

References

ACTFL-NCSSFL. (2017). *NCSSFL-ACTFL can-do statements*. Retrieved May 5, 2024, from www.actfl.org/resources/ncssfl-actfl-can-do-statements

Bishop, R. S. (1990). Mirrors, windows, and sliding glass doors. *Perspectives*, *6*(3), ix–xi.
Byram, M. (1997). *Teaching and assessing intercultural communicative competence*. Bristol, UK: Multilingual Matters.
Byram, M. (2008). *From foreign language education to education for intercultural citizenship: Essays and reflections*. Clevedon: Multilingual Matters.
Byram, M. (2021). *Teaching and assessing intercultural communicative competence* (2nd ed.). Clevedon: Multilingual Matters.
Byram, M., & Wagner, M. (2018). Making a difference: Language education for intercultural and international dialogue. *Foreign Language Annals*, *51*(1), 140–151.
Keene, E. L., & Zimmerman, S. (1997). *Mosaic of thought: Teaching comprehension in a reader's workshop*. Portsmouth, NH: Heinemann.
Nation, P. (2007). The four strands. *Innovation in Language Learning and Teaching*, *1*(1), 2–13.
Wiggins, G., & McTighe, J. (2005). *Understanding by design*. Alexandria, VA: Association for Supervision and Curriculum Development.

7 "Mùlán Joins the Army" 《木兰从军》 (Mùlán Cóngjūn)

Teaching the Folktale of Mulan through the Lens of Global Feminism

- **Language Proficiency Level:** Advanced low; can be adapted lower for intermediate high or higher for advanced-mid;
- **ICC Developmental Goals:** Understand women's roles in society; compare textual and visual representations of Mulan and connect them with perspectives;
- **High School/AP Theme:** Families and communities – roles within families; personal and public identities – women who are heroes and national figures;
- **Suggested College Course:** Chinese Culture through Classic Stories;
- **Suggested Instructional Time:** Three lessons, about one instructional hour each; followed by a week-long midterm project.

1. Introduction

People in the West typically learn of Mulan as Disney's "Asian princess," whose abilities and inner strength were suppressed in the traditional Chinese patriarchal society (Wang, 2020, 2022; 王卓昇, 2020). Following the Disney narrative, Mulan ran away from home, fought valiantly in the army disguised as a man, only to suffer shame and ostracization when she accidentally revealed her female identity. She ultimately earned respect and acceptance from her male companions by saving the emperor and the nation from foreign invasion. However, the original story of Mulan, recorded in an ancient folk song in the Southern and Northern Dynasties period of China known as 《木兰辞》 (*Mùláncí*, *The Ballad of Mulan* or *the Song of Mulan*) tells a simple story of a young female military general supported by her community and respected by her fellow soldiers where the final revelation of her female identity was perceived as a marvel rather than a betrayal. Guided by critical perspectives on popular media's representations of Mulan (Wang, 2020, 2022; 王卓昇, 2020), utilizing insights on the structure of epic narratives (Labov & Waletzky, 1967/1997), and drawing on the framework of global feminism (Ferree, 2006), this unit demonstrates how language teachers can develop students' critical thinking on gender roles cross-culturally and consequently develop knowledge and perspectives essential for intercultural communication. The unit culminates in a collaborative narrative project where students research a female historical figure of their choosing and create a digital book together celebrating women who made history on a global scale. This unit can also commemorate Women's History Month in March in the United States if the course schedule falls during the spring semester.

2. Contextualizing the Topic

The lessons illustrated in this chapter originate in a college-level Chinese foreign language course titled "Chinese Culture through Classic Stories." It is an advanced-level Chinese language class designed with theoretical conviction that the teaching of the Chinese language should be integrated with the teaching of culture and literature. The course is designed to serve a broad range of students, including both students from non-heritage backgrounds who study Chinese as a foreign language and students from a variety of heritage backgrounds (see a similar context discussed in chapter 5). In this class, "stories" are the main literary vehicle through which Chinese culture is made concrete and can be used to engage students from a mix of backgrounds, prioritizing students' own interpretations and creative efforts. It is this intercultural space – namely, stories as constructed in their original cultural contexts and told and retold for different audiences and understood in students' own worlds – that creates opportunities for students to develop intercultural communicative competence.

The course takes place in a 15-week semester and is designed for students typically enrolled in their fourth year of study who have already completed three years of formal Chinese learning in the classroom. Students select the course to fulfill their Chinese Minor requirement or for a general elective out of personal interest. The course follows a thematic organization using selected stories with intentionally diverse themes; for example, allegories from Chinese philosophical traditions offer a peek into contrasting Chinese cultural values, such as the Confucian school versus the Daoist school; excerpts from classic Chinese novels give students a taste of the most well-known epics that would otherwise be not accessible to foreign language students (see chapters 2, 3, and 4); and various other classic stories, such as 《桃花源记》 (Táohuāyuánjì, 'Story of the Peach Blossom Land'), and 《嫦娥奔月》 (Cháng'é Bēnyuè, 'Cháng'é Ascending to the Moon') (see chapter 5). A commonality across the thematic units is that the selected stories have literary origins, such as poetry, narrative prose, and novels. Most of the stories are rewritten by the instructor into modern Chinese to be accessible to Chinese language learners, whereas the stories' literary origins are also presented to students verbatim as samples of classic Chinese literature; students are often intrigued to learn that the stories they are studying originated in ancient times, and they become more aware of the fact that the cultural contexts that gave birth to canonical stories continue to change due to changing social conditions. The particular lesson unit we outline here takes scholarly insight from research on epic narrative structure (Labov & Waletzky, 1967/1997). In addition, global feminism is selected as an interpretive frame to modernize and make relevant the Mulan story.

3. The Story of Mulan through the Lens of Global Feminism

Feminism advocates for understanding women's experience from a woman's perspective (Ferree, 2006). In a male-dominant society, feminism is a lens through which to raise awareness of the lived experiences of women under the social conditions of submission and subjugation to male dominance. Global feminism elevates feminist perspectives to a global scale where "women help women," transcending ethnic, racial, and national boundaries.

For the Chinese people, the name Mulan is connected with idiomatic expressions such as "替父从军" (tì fù cóng jūn) and "代父从军" (dài fù cóng jūn, 'join the army in one's father's place'). In this context, Mulan is a symbol of nationalism as well as family duty. In the story of *Mùláncí*, Mulan received the highest commendation from the emperor but chose to return to her home life without hesitation despite offers of high office and material rewards. Mulan's behaviors represent a variety of Confucian cultural ideals for women: to be brave and patriotic in times of national crisis and to be virtuous and devoted in the home domain in times of peace. Gradually, the heroic story of Mulan was subjugated to the dominant patriarchal social order and Mulan's image became entangled with sexual fantasy in the late Ming period in popular media genres such as operas (Wang, 2020).

In the Western world, Mulan is known through the Disney animation film *Mulan* (1998). Targeting young children and teens in the US, the Disney-style dramatization of Mulan offered catchy songs, tropes of disguised identity, and dramatic turns of events. The narrative utilizes the US society's dominant cultural values of individualism, self-discovery, and the pursuit of happiness. The various conflicts and their resolutions imagined for Mulan, as well as the romantic undertone between Mulan and her captain, constitute an entertaining "coming of age" story of Mulan for the Western audience. Teens resonate with the story and sympathize with Mulan's conflicts between her true self and her oppressive patriarchal community where a woman is valued for their domestic virtue and femininity that bring honor to the family. The cultural values of individualism and the pursuit of happiness merge with the Westernized understanding of the Chinese patriarchal social values of suppression of individuality, male dominance, and filial piety.

Disney's *Mulan* (1998) is a product of its time as well as the mainstream American culture at the time. The supporting characters are constructed at the expense of racial stereotypes against minority groups (e.g., the letters to home written by Mulan's guardian cricket were ostensibly in gibberish Chinese recognizable as a Chinese restaurant take-out menu [see Wang, 2020, 2022]; Mushu the dragon, ostensibly named after a dish in a traditional Chinese American restaurant, is portrayed as loyal and kind, but vain and silly, speaking in an African American Vernacular accent [Lippi-Green, 2012]).

Disney's narrative of Mulan has morphed from *Mulan* (1998) to a feminist remake of the same name by New Zealand filmmaker Niki Caro in 2020. Wang (2020, 2022) argues that Caro's remake of *Mulan* in many ways was intended to correct the 1998 version's male-dominant perspective and refrain from exploiting stereotypes at the expense of minority cultures. Under Caro's directorship, Mulan defined her choice on her own terms, without the validation of her male partners. In Caro's film, Mulan's talents and strengths were naturally hers, waiting to be revealed and released when she was ready, and in this process she was protected and mentored by the male members of her community, including her father, her general, and her military companions. Caro's storyline replaced the Mushu dragon with a silent but powerful phoenix and a powerful witch who in many ways was similar to Mulan, except she suffered the fate of ostracization by her own people due to their fear of women with formidable strength. The witch chose to sacrifice her own life to help Mulan grow into a warrior, thus embedding the story of Mulan in the context of global feminism (Wang, ibid.).

These different versions of Mulan demonstrate that stories are the products of their times and social conditions as well as the advocacies and ideologies of the story maker. In this unit, we adopt a feminist perspective on who Mulan is, largely based on the analysis of Wang (ibid.) that Mulan is a woman who, through intellect, skills, hard work, and persistence, successfully breaks the norms of a field traditionally dominated by men. This general framework helps us to see Mulan outside of the literary narrative context – that is, women like Mulan make their place not only in the army but also in other traditional fields dominated by men, such as sports, politics, diplomacy, and science. Through this conception of Mulan, we transcend national, ethnic, and radical boundaries and can teach Mulan productively for intercultural communicative competence merging with a global feminist perspective.

4. Methodology Highlight: Narrative Analysis

While global feminism provides a general framework for the focus of the unit as to what kind of story is the story of Mulan, we also need a toolkit to study and compare the different versions of the classic folktale.

Narrative analysis is an interdisciplinary area that focuses on the structure and use of narratives. Labov and Waletzky (1967/1997) identified that stories often have the following structural components: an abstract that gives an overview of what the story is about; orientation that establishes the time, place, and main characters for the necessary background and context of the story; complicating action where the main events and actions take place, usually a series of connected events resulting in a problem or conflict waiting to be resolved; resolution where the outcome of the story resolves the building tension in the story and brings it to its closure; and the coda that appends to the resolution in the form of a moral reflection or a recap, such as the fairy tale cliché ending "they lived happily ever after." Throughout these stages, the narrator evinces their evaluations of and attitudes toward the persons and events; subjective evaluations are spread out in the storytelling and are particularly noticeable in the complicating action and resolution. Figure 7.1 illustrates these components of a canonical narrative.

Using the framework of narrative analysis, the variations of the Mulan story can be compared at the juncture of these core components. For example, the original story told in *Mùláncí* lacks an orientation stage. The narrative poem directly starts with Mulan sitting in front of a loom; instead of weaving, she sighs heavily. This leads to the complicating event that there have been urgent conscription orders where each household is to send one male to the northern border to fight against foreign invasion. Her elderly father is too old to serve; her younger brother is too young. One resolution at this stage is that Mulan decides to take her father's place and departs the home dressed as a man in her newly

"Mùlán Joins the Army"《木兰从军》 165

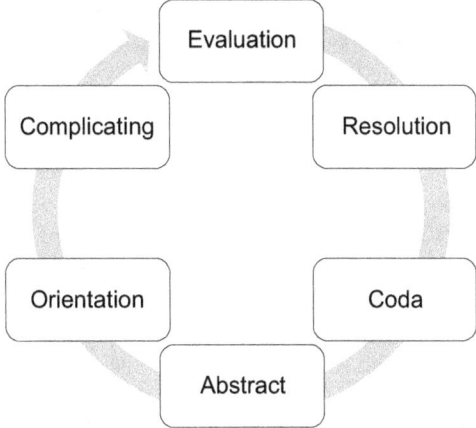

Figure 7.1 Components of a canonical narrative, adapted from Labov and Waletzky (1967/1997).

purchased military attire. The poem largely takes the perspective of Mulan as she travels to the northern border. We see Mulan camping by the Yellow River and at the foothill of the Heishan Mountain imagining her elderly parents' loving calls to her. The military journey, which spans more than ten years, is described in broad strokes in a few very quick verses: galloping soldiers, deaths, victories, and glories. The entire military journey constitutes a complicating action. Returning as a hero, Mulan is received by the emperor, who commends her with the highest position and wealth, only to be rejected by Mulan, who asks instead to have a fast ride to return home. Detailed, vivid descriptions resume toward the end of the poem, describing Mulan reuniting with her family and revealing her female identity to her fellow soldiers. The poem concludes with a rhetorical question in Mulan's voice:

雄兔脚扑朔 xióngtù jiǎo pūshuò,
雌兔眼迷离 cítù yǎn mílí,
双兔傍地走 shuāngtù bàng dì zǒu,
安能辨我是雌雄? ān néng biàn wǒ shì cíxióng?

[The male hare's feet kick,
the female hare's eyes squint,
when two hares run side by side on the ground,
who can distinguish which one is male and which one is female?]

In the context of the poem, this rhetorical question is a direct quote from Mulan, who proudly reveals her identity as a woman. The broad strokes of the military years are in sharp contrast with the minute details of experiences from Mulan's experience revealing Mulan's own feelings and observations. Thus through narrative analysis, comparing the parts that are detailed and the parts that are fleeting, we can argue that the original folk song was told from Mulan's perspective, a feminist portrayal of Mulan.

Disney's 1998 animation film changes the setting to a village where Mulan is a tomboy and her father is a former soldier with an old injury. The long orientation stage of the story, while necessitated by the length of a film compared to a folk song, also works to foreshadow the conflicts within Mulan, between Mulan and her family, and between Mulan and her community. The complicating action is complex, involving both the arrival of government officials with contemptuous airs announcing conscription orders and the family's pressure on Mulan to uphold female virtues and get married for the honor of the family. In the original story, Mulan took on the disguise of a man with the consent of her family and said farewell to her parents properly before departing. In the Disney story, she ran away in a conflicting act of defiance toward her parents and a filial act of helping her family. Thus, deceit and identity conflict, waiting to be resolved, drive the story. The final resolution in the original folk song is an elaborate description of Mulan changing into her favorite feminine attire, and upon the cries of marvel from her military peers, she playfully retorts the lines quoted earlier. The final resolution of the narrative in the 1998 animated film sees a trepid Mulan coming home, bringing her father the sword that epitomizes the honor she has now earned for the family, only to be met with her father's embrace that shows he loved her all the same. The happy ending is further enhanced, with a hint at a sequel in the making, with the arrival of her captain. There are also numerous complicating actions within the military journey that came to their respective resolutions. These detailed, focused depictions serve entertaining values, absent from the original narrative poem.

Caro's 2020 live-action remake largely follows the plot of the 1998 animated film. What did change in the narrative arc are the numerous complicating actions revolving around Mulan's hidden identity only because she is not yet ready to reveal it. The addition of the witch character alludes to the alternative destiny of a powerful woman fated to be abandoned and ostracized by her own people. Mulan's rejection of the witch's offer to join her and her persistent loyalty to her own people ultimately earned the witch's respect.

While it is not necessary for students who are learning Chinese as a second or heritage language to be presented with a detailed description of how a story develops as guided by narrative analysis, the perspective of narrative analysis helps to narrow our instructional focus on aspects of the story across different variations.

Details on implementing this approach are discussed in section 6.

5. Curricular Modeling

The unit is constructed in three stages. First, students work together to create a profile of previous knowledge and experience with the Mulan story. This choice is due to the mixed-level class where students will have different knowledge and sensibility about the Mulan story. Through a class poll activity, students practice speaking Chinese while activating their background knowledge about the Mulan story. Students also see several juxtaposed images of Mulan, which stimulates students' critical thinking about who Mulan is.

After students have gotten familiar with the story through the input text, they identify the key elements of the story as guided by narrative analysis (e.g., orientation, complicating action, resolution, and coda and evaluation). In the second stage, excerpts from various media representations of the Mulan story are played and discussed, focusing on how the various versions of the story differ. The third stage of the unit broadens the context of the discussion to normative gender roles in society and asks students to relate Mulan to other women across cultures who have made history because of their success in traditionally male-dominated fields.

The final component of the lesson is a stand-alone week where students collaborate in making a digital storybook on the theme of Mulan-like women around the world, which further pivots on global feminism and narrative analysis. For classes that do not have a stand-alone week, an alternative project is described that can be done outside of class in the format of a podcast.

5.1. Learning Outcomes

The following learning outcomes illustrate the expected outcomes for both the course and for the unit. The overall outcomes situate language skills development in ICC skills development and vice versa. The common consideration is how the course-specific learning outcomes, language performance descriptor, and ICC developing goals relate to one another and are exemplified in the class activities. The learning outcomes provide the most important compass for backward design and criteria for assessing students' achievements of the learning outcomes.

Learning Outcomes as Part of the "Chinese Culture through Classic Stories" Course

The overall class goal is to provide you with (1) an explicit knowledge about Chinese myths and fables that have shaped the Chinese culture and (2) skills for advanced communication in Chinese. Overall, you will develop:

- better understanding of Chinese myths and fables;
- skills in discussing myths and fables related to their cultural meaning and relating them to your own understanding of cultural differences;
- the ability to tell stories and comment on them in standard Mandarin Chinese in oral and written modes;
- better knowledge of idioms, including their historical meaning and current usage;
- fluency, accuracy, and comprehensibility in overall spoken and written communication in Mandarin Chinese; and
- confidence, knowledge, and skills for navigating intercultural communication.

The corresponding language performance goals are written in the "can do" format of "I can . . ." to make learners understand from their perspectives what they can achieve in this unit (ACTFL-NCSSFL, 2017).

Language Performance Objective (Can-Do Statements)

- I can follow the main story of Mulan based on the Chinese folk song and can offer supporting details across major time frames in the fictional narrative. (Interpretive)
- I can describe and present the basic facts about the folk song Mùláncí. (Interpretive; Presentational)
- I can tell the story of Mulan in writing and speaking through organized paragraphs. (Presentational)
- I can understand the common idioms in modern Chinese that relate to the Mulan story. (Interpretive)
- I can apply the lessons learned to describe and share my views on another historical figure. (Interpersonal)

The corresponding ICC development goals are written based on the four aspects of ICC: knowledge, attitude, skills, and critical cultural awareness (Byram, 2008, 2021; Byram & Wagner, 2018; inter alia).

Intercultural Communicative Competence Developmental Goals

- **Knowledge:** I can describe fully the story of Mulan as originally told in the folklore and can describe the Western version of Mulan. I can explain the perspectives and values illustrated in each of the variations and the core values of Mulan as relevant to equal rights for women on a global scale.
- **Attitude:** When describing the variations of the Mulan story, I can see the relationships between gender roles and dominant cultural values, thus keeping an open mind about the differing perspectives and values that motivate conflicting understandings of Mulan and different versions of the Mulan story.
- **Skill:** I can relate Mulan's story to the female figures in my own culture. I can contrast different views about gender roles in society and discuss the limitations and even the harmfulness of stereotypes about gender roles.
- **Critical Cultural Awareness:** I understand that the Mulan story can be told from different perspectives. I am more aware of a woman's perspective and of the challenges that women face in a male-dominant society.

5.2. Materials

A. PowerPoint Lecture Slides and Student Handouts

- Introduction to variations of the Mulan story within Chinese society and in the West

- Activating background knowledge
- Templates for a Jeopardy! game, a debate, and other collaborative activities for critical thinking and story comprehension
- Handouts to structure activities relating the Mulan story to gender roles in modern society

B. Video Materials
- Clips from *Mulan* (1998), *Mulan* (2020) and Chinese domestic renditions
- A recitation of *Mùláncí* in Chinese from YouTube
- Clips from various media interviews on Mulan and on gender roles

C. Preview Packet
- The full text of 《木兰从军》 with vocabulary list, comprehension questions, and selected grammar patterns
- Online supplement: New words in two sets, one with Pinyin and one without Pinyin, hosted on Quizlet.com
- Online supplement: Self-paced quiz to assess initial story comprehension

D. Enrichment Packet
- Notes on the evolution of the Mulan story
- Notes on the various film adaptations of Mulan
- Information on the period of Northern Wei as background for the Mulan story
- Notes on the impact of the Mulan story on Chinese language
- Notes on English translation of the Ballad of Mulan

E. Study Packet
- Revisiting the story text told in the preview packet, accompanied by learning materials focused on specific language proficiency outcomes and the ICC learning outcomes of the unit
- Slang and expressions with gender bias
- Discussion questions on gender stereotypes

F. Project Guides
- Biography e-book project guideline, a model for the project, and its assessment rubric
- Podcast Project guideline and and its assessment rubric

5.3. *Suggested Learning Activities*

This sample unit is budgeted for three instructional hours, followed by a stand-alone midterm project week. The sample lessons and activities are geared toward advanced-low college students who are serious about Chinese learning and are mature enough to engage in critical discussion. As a college-level class, contact hours are limited and much of the learning is expected to take place outside of class. The lessons use flipped instruction principles so that students can efficiently complete guided learning activities outside of class hours, aided by media technology and self-paced flexibility for language needs. The class time builds on the assumption that students have completed the homework assignments on time and are ready to perform, discuss, and collaborate in class.

Lesson 1: Schema Activation; Who Is Mulan; Images of Mulan

> Objectives: activate students' prior knowledge; raise awareness of current language proficiency for discussing the Mulan story; develop an introductory knowledge of the sociocultural and historical context of *Mùláncí*.

Because Mulan's story is relatively familiar to students, but its historical context, social context, and critical positions from the global feminist approach are not familiar, the first set of materials engages students by activating their prior knowledge about the story, gauging their language proficiency for being able to tell and discuss the story, and connecting students with their own initial experience with the Mulan story.

Activity 1: Activating Schemata: Introduction to the Mulan Story (Estimated Time: 25 Minutes)

- Assign students to work with a partner and each pair is assigned a question from the class poll handout. Students walk around the room to poll everyone and tally the results. The questions on the poll ask for individual experiences and details in the story that students may not recall or know. Some of the questions are designed to raise students' awareness that folk knowledge of the Mulan story differs from historical facts.
- Each pair reports back to class the results of their poll.
- Teacher gives a summary of students' poll results.

Activity 2: Introduction to the Historical Background of the Mulan Story (Estimated Time: 20 Minutes)

- Lecture on the historical background of the story of Mulan using the lecture slides interspersed with discussion questions.
- Explain the cultural significance of *Mùláncí*.
- Listen to the video recitation of *Mùláncí*.

Assigning Homework (5 Minutes)

- Assign the preview packet and the enrichment packet.
- Instruct students to study the story in the preview packet and become familiar with the story's cultural background based on the enrichment packet.
- Instruct students to study new vocabulary introduced using Quizlet.
- Before the next class, students are required to complete an online self-paced quiz with comprehension questions, vocabulary exercises, and cultural knowledge tasks.

Lesson 2: Story Plot Clarification; Identifying Literary Devices; Cultural Concepts

> Objectives: review vocabulary and cultural knowledge about the story of Mulan; clarify story plot guided by narrative structure; practice speaking while personalizing and diversifying perspectives on cultural concepts utilizing clips from film renditions of the story of Mulan.

After completing the preview packet, students should come to lesson 2 already familiar with the story's contents and related vocabulary. The first Jeopardy! game helps students to re-activate what they have learned from the preview packet. The varied degrees of challenges in the Jeopardy! game are designed for the mixed backgrounds of students. This game format is low-risk and engaging for students, fostering a collaborative learning environment across different proficiency levels. After the game, students use a handout to structure focused critical discussion. As students exchange ideas among themselves, the teacher monitors students' language use and answers any questions students may have. The first part of the group discussion handout is devoted to noticing and recalling stages in the story plot that correspond to the canonical narrative components. This structural awareness helps later when watching comparable clips from the several film versions of *Mulan*. Once the story plot is well understood, the remaining time is designated for critical discussion and noticing of literary devices in the original poem.

Activity 1: Using a Jeopardy! Game to Review Story Plot (Estimated Time: 10 Minutes)

- Make it clear to students that some of the questions are directly from the preview packet and others are included as surprise questions.
- Emphasize that the goal is not to win but to collaborate and have fun.
- Play the game.
- Announce the winner and provide a small reward.

Activity 2: Group Discussion (Estimated Time: 20 Minutes)

- Students can stay with the same group from the Jeopardy! game.
- Assign the discussion handout. The discussion handout is geared toward further clarifying the story plot and raising students' awareness of variations of the story for different audiences based on the narrative analysis approach.
- Some of the discussions may be challenging for students depending on their maturity level and critical-thinking skills. Teacher can choose to focus on the questions that are more factual (for example, comparisons of film critiques from Douban and Rotten Tomatoes) or venture into the critical questions. The discussion questions on the literary devices tend to be interesting for students who otherwise would not have noticed them.

- Similar to other group discussion activities, the teacher takes on the role of a facilitator. Each group should nominate a representative to report back to the class, and the teacher should integrate their summaries and implicitly model for students through recasting students' summaries into more complete contents and more accurate choices of sentence patterns and vocabulary.

Activity 3: Discussing Film Adaptation (Estimated Time: 20 Minutes)

- Activity 2 has prepared students to watch and discuss comparable clips from different film renditions of *Mulan*. Brief movie clips are available on YouTube. Depending on what has been discussed in activity 2, the teacher can choose comparable segments or focus on the two versions of *Mulan* (2020) and Mulan (1998).
- As demonstrated in the sample discussion handout, the teacher can prompt discussions on cultural concepts such as 三从四德 (Sāncóngsìdé), 气 (qì, 'energy') and 面子 (miànzi, 'face'), leading to a critical discussion on gender and cultural stereotypes that relate to what students have read in the enrichment packet.

Assigning Homework for Lesson 3

- Instruct students to use the study packet to review the story, reinforce vocabulary and study grammar patterns.
- The study packet also guides students to reflect on gender roles and gender biases in modern society and build cross-cultural perspectives.

Lesson 3: Gender Roles, Gender Biases, and Modern-Day Mulan

> Objectives: foster an understanding of Mulan as a symbol for women who make history; raise students' awareness of gender bias and stereotypes in society and in language; explore intercultural perspectives with a focus on gender roles.

This lesson helps students to use the language actively in the process of exploring intercultural perspectives with a focus on gender roles as have evolved in the Chinese society and globally. This lesson connects the story of Mulan with the contemporary society where every working woman is potentially a Mulan-like character facing gender biases in the workplace and at home. This lesson helps to solidify students' cross-cultural understanding of Mulan.

Activity 1: Discussing Gender Roles and Gender Bias (Estimated Time: 25 Minutes)

- Aided by the exercises and questions on the handout, students discuss gender bias, and stereotypes as well as those reflected in language.

- Have the speaking task in the study guide projected on the slide. Students work in groups to share their tentative ideas for the speaking task. In so doing, students reflect on the meaning of International Working Women's Day (March 8) and discuss its rebranding as 女神节 ("Goddess Day") to fuel consumerism.
- Regroup students into whole-class discussion; ask volunteers to share from the group discussions.

Activity 2: One-Minute Debate (Estimated Time: 20 Minutes)

- Students are put into groups of three or four. Depending on the size of the class, you can have four groups who take turns and play the game in two parts.
- Explain the format and purpose of the activity. Assure students that there are no right or wrong answers and ensure that the classroom is a safe place to practice Chinese with meaningful contents.
- Explain that the format of the one-minute debate is meant to provoke thinking from both sides of a controversial issue.
- Play the one-minute debate, with the teacher in role of a host and facilitator.
- If you have students who are more advanced than others, you can assign a penal of student judges to comment and determine which group wins the debate.

Assigning Homework (5 minutes)

- Instruct students to complete the self-paced quiz for the study packet.
- Students complete the speaking task for the unit.
- Depending on whether you will have a midterm project week or not, you can adjust the unit-final assessment. As demonstrated in this unit, the unit-final tasks did not include a writing assignment because students will engage in writing in the upcoming collaborative digital book project.

5.4. Assessment

Similar to chapter 5, assessments of language and ICC goals are conducted outside of class at students' own pace in the rehearsed condition. This choice differs from some of the other chapters where the third hour is spent on performance assessment in class. This design, of self-paced assessment outside of class, is geared toward a multi-level class. When students come from a mixture of heritage and non-heritage backgrounds, having the same assessment in a spontaneous time-sensitive manner is both unrealistic and creates a high-anxiety condition for non-heritage learners.

Formative Assessments

- Formative assessments include group communicative tasks in class and the self-paced quiz questions in the preview packet and the study packet.

- These assessments are completed by students at their own pace where the feedback helps them to gauge how well they are learning.

Summative Assessments

- Depending on whether you have time for a midterm project or will opt for a unit-final speaking task and/or a writing task, the summative assessment is conducted in the rehearsed interactional condition based on summative assessment rubrics.
- The two project options are explained in detail in section 7 and their guidelines are available among the online supplements for this chapter.

6. Implementing Narrative Analysis

Techniques from narrative analysis are incorporated in the group discussion handout for reviewing the story plot. Students are to answer questions in Chinese that distill the story down into its core components. They are also incorporated in the selection of film clips so that without class time to watch the entire films, a few minutes, selected using narrative analysis as a guide, scaffold students to critically discuss the comparable structural elements and relate the story's renditions to the social contexts and audience expectations that mold the stories.

As will be discussed in section 7, narrative analysis is also incorporated in the design of the collaborative e-book project. Mirroring how we have approached the Mulan story, where the focus zeroes in on canonical components of the epic story, in the biographic e-book that students co-create, students each produce five sections depicting the female hero of their choosing. Each component focuses on an orientation, a vivid visual description, a scene of tension (that corresponds to either a complicating action or a resolution), and an imagined dialogue (which brings out the writer's evaluative stance). Thus, the biography e-book, within its limited space, allows students to both practice advanced language skills, such as interacting, narrating across major time frames, providing detailed visual descriptions, and describing a concrete scene, and express intercultural understanding.

7. Projects and Student Sample Work

Throughout the Mulan unit, students not only study the Mulan story but also start to understand a feminist perspective on Mulan as a cultural symbol for women's achievements and struggles in a male-dominant society. Through the variations derived from the original Mulan story, students come to understand that stories are influenced by the dominant ideologies and cultural values of a specific time and place. In addition, students start to have the language for discussing gender biases in everyday situations. To take advantage of the students' deeper intercultural understanding and a global perspective on women's experiences with local conditions, the week immediately following the unit can be a stand-alone project week. This week is organized around students jointly completing an e-book on the theme

"Mùlán Joins the Army" 《木兰从军》   175

of Mulan-like heroes around the world. The project leverages the students' ability to work individually as well as collaboratively to demonstrate advanced-level language skills for ICC developmental goals.

The e-book project is a whole-class biography where each student chooses a female character from their own culture and writes a profile on her. The length of the final product will depend on the size of the class, but, ideally, the book should contain no more than ten historical figures for readability; if the class size is larger, students can work in pairs. In the age of Wikipedia and AI-powered chatbots, such as ChatGPT, it may be tempting for students to opt for existing information. The design of the project thus focuses away from a traditional biography.

Each page requires some text along with some visual representation for the text described as follows:

1) **The first page** includes a choice of an image that best represents the character of the student author's choice, and students are required to vividly describe the appearance of the character in the image.
2) **The second page** features the student author's creation and explanation of a word cloud based on four to five keywords in Chinese that they believe best represent the characteristics of their chosen character. This design requires students to digest the information they've researched about the character and summarize it in their own words filtered through their own reason for choosing this character.
3) **The third page** requires students to create a graphic timeline of the biography of the character of their choice, which helps students to not simply repeat information from research but personalize the information in their own words. They must use words and phrases that they understand and create the graphic timeline with facts without using long sentences. This helps them to practice the speaking skills they will need during the presentation stage of the e-book.
4) **The fourth page** asks students to depict a critical moment from the person's life that necessitates some dramatic, complicating action where tension builds up before the resolution or release of that tension. Students learn to approach the individual as a real person who experienced moments of conflicts and deliberation, just like Mulan. The choices the students make reveal their understanding of culture and of the relationship between personal choice and social conditions – the very essence of pragmatic understanding across culture.
5) **The fifth and last page** asks students to imagine that they can travel back in time to meet the person they are describing and think of a question they want to ask her. They are then asked to imagine how the person would answer and script a dialogue of this fictional interaction. This asks the student to both embody themselves in face-to-face contact with a historical person and adopt the perspective of the historical person.

Throughout the project week, students create parts of the e-book as homework, present and comment on each other's drafts, and receive peer feedback. The last hour of the project week is dedicated to a presentation in class where students showcase a page from their book that they are most proud of and have a "book launch" celebration (detailed guideline and model for this project are available in the online supplements for this chapter).

The Mulan unit can be intentionally placed in March so that the stand-alone project coincides with the International Working Women's Day on March 8 and Women's History Month in March (in the US). The final product, the e-book, can be published online with the students' consent. Ideally the e-book is a bilingual version, such that a broad audience can read it.

To give you a view of how the e-book project connects to the language and ICC goals of this unit, below were two pages a student created to feature 宋美龄 (Soong Mei-ling) as a Mulan-like character who made history in the traditionally male-dominant realm of politics.

(Page 1 of the biography; to accompany a photographic image of the character)

宋美龄是中华民国第一夫人。1897年3月在上海出生。她的父亲"查理"宋是卫理公会的牧师和商人，她的母亲是虔诚的基督教徒，对孩子要求很严格。这张照片是我从谷歌图片上找到的。 照片里的她把黑色头发利落梳起来。在她所有的照片中都把头发梳起来。她眉清目秀，笑容温和， 圆圆的脸。穿着黑色的旗袍和人造皮草外套。照片的背景是白宫外，有绿色的树和草坪。她跟埃莉诺·罗斯福坐在一起。埃莉诺的灰白色的头发整齐地卷曲的。也穿着人造皮草外套和珊瑚色连衣裙。她戴着珍珠项链，然而美龄戴耳环。照片里，美龄和埃莉诺看起来在40多岁。

[Soong Mei-ling was the First Lady of the Republic of China. She was born in Shanghai in March 1897. Her father, "Charlie" Song, was a pastor and businessman in the Methodist Church, while her mother was a devout Christian with strict expectations for her children. The photo I found on Google Images shows her with neatly combed black hair. In all her pictures, she wore her hair combed up. She had delicate features, a gentle smile, and a round face. She was dressed in a black qipao and a faux fur coat. The background of the photo was outside the White House, with green trees and a lawn. She was sitting with Eleanor Roosevelt, who had neatly curled gray-white hair. Eleanor was also wearing a faux fur coat and a coral-colored dress. She wore a pearl necklace, while Mei-ling wore earrings. In the photo, Mei-ling and Eleanor appeared to be in their 40s.]

(Page 4 of the biography; to accompany two images one from *Mulan* [1998] and one from Soong Mei-ling's speaking to the US Congress)

我选择的特殊的瞬间是她访问华盛顿特区收到了起立鼓掌的时候。那天她的发言被称为《中国第一夫人在美国国会讲话》。从火车上出来后，美龄受到美国第一夫人罗斯福夫人的欢迎。 她还被送上了一束花，并护送着她到罗斯福先生的车上。 到达白宫后，参议员和立法者都渴望与她握手。没有很多人被欢迎进入白宫，更不用说在美国代表面前讲话。她发言以后，全场起立鼓掌，这个场景有点儿像1998年《花木兰》的电影里面，皇帝说：我听说过很多有关你，花木兰，你偷走了父亲的盔甲，逃离家园，假扮一名士兵，欺骗了您的指挥官，羞辱了中国军队，摧毁了我的宫殿，而且 . . . . . 可是你救了我们所有人。包括皇帝在内。所有人都向她鞠躬，因为他们尊重她。

[The particular moment I chose was when she visited Washington, DC, and received a standing ovation. On that day, her speech was titled "Speech of the First Lady of China at the US Congress." After coming out of the train, Mei-ling was welcomed by the US First Lady, Mrs. Roosevelt. She was also presented with a bouquet of flowers and escorted to Mr. Roosevelt's car. Upon arriving at the White House, senators and legislators were eager to shake hands with her. Not many people were welcomed into the White House, let alone to speak before the US representatives. After her speech, the entire audience stood and applauded. This scene is somewhat reminiscent of the 1998 movie *Mulan*, where the emperor says, "I've heard a great deal about you, Mulan. You stole your father's armor, ran away from home, impersonated a soldier, deceived your commanding officer, dishonored the Chinese army, destroyed my palace, and . . . you have saved us all. Including the Emperor himself," and everyone bowed to her out of respect.]

If you do not have space for a stand-alone project week, we've also used a mini talk show podcast project which is more flexible for a larger class size and limited contact hours. Students work in pairs and are responsible for coming up with their own questions for the length of the interaction required while emulating the genre of a talk-show podcast program. Like a real talk show podcast program, to prepare for the final recording the paired students will have planned their talking points, compared notes, and measured the length of each turn and worked out the transitions between questions (the sample project guideline is available in the online supplements for this chapter). Instead of a creative project like the e-book, the podcast project works at the student's own pace, and the guidelines are specific to give students the chance to build a fluid conversation through practice and rehearsing together.

The two projects are distinct in their respective foci, the amount of research needed, and the language skills practiced (conversation skills versus writing and presentation skills). Teachers can choose what works the best for their students' interests and levels. Following backward design principles, teachers can first decide on the final project, which is the central method of summative assessment, and then adjust the input and practice in the Mulan unit by, for example, spending more efforts practicing conversation skills on contemporary gender issues, or focusing more on developing pertinent writing skills (such as writing biographical sketches, describing a person's appearance in a photograph, scripting an imagined dialogue, describing actions in a specific scene, etc.).

8. Teacher's Reflections

Stories may perpetuate ethnic and gender stereotypes for entertaining the masses; stories may also reveal experiences and perspectives from the underrepresented that open possibilities for change. How we tell a story matters. From a global feminist perspective, this unit constructs the story of Mulan as a cultural symbol for women's struggles and achievements that transcends time (past, present, and future), space (East and West), and professional fields. This unit gives students a structure where their own perspectives and experiences can connect with a traditional Chinese folktale, leading to greater intercultural understanding.

Overall, a feminist perspective on Mulan may not be a familiar perspective, and thus, careful scaffolding is necessary and important. Students need sufficient knowledge before they can engage in critical discussion. The initial lesson and the preview packet as well as the enrichment packets are geared toward the goal of scaffolding and building critical discussions with sufficient cultural knowledge and knowledge of the story itself.

Appendices: Sample Teaching Materials

Additional supplemental materials, including the e-book project guideline and grading rubric, a model for the e-book project, and the talk show project guideline, as well as student activity handouts can be requested by scanning this QR code.

Appendix 7.1: Preview Packet

《木兰从军》 预习作业 (Preview Packet)

1. 课文 Lesson Text

《木兰从军》

织布机发出"唧唧！唧唧！"的声音，木兰坐在织布机前，对着门外织布。不一会儿，听不到织布机的声音了，只听到木兰在叹气。

"木兰啊，你在想什么？你在回忆什么？"

"我没有在想什么，没有在回忆什么。昨天,家里收到了征兵文书，一共有12卷，每一卷上都写着父亲的名字。父亲没有长子，我没有哥哥，我要去买一匹骏马，配一副马鞍，代替父亲去前线战斗！"

木兰去东市买了骏马，去西市买了马鞍，去南市买了马的辔头，去北市买了一条长鞭。第二天一大早，女扮男装的木兰告别了父母，一路向北，纵马飞奔，天黑前就来到了黄河。晚上木兰睡在黄河边，听不到父母呼唤自己的声音，只听到黄河水在身边哗哗地流着。

第二天一大早，木兰离开黄河，继续一路向北，纵马飞奔，天黑前就来到了黑山头，这里离前线很近，木兰听不到父母呼唤自己的声音，只听到燕山脚下敌人的战马发出啾啾的叫声。

"Mùlán Joins the Army" 《木兰从军》 179

　　白天，木兰和战士们纵马飞奔，在崇山峻岭间战斗。夜晚，寒冷的空气中传来守夜人打更的声音，星星和月亮闪着冷冷的光，照在战士们银色的盔甲上。
　　一晃十年过去了，战争终于结束。战士们有的为国捐躯，有的胜利归来。木兰胜利归来，见到了国家的君王。君王坐在高高的大堂上，按每个战士的战绩赐给官位和财富。木兰战绩赫赫，君王把丰厚的财富赐给木兰，并请木兰做国家的尚书郎。
　　木兰不为所动，对君王说：
　　"我不想做尚书郎，请您赐给我一匹日行千里的好马，让我早日回到家乡。"
　　"木兰回来了，木兰回来了！"
　　村子里的人都奔走相告，父母听说女儿回来了，互相搀扶着来到城门外迎接木兰。姐姐听说妹妹回来了，打扮得漂漂亮亮的，等着妹妹。弟弟听说姐姐回来了，磨刀霍霍，杀猪宰羊。
　　木兰一回到家就打开东边的门，坐上西边的床，脱下军人的衣服，穿上旧时的衣裙，梳起云朵一样的头发，对着镜子贴上美丽的花黄。木兰从屋子里走出来，她的战友们都大吃一惊！
　　"我们在一起生活了十年，竟然不知道木兰是女郎！"
　　雄兔喜欢蹬腿，雌兔喜欢眯眼，可是，当两只兔子同时在地面上奔跑的时候，谁又能分辨得出哪一只是雄兔、哪一只是雌兔呢？

Language Coding Key

<u>Underlined</u>: new vocabulary
Bold: useful grammatical patterns

2. **New Words from the Lesson Text** 课文里的生词

1)	织布机	zhībùjī	weaving machine, loom
2)	叹气	tànqì	sigh
3)	回忆	huíyì	remember
4)	征兵文书	zhēngbīng wénshū	conscription paper
5)	长子	zhǎngzǐ	eldest son
6)	骏马	jùnmǎ	a horse
7)	代替	dàitì	replace
8)	前线	qiánxiàn	war front
9)	战斗	zhàndòu	combat
10)	战士	zhànshì	soldier
11)	战友	zhànyǒu	fellow soldier
12)	马鞍	mǎ'ān	saddles
13)	辔头	pèitóu	bridle
14)	长鞭	zhǎng biān	a long whip
15)	告别	gàobié	bid farewell
16)	呼唤	hūhuàn	call out

17)	黑山头	hēishān tóu	head of Black Mountain
18)	敌人	dírén	enemy
19)	战马	zhànmǎ	war horse
20)	盔甲	kuījiǎ	armor
21)	寒气	hánqì	chill
22)	守夜人	shǒuyè rén	night watchman
23)	打更	dǎ gēng night	(watchman) sounding the gongs
24)	一晃	yīhuàng	time flies
25)	终于	zhōngyú	finally
26)	按	àn	according to
27)	赐给	shǎnggei	give reward to
28)	尚书郎	shàngshūláng	highest official post, prime minister
29)	早日	zǎorì	as early as possible
30)	家乡	jiāxiāng	hometown
31)	迎接	yíng jiē	meet
32)	磨刀	mó dāo	sharpen the knife
33)	脱下	tuō xià	take off
34)	梳起	shū qǐ	comb up
35)	贴上	tiē shàng	to put on
36)	花黄	huā huáng	flower decoration
37)	雄兔	xióng tù	male rabbit
38)	蹬腿	dēngtuǐ	kick
39)	雌兔	cí tù	female rabbit
40)	眯眼	mī yǎn	squint
41)	奔跑	bēnpǎo	run
42)	分辨	fēnbiàn	distinguish

Four-Character Expressions in the Story

43)	女扮男装	nǚ bàn nánzhuāng	women dressed up in men's clothing
44)	替父从军	tì fù cóngjūn	join the army in one's father's place
45)	一路向北	yīlù xiàng běi	all the way north
46)	纵马飞奔	zòng mǎ fēi bēn	gallop
47)	燕山脚下	yànshān jiǎoxià	at the foot of Yanshan Mountain
48)	崇山峻岭	chóngshānjùnlǐng	great and dangerous mountains
49)	为国捐躯	wèi guó juānqū	die for one's country
50)	胜利归来	shènglì guīlái	return victoriously
51)	战绩赫赫	zhànjì hèhè	great military record
52)	不为所动	bù wéi suǒ dòng	unmoved
53)	日行千里	rì xíng qiānlǐ	travel thousands of miles
54)	奔走相告	bēnzǒu xiāng gào	running to tell each other
55)	互相搀扶	hùxiāng chānfú	support each other
56)	磨刀霍霍	Mó dāo huòhuò	sharpening the knife energetically
57)	杀猪宰羊	shā zhū zǎi yáng	slaughter pigs and sheep

3. 生词练习

a. **Match the Fixed Expressions on the Left to Their Colloquial Paraphrase on the Right**

替父从军	女性扮成男性，穿着男性的服装。
崇山峻岭	骑着马，像飞一样
为国捐躯	一天就可以走一千里
不为所动	为了自己的国家，死在战场。
女扮男装	高大的山和岭
纵马飞奔	跑着互相告诉好消息
日行千里	很多的战绩
战绩赫赫	不被打动
奔走相告	代替自己的父亲去战斗

b. **Fill Out the Blank with the Appropriate Grammar Word**

- Marking the goal, direction, or location of an action (来/回/看/想+到，脱+下，穿+上，打+开，梳+起，贴+上)
- Marking the location of an action (V+在 … 上；从 +location +出来)

A. 夜晚，寒冷的空气中传来守夜人打更的声音，星星和月亮闪着冷冷的光，照( )战士们银色的盔甲( )。（shine onto ...）
B. 父母听说女儿回来了，互相搀扶着来( )城门外迎接木兰。(at)
C. 木兰一回( )家就打( )东边的门，坐(上)西边的床，脱( )军人的衣服，穿( )旧时的衣裙，梳( )云朵一样的头发，对着镜子贴( )美丽的花黄。木兰( )屋子里走( )，她的战士朋友们都大吃一惊！

4. 课文理解 Text Comprehension

a. **Answer the Following Questions in Full Sentences Based on the Story You Read**

1) 木兰家里有几口人，他们是谁？
2) 故事刚开始的时候，木兰在做什么？她为什么叹气？
3) 为了帮家人，木兰打算怎么做？她去了哪些地方，买了哪些东西？
4) 木兰什么时候出发去前线的？往什么方向走的？一路上经过了哪些地方？
5) 木兰在路上想念她的父母吗？你怎么知道的？
6) 木兰在军队里做得怎么样？白天做什么？晚上做什么？
7) 木兰在前线战斗了多少年？
8) 木兰见到君王了吗？
9) 君王赐给木兰什么？木兰怎么说？
10) 木兰回到家之前，家人都在做什么？
11) 木兰一回到家就做什么？
12) 木兰穿上原来的衣服出来见战友们，战友们怎么说？木兰怎么说？

b. Listen to the original *Mùláncí* recited in the video here: https://youtu.be/oQEI5PKMjgI

Recite along with the text in the Enrichment Guide to appreciate the rhythmic form of the original poem.

5. Cultural Enrichments 文化延展

Read the Enrichment Guide. Be ready to answer the knowledge quiz online.

Appendix 7.2: Enrichment Guide

《木兰从军》 Enrichment Guide

1. 故事介绍 Background

《木兰从军》 is a story adapted from the ancient folk song 《木兰辞》 (*Mùláncí*, 'The Ballad of Mulan'). This beautiful 民歌 (míngē, 'folk song') is likely of a non-Han Chinese origin judging by the horse-riding skill of Mulan and the address term used in the poem 可汗 (Kèhán, Khan) for the leader of the state. 《木兰辞》 first appeared in 《乐府诗集》 (Yuèfǔ Shījí, 'Yuèfǔ Poetry Collection'), compiled by 郭茂倩 (Guō Màoqiàn) of the Northern Song Dynasty (北宋 Běi Sòng). Working for the government's music bureau (乐府 Yuèfǔ), Guō Màoqiàn collected more than 5,000 folk songs and poems covering the Han Dynasty (汉朝 Hàn cháo), the Wei State (魏国 Wèi guó), the Jin Dynasty (晋朝 Jìn cháo), and the Southern and Northern Dynasties (南北朝 Nánběi cháo). These sung poems and folk songs reflected the everyday lives of ordinary people in those periods.

Mùláncí tells the story of a young woman of the Northern Wei period (北魏 Běi Wèi) who disguised herself as a man to serve in the army in her father's place (the story gave rise to such fixed expressions as 女扮男装 [nǚ bàn nánzhuāng, 'women dressed in men's clothing'], 替父从军 [tì fù cóngjūn, 'join the army in one's father's place']). The setting of 《木兰辞》 is likely during the Northern and Southern Dynasties (南北朝 Nánběi cháo, AD 420–589). During this time, Mulan's country was constantly attacked by the nomadic tribes residing beyond the northern borders.

Characters, Times, and Places from the Introduction Text

1)	乐府	yuèfǔ	music bureau
2)	诗集	shījí	collection of poems
3)	木兰辞	mùláncí	The Ballad of Mulan
4)	南北朝	nánběi cháo	Northern and Southern Dynasties
5)	民歌	míngē	folk song
6)	北魏	Bei Wèi	State of Northern Wei
7)	郭茂倩	Guō Màoqiàn	compiler of Yuefu poetry
8)	北宋	Běi Sòng	Northern Sòng Dynasty

9)	汉朝	Hàn cháo	Han Dynasty
10)	晋朝	Jìn cháo	Jin Dynasty
11)	魏国	Wèi guó	the State of Wei
12)	女扮男装	nǚ bàn nánzhuāng	women dressed in men's clothing
13)	替父从军	tì fù cóngjūn	join the army in one's father's place

2. 中国本土对木兰故事的改编 Adaptations of the Mulan Story within Chinese Domestic Audience

In China, Mulan's story is often retold in dramatic forms during foreign invasions to boost morale and patriotism. For instance, the 1939 feature film 《木兰从军》 (*Mulan Joins the Army*) directed by 卜万苍 (Bǔ Wànchāng, 1903–1974) was produced during Japan's invasion of China. The film used Mulan's image to rally morale against the foreign invasion. In 1951, two years after the founding of the People's Republic of China, Mulan was adapted into a local opera form 豫剧 (Yu Opera or Henan Opera) praising women's equal role in supporting war efforts.

3. 迪斯尼对木兰故事的改编 Disney's Adaptations: *Mulan* (1998) and *Mulan* (2020)

In 1998, Disney released *Mulan*, an animated film that introduced the first "Asian princess," deviating from the traditional royal lineage portrayed in classics like *Snow White* and *Sleeping Beauty*. The story is an adaptation of the Chinese legend of Mulan for the English-speaking Western audience. The animated classic highlights Mulan's defiance of Confucian gender roles, portraying her as equal to men and self-reliant, evolving into a skilled and brave warrior. The metaphor of the pink magnolia flower symbolizes Mulan's family name (花 Huā) and symbolizes her blooming into her true self.

While commercially successful and an instant classic, the film faced criticism for crude jokes at the expense of minority cultures and a questionable portrayal of women. Disney's 2020 remake of *Mulan*, directed by feminist New Zealand filmmaker Niki Caro and using real actors, largely follows a similar plot. Much of the storyline revolves around Mulan feeling ambivalent until she no longer hides her identity – not just a woman disguised in men's clothing but also a powerful individual destined to be a legendary warrior. In comparison to the animated version, Niki Caro's adaptation aimed to be culturally respectful, paying tribute to the power of Chinese culture in nurturing and protecting its own.

The Mushu dragon in *Mulan* (1998) was removed due to severe criticism for cultural appropriation, perpetuating stereotypes. In its place, a silent phoenix, symbolizing powerful but silent protection from Mulan's own community, was introduced. Another female supporting role is also added, a foreign witch comparable to Mulan in her skills and strength but abandoned by her own people for fearing her supernatural talents. In the end, the witch sacrificed herself to save Mulan, underscoring the film director's feminist take on the legend where women support each other on a global scale.

The absence of songs and the deviation from the entertaining tropes in the 1998 animated film disappointed those accustomed to such elements. The Chinese-speaking audience also criticized the numerous attempts in *Mulan* (2020) to iconize clichés of Chinese traditional culture without a deeper understanding of them. Certain stereotypes from the original film persist, such as the largely bland, even caricatured supporting roles. However, as Wang (2020, 2022) argued, *Mulan* (2020) positions the heroine as respected and protected by her own community, which is a remarkable improvement from *Mulan* (1998).

4. 木兰姓花吗？Was Mulan's Family Name Huā?

The flower symbolism is most prominently used in *Mulan* (1998), where the magnolia is indicative of Mulan's feminine identity. On the other hand, historically, Mulan did not have a surname in earlier forms of the legend. Later she was given the family name "魏" (Wèi) plausibly due to her living in the time of the State of Wei in the Southern and Northern Dynasties. Later, the name "花" (Huā, 'flower') was invented for her in a well-circulated play about Mulan written by the painter and playwright Xue Wei of the Ming Dynasty (明朝的徐渭), sexualizing Mulan as a "flower" (Wang [2020] provides a critical analysis of this evolution).

5. 木兰是哪里人？Where Did Mulan Live?

The story of Mulan does not specify a particular region. 《木兰辞》 does not provide details about her specific place of birth or hometown. The poem did portray her as skilled in horse riding and fighting at northern borders– therefore she was likely a resident of the Northern Wei period (北魏, 386–534 CE) where the ruling group was 鲜卑 (Xiānbēi), an ancient nomadic ethnic group in East Asia, primarily inhabiting the northeastern regions. At certain points in history, the Xiānbēi migrated southward into northern China, establishing independent polities, notably the Northern Wei Dynasty.

Different adaptations of the story may have different settings, becoming a source of debate regarding the adaptation's cultural authenticity. When *Mulan* (2020) was released, it received negative reviews from the Chinese audience. Many critiques expressed dissatisfaction with the film's lack of cultural authenticity. For instance, in the movie, Mulan is depicted growing up in 土楼 (Tǔlóu), a unique architectural style found in the Fujian province in southern China. This location contradicts Mulan's story, which is more plausible in northern terrains, given its theme of battling at northern borders, passing by the Yellow River, and crossing the Yan mountains as Mulan journeyed her way to the battlefield.

6. 北魏的时代特点 Characteristics of the Northern Wei Period

If Mulan lived during the period of the State of Wei (known as "Northern Wei"), the legend of Mulan would be connected with the historical context of that time, featuring tumultuous wars and foreign invasions at the northern borders. The most prominent characteristic of the Northern Wei period is that it is but one era in the so-called Southern and Northern Dynasties, where China was divided into multiple independent states.

During the Southern and Northern Dynasties, the dissemination of Buddhism in China experienced significant growth. Emperor Ming of Northern Wei played a crucial role in this by adopting Buddhism as the state religion, contributing to its widespread acceptance. In the Mulan legend, when Mulan returns home from war, she reverts to her female clothing, adorning her face with decorative pasties called 花黄 (huāhuáng). These pasties are golden-yellow paper cut into intricate patterns like stars, moons, flowers, and birds. This aesthetic trend was influenced by Buddhism, evident in the facial adornments of Buddhist figures in murals and paintings of the time.

The political divisions, cultural diversity, the spread of Buddhism, and the influence of nomadic cultures in the north during this period contributed to a more expansive cultural milieu for Mulan where women's roles extended beyond the home domain.

7. "忠勇孝悌" vs. "忠勇真" Different Cultural Virtues Portrayed in Various Adaptations of Mulan

Within the Chinese domestic audience, the traditional Mulan story is often said to represent the four tenets of Chinese Confucianism "忠勇孝悌":

- 忠 (zhōng): loyalty or faithfulness to one's country, family, and friends
- 勇 (yǒng): courage or the quality of being brave in the face of difficulties and dangers
- 孝 (xiào): the virtue of respect and obedience to one's parents
- 悌 (tì): sibling responsibility (The traditional concept of 悌 is exclusively on brotherly bonding, but it has been extended to connoting harmony and friendship among peers.)

These virtues have long served as a moral compass within traditional Chinese Confucian society. However, some of these virtues can be used to perpetuate harmful norms that subject women to male dominance. *Mulan* (1998) caricatures Mulan's community with song lyrics and dialogue lines asking Mulan to follow the Confucian teaching of "三从四德" (literally, three areas of obedience and four areas of virtue – obedience to one's father, husband, and brothers and upholding virtue in character, speech, appearance, and domestic duties). For the modern audience, the patriarchal order of restricting women's values to the home domain is archaic. Not surprisingly, Disney's 2020 remake alters these virtues, changing them into three tenets: "忠勇真" (loyalty, courage, truthfulness). Mulan's sword, inherited from her father, bears this three-virtues inscription and features prominently in movie posters. This modification in word choice reflects *Mulan* (2020) as an effort to honor the native culture that inspired the Mulan story while considering the sensibilities of its Western audience.

8. 木兰的故事对中文的影响 The Impact of the Legend of Mulan on Chinese Language

The legend of Mulan and particularly the classic folksong 《木兰辞》 have supplied numerous phrases that continue to be understood and used in modern Chinese. Below are some of them:

中文 Chinese	翻译 Translation
谁说女子不如男 Shuí shuō nǚzǐ bù rú nán	"Who says women are not as good as men?" (This phrase is a verse from the 1951 Yu Opera adaptation of Mulan).
扑朔迷离 pū shuò mí lí	"confusing and bewildering" or "mysterious and unpredictable" This phrase, originated in the last section of 《木兰辞》, describing the distinct behaviors of the male and female hares, now is used to describe a situation or a situation that is unclear, intricate, or hard to fathom, creating confusion and uncertainty.
现代花木兰 xiàndài Huā Mùlán	"Modern Mulan" This phrase characterizes a woman who exhibits similar qualities of bravery, strength, and determination in the face of challenges.
替父从军 tì fù cóng jūn 代父从军 dài fù cóng jūn	"Joining the military in one's father's place" This fixed expression doesn't have broad usage in modern Chinese, but it instantly evokes the image of Mulan.
巾帼英雄 jīn guó yīngxióng	"women heroes" The word "巾帼" refers to women's headgear. This phrase describes women who exhibit heroic qualities.
女扮男装 nǚ bàn nán zhuāng	"dressed as a man" This phrase is in reference to Mulan disguising herself as a man and can be referred neutrally to any occasion where a woman adopts a man's clothing to pretend to be a man.
万里赴戎机, 关山度若飞 wàn lǐ fù róng jī, guān shān dù ruò fēi	This fixed expression, originally describing Mulan riding thousands of miles in battles, crossing mountains as if flying, now describes military gallantry with poetic imagery.
木兰不用尚书郎 Mùlán bùyòng shàngshū láng	"Mulan rejected the emperor's offer of a high-ranking position." This phrase evokes the image of indifference to titles and honors.
磨刀霍霍 mó dāo huò huò	This phrase originally depicts Mulan's younger brother sharpening the butcher knife to prepare a feast for his sister's glorious return. Now it is used to describe enthusiastic preparation for an important occasion.
将军百战死, 壮士十年归 jiāngjūn bǎi zhàn sǐ, zhuàngshì shí nián guī.	"Generals die after a hundred battles, brave warriors return after a decade." This verse now is a cliché to describe the scale and tragedy of war.

9. 《木兰辞》的翻译 Mùláncí Translated in English

A well-known version of the English translation of 《木兰辞》 is by 许渊冲 (Xǔ Yuānchōng, 1921–2021), a renowned translator celebrated for his translation of Chinese classical poetry into both English and French. His translation approach stirred controversy, as he emphasized the importance of capturing not only the literal meaning but also the essence of the original text. He advocated for a "domestication" of translation, where the translated work seamlessly integrates with the target language's cultural nuances, preserving not only the meaning but also the aesthetic qualities in terms of sounds, rhythms, and deeper cultural metaphors. His renowned translation of *Mùláncí* serves as a prime example of this distinctive translation method.

You can listen to a recitation of *Mùláncí* at this link:

https://youtu.be/WpgyS2EHK3U

You can read the full translation in English of multiple versions at this link:

http://ex.chinadaily.com.cn/exchange/partners/82/rss/channel/language/columns/v0m20b/stories/WS5d3fee11a310d83056401cb5.html

Appendix 7.3: Study Packet

Study Packet

Study these words using Quizlet. Be ready to use these words in class.

1)	女性	nǚxìng	female
2)	男性	nánxìng	male
3)	女性主义	nǚxìng zhǔyì	feminism
4)	男权社会	nánquán shèhuì	male-dominant society
5)	父权社会	fùquán shèhuì	patriarchal society
6)	性别	xìngbié	gender
7)	歧视	qíshì	discriminate against
8)	偏见	piānjiàn	bias
9)	刻板印象	kèbǎn yìnxiàng	stereotype
10)	男女平等	nánnǚ píngděng	gender equality
11)	职业	zhíyè	profession
12)	3.8国际劳动妇女日	3.8 Guójì láodòng fùnǚ rì	3.8 International Working Women's Day
13)	平权运动	píngquán yùndòng	equal rights movement
14)	差异	chāyì	difference
15)	进步	jìnbù	progress
16)	退步	tuìbù	regress

"Mùlán Joins the Army" 《木兰从军》

1. Match the Four-Character Idioms with Their Paraphrase

女性主义	女性扮成男性，穿着男性的服装
父权社会	骑着马，像飞一样
刻板印象	一天就可以走一千里
平权运动	为了自己的国家，死在战场
替父从军	高大的山和岭
女扮男装	跑着互相告诉好消息
崇山峻岭	很多的战绩
为国捐躯	追求民族、种族、性别，人人平等
战绩赫赫	代替自己的父亲去加入军队
不为所动	不被别人或者事情改变自己的想法
日行千里	把父亲和男性看得更重要的社会
奔走相告	对人或者事情的固定的（不好的）印象
纵马飞奔	理解女性在父权社会的困难，支持女性独立

2. 这些词，中文怎么说？

_____ _____
(gender)   (women)

_____ _____
(female)   (male)

_____ _____
(male-dominant society) (patriarchal society)

_____ _____
(difference) bias)

_____ _____
(stereotype) (discrimination)

_____ _____
(feminism)   (3.8 International Working Women's Day)

_____ _____
(regress)   (progress)

3. Gender Bias in Language

下面的流行语，哪些你认识？哪些是有性别歧视的？同样的意思，有不歧视的表达吗？ Among these slang terms, which ones do you recognize? What do these expressions mean? Which ones have gender bias? Are there alternative expressions for the ideas without expressing bias?

小鲜肉	大女主
男人婆	娘娘腔
头发长，见识短	婆婆妈妈
男主外女主内	女强人
上得厅堂，下得厨房	好男人/好女人
妇孺皆知	老男人/老女人

剩女   钻石王老五
(别的例子)

_____   _____

4. Padlet Speaking and Recording

Pay attention to your pace, word groups, tones, and pronunciation. Be as fluent, accurate, and natural as you can for part 1. Be thorough and detailed, and incorporate class materials for part 2.

Part 1: Record the lesson text (alternatively, record your recitation of the folk song Mùláncí)
Part 2: 说说你的想法. Pick **two topics** from the following list. Expressing your ideas. Give concrete examples. Formulate a coherent commentary.

1) 你觉得，常常跟女性联系在一起的职业有哪些？这样的联系，是实际情况，还是刻板印象？
2) 你所在的行业或者领域里，有什么样的刻板印象吗？有性别方面的刻板印象吗？
3) 你被人以性别评价过吗？
4) 你所从事的领域和着行业里，有木兰这样的人物吗？
5) "三八国际劳动妇女日"现在变成了"女神节"，这一天，在中国，女性可以放半天假，会收到鲜花和礼物，半价购物。这样看来，女性的地位提高了吗？

References

ACTFL-NCSSFL. (2017). *NCSSFL-ACTFL can-do statements*. Retrieved June 1, 2022, from www.actfl.org/resources/ncssfl-actfl-can-do-statements
Byram, M. (2008). *From foreign language education to education for intercultural citizenship: Essays and reflections*. Clevedon: Multilingual Matters.
Byram, M. (2021). *Teaching and assessing intercultural communicative competence* (2nd ed.). Clevedon: Multilingual Matters.
Byram, M., & Wagner, M. (2018). Making a difference: Language education for intercultural and international dialogue. *Foreign Language Annals*, *51*(1), 140–151.
Ferree, M. M. (2006). Globalization and feminism: Opportunities and obstacles for activism in the global arena. In M. M. Ferree & A. M. Tripp (Eds.), *Global feminism: Transnational women's activism, organizing, and human rights* (pp. 14–45). New York University Press.
Labov, W., & Waletzky, J. (1967/1997). *"Narrative analysis": Essays on the verbal and visual arts* (J. Helm (ed.), pp. 12–44). Seattle: University of Washington Press. Reprinted in *Journal of Narrative and Life History*, *7*, 3–38, 1997.
Lippi-Green, R. (2012). *English with an accent: Language, ideology and discrimination in the United States* (2nd ed.). Abingdon, UK: Routledge.
Wang, Z. (2020). Cultural 'authenticity' as a conflict-ridden hypotext: Mulan (1998), Mulan Joins the Army (1939), and a millennium-long intertextual metamorphosis. *Arts 2020*, *9*, 78.
Wang, Z. (2022). From Mulan (1998) to Mulan (2020): Disney conventions, cross-cultural feminist intervention, and a compromised progress. *Arts*, *11*(5).
王卓异 (2020, October 15). 迪士尼"读不懂"中国文化？真人版电影《花木兰》的"魔改"争议. 《凤凰周刊》总第738期.

8 "Sàiwēng Lost His Horse" 《塞翁失马》 (Sàiwēng Shīmǎ)

Teaching Traditional Idiom Story through the Six Thinking Hats Technique

- **Language Proficiency Level:** Intermediate low to high;
- **ICC Developmental Goal:** Willingness to question the value in one's own environment;
- **High School/AP Theme:** Families and communities – social values; personal and public identity – self-image;
- **Suggested High School Course:** Chinese 4, AP Chinese Language & Culture;
- **Suggested College Course:** Chinese Communication and Composition; Advanced Chinese Language and Culture; Advanced Chinese Language and Culture through Stories;
- **Suggested Instructional Time:** Seven 50-minute lessons.

1. Introduction

This chapter invites students to embark on a transformative journey that transcends mere words, guiding them through the enchanting realm of Chinese idioms where age-old wisdom and cultural insights spring to life through the language. Their exploration will commence by uncovering the unique traits distinguishing Chinese idioms from their English counterparts. Subsequently, students will immerse themselves in the intriguing fable/idiom story of 《塞翁失马》 (Sàiwēng Shīmǎ, 'Sàiwēng Lost His Horse'), engaging in thought-provoking discussions centered around the transformative power of seemingly adverse and favorable circumstances. Drawing parallels between the story and their own experiences, students will navigate the intricacies of change and perspective, employing the Six Thinking Hats technique as their guide (De Bono, 1985).

The Six Thinking Hats technique, a creative thinking tool dividing different cognitive styles into six distinctive "hats" (logical, emotional, cautious, optimistic, creative, and controlling), will serve as the conduit for their exploration. By donning each hat, students will ensure comprehensive coverage of viewpoints while dissecting specific questions and topics. As they adopt various roles within their teams, students will ensure a holistic analysis, embracing a diversity of perspectives and thinking styles.

Upon exploring the narrative 《塞翁失马》 (Sàiwēng Shīmǎ, 'Sàiwēng Lost His Horse'), a project will follow suit, providing students with the opportunity to expand their exploration of Chinese idioms and connect it with their previous knowledge. Applying the Six Thinking Hats technique, refined through their initial engagement with the "Sàiwēng Lost His Horse" idiom, they will immerse themselves in a realm of idiomatic expressions and fable stories, delving further into the cultural tapestry in connection with their own previous knowledge and making text-to-text, text-to-self, and text-to-world connections (refer to chapter 6 for details about the connection strategy).

2. Contextualizing the Topic

The Chinese program in our high school has been developing its own thematic units for all levels for more than ten years, except for AP Chinese Language and Culture, which gives the teachers more freedom to include the latest materials. Overall, student feedback suggests that the emerging curriculum gives them a greater sense of engagement and accomplishment in learning. As a result, the number of students in our Chinese language program has been steadily increasing. The unit illustrated in this chapter is used in a high school Chinese world language course titled *Chinese Four Accelerated*, which is also a one-year dual-credit course. More than 90% of the students are heritage speakers who have Chinese learning experience before entering high school. They are placed into different levels based on their placement test results using the ACTFL Assessment of Performance toward Proficiency in Languages® (AAPPL). Two higher-level Chinese courses followed *Chinese Four Accelerated*: *AP Chinese Language and Culture*, and *Chinese Six: Chinese Literature, Media, and Culture*. The course *Chinese Four Accelerated* covers current and historical figures, customs and traditions, environment protection, teenagers' lives, and Chinese movies. Our movie unit includes three movies that help students to explore culture and history from different perspectives. The film *Ne Zha* enables students to delve into Chinese mythology; the movie *Red Cliff II* showcases a part of ancient Chinese history; and *To Live* guides them to experience Chinese people's lives in modern history.

This idiom unit takes place right after the movie *To Live* since the implied meaning in the fable/idiom story of "Sàiwēng Lost His Horse," the transformation between good and bad events is possible, is well exemplified in the characters' lives in the movie *To Live*. With the idiom project following the debrief of "Sàiwēng Lost His Horse," students are invited to encounter the realm of Chinese idioms and implied wisdom.

3. Methodology Highlight: Six Thinking Hats Technique

The Six Thinking Hats technique is a structured and systematic approach to thinking and problem-solving developed by Edward De Bono (1985). It involves wearing metaphorical hats, each of which represents a different mode or perspective of thinking (see the following for the hat colors and their representations). These hats guide individuals or groups through various ways of looking at a situation, encouraging them to consider different angles, explore diverse viewpoints, and make more comprehensive decisions. In this idiom unit, students will wear the six different hats when role-playing the idiom story. This approach assists them in thinking about the story twists in "Sàiwēng Lost His Horse" from different perspectives and provides them with an innovative way to practice the target language to express their ideas. This process nurtures their creativity and engages them more in the learning process, contributing to the elevation of their language proficiency.

Hat Color	Representation
White	objective and factual thinking
Red	feeling and emotions
Black	negative thinking
Yellow	positive thinking
Green	creative and innovative thinking
Blue	the big picture/process control

4. Curricular Modeling

We offer the following complete set of materials ready for use in the classroom along with accompanying activities. These materials and suggested activities support and are guided by the learning outcomes described for the robust use of backward design principles (Wiggins & McTighe, 2005).

4.1 Learning Objectives and Primary Performance Assessments

Learning objectives are composed of two parts: language performance objectives and intercultural communication competence objectives. All of the learning objectives are written in the "can do" format of "I can . . ." to make learners understand from their perspectives what they can achieve in this unit (ACTFL-NCSSFL, 2017).

Language Performance Objectives (Can-Do Statements)

- I can follow the main story and identify some supporting details of "Sàiwēng Lost His Horse" and the idiom of my choice from the idiom project. (*Interpretive*)
- I can tell in writing and speaking the story of "Sàiwēng Lost His Horse" and the idiom that my team chose as our project focus. (*Presentational*)
- I can apply the idioms learned to make text-to-text, text-to-self, and/or text-to-world connections. (*Presentational*; *Interpersonal*)
- I can apply the Six Thinking Hats technique to analyze significant events. (*Presentational*; *Interpersonal*)

The corresponding ICC development goals are written based on four aspects of ICC known as KASA: knowledge, attitude, skills, and critical cultural awareness (Byram, 2008, 2021; Byram & Wagner, 2018; inter alia).

Intercultural Communication Competence Objectives

- **Knowledge:** I can describe fully the story and the moral of "Sàiwēng Lost His Horse" and the idiom of my choice from the idiom project.
- **Attitude:** When describing "Sàiwēng Lost His Horse" and the idiom of my choice from the idiom project, I value and appreciate the practice and wisdom exemplified in the idiom stories and show curiosity to further explore the perspectives related to the practice.
- **Skill:** I can relate the idiom stories to my own experiences (text-to-self), the ones from other stories, articles, or movies (text-to-text), or the experience in the world around me (text-to-world). I can also apply the Six Thinking Hats technique to analyze the significant event(s), especially the ones that involve people from different cultural and ethnic backgrounds.
- **Critical Cultural Awareness:** I am aware of the different perspectives and values embodied in the idioms from different cultures. I am also aware of the perspectives and values represented in the idioms from my own culture.

The associated language performance objectives are also expressed using the "can do" framework, phrased as "I can . . ." statements. This approach helps learners grasp what they can accomplish in this unit from their own viewpoints (ACTFL-NCSSFL, 2017).

4.2 Teaching Materials

The classroom-ready materials are presented in the appendices immediately following this chapter for your convenience. Additionally, you can download the same materials, along with supplementary resources in an adaptable digital format, including all worksheets, from the chapter's online supplements folder (refer to the appendices section).

A. Unit Plan: Provides students with an overview of what will be covered, as well as the assessment methods, major learning vocabulary/structures, and other related resources.
B. Google Slides
- Comparing and contrasting Chinese and English idiom.
- Introduction of the story of "Sàiwēng Lost His Horse."

Table 8.1 Primary Performance Assessment for the "Sàiwēng Lost His Horse" Unit

Communicative Modes	Language Performance Assessment
Interpretive Mode	• I can identify the main point and some details in reading selections about the idiom "Sàiwēng Lost His Horse" and those from the idiom project. • I can identify the main point and some details that students made in the writing about the idiom and the text-to-text, text-to-self, and text-to-world connections.
Presentational Mode	Writing prompt: You volunteer to teach little kids Chinese in a Saturday Chinese school. This coming weekend, you will teach them the idiom "Sàiwēng Lost His Horse." It is your first-time teaching, so you are pretty nervous and decide to write down the rough script of what you will teach them. Your script draft should include, but not be limited to: • a retelling of the story of "Sàiwēng Lost His Horse." (Make sure to have a beginning, middle [including the three twists], and an ending. Use a narrative format, not a dialogue format.) • the moral that the idiom tells us. • connections to the character, story, or the moral of the story using your own experiences or those you are familiar with, as well as to other texts, movies, or the world around you. (You can use your own examples to help guide your students in sharing their personal connections later.)
Interpersonal Mode	I can participate in a simulated conversation by responding to a series of six questions related to "Sàiwēng Lost His Horse" and the idiom project.

- Utilizing practical examples related to students to illustrate how the Six Thinking Hats technique can be applied for a multifaceted approach to problem-solving.
- Incorporating the Six Thinking Hats technique, perform the story of "Sàiwēng Lost His Horse."
- Focusing on vocabulary and sentence structure exercises, preparing students to practice fluent storytelling, story writing, and make text-to-text, text-to-self, and text-to-world connections.
- Team idiom project instruction and template.

C. Video Materials: "Sàiwēng Lost His Horse"
D. Handouts:

- Chinese and English Idioms Comparisons and Contrasts: Provides definitions of idioms in Chinese and offers examples to enable students to compare and contrast Chinese and English idioms in terms of their literal and implied meanings, the length of the idioms, whether there is a backstory to the idioms, and more.
- Preview Packet: Includes vocabulary, structures, the story "Sàiwēng Lost His Horse," and related practice questions.

- Study Packet: Includes practice exercises complementary to classroom sessions, such as the GIST activity and the Six Thinking Hats technique, to help retell the story of "Sàiwēng Lost His Horse."
- Idiom Project: Includes the requirements for the idiom project and a worksheet for students to take notes when other teams present their idioms.
- Review of Idioms and Idioms in Context: Includes practice exercises to reinforce the idioms learned through the idiom project. The practice encompasses multiple-choice questions, exploration of literal and implied meanings of idioms, placing idioms in context, and more.

E. Unit-Final Communicative Tasks
- Speaking assessment prompts
- Essay prompts
- Interpretive reading assessment
- Assessment rubrics

4.3 Suggested Lessons and Activities

The sample lessons and activities are geared toward high school students who are in the fourth level of taking Chinese courses as an elective course to meet their high school graduation requirement and/or college admission requirement for world languages. Students engage in a daily 50-minute Chinese class, where primary learning occurs within the classroom. To reinforce their understanding, a 10–20-minute homework assignment is given each day, allowing them to review the material covered. The unit commences by introducing Chinese idioms, followed by a comparative analysis with their English counterparts. Equipped with this foundational knowledge, students are then guided to immerse themselves in the intricacies of the idiom and the tale of "Sàiwēng Lost His Horse." To navigate the twists within the narrative effectively, the Six Thinking Hats technique is employed. Additionally, the strategy of making connections is woven into the instruction, aiding students in relating the material to their existing experiences and knowledge. The unit reaches its culmination with an engaging idiom project.

The study of "Sàiwēng Lost His Horse" imparts a practical understanding of both the Six Thinking Hats technique and the connection-making strategy. Additionally, it furnishes students with a tangible model for their collaborative idiom project. By intertwining focused language learning with these techniques and embedding targeted language practice ahead of the final assessments, students achieve an elevated level of performance. This contrasts markedly with scenarios where the Six Thinking Hats technique and the connection-making strategy are not incorporated, underscoring their positive impact.

This unit on idioms follows the movie unit *To Live*, which serves as an excellent introduction to the fable/idiom "Sàiwēng Lost His Horse," as the destinies of the characters in the movie constantly shift between favorable and unfavorable circumstances for various reasons. After viewing the movie *To Live*, students have a wealth of topics at their disposal that they can use to respond to the two questions regarding the transitions between good and bad luck. This process demonstrates how learners can establish text-to-text connections, ultimately motivating them to incorporate rich stories and personal experiences into their text-to-self and text-to-world connections. For students who have not had the opportunity to watch the movie *To Live* prior to encountering the idiom "Sàiwēng Lost His Horse," presenting them with examples of such transitions will provide them with a clear understanding of the types of connections they can form.

The following are the main activities for this unit.

Activity 1: Chinese and English Idioms Comparisons (Period 1, Estimated Time: 45 Minutes)

Materials: unit plan, Chinese/English idioms comparisons

- Begin the class by having students brainstorm idioms that they know, which can be from any culture.
- Students provide a definition of Chinese idioms before the teacher shares with them a sample definition.
- Compare and contrast Chinese and English idioms in terms of their literal and implied meanings, the length of the idioms, whether there is backstory to the idioms, and more.
- Conclude the activity by introducing the background of the fable/idiom story "Sàiwēng Lost His Horse."
- Distribute the teacher-made unit textbook to students, which comprises the unit plan and the study packets, along with other necessary materials.

Activity 2: Learn "Sàiwēng Lost His Horse" with the GIST Activity (Period 2, Estimated Time: 45 Minutes)

Materials: study packet, worksheets

- Start the fable/idiom story by inviting students to discuss the following questions: Under what circumstances can seemingly negative events transform into positive outcomes? Conversely, when might ostensibly positive situations take a turn for the worse? Do you possess or are you aware of experiences similar to those of Saiweng?
- After playing the video of "Sàiwēng Lost His Horse," have students practice Q&A in pairs to familiarize themselves with the story line and new vocabulary.
- Use the activity "The Gist" to retell the fable/idiom story "Sàiwēng Lost His Horse" verbally following these steps:
    - Have students generate 15–20 key vocabulary words to retell the story. (Teachers can provide students with the keywords if students are struggling to generate them.)
    - Have students share their key vocabulary with each other.
    - Using their own vocabulary, retell the story of "Sàiwēng Lost His Horse."

Activity 3: Learn 《塞翁失马》 "Sàiwēng Lost His Horse" with the Six Thinking Hats Technique (Period 3, Estimated Time: 45 Minutes)

Before using the Six Thinking Hats technique to explore "Sàiwēng Lost His Horse" further, practice it using examples that students are familiar with since this technique may be new for the majority of the students. The following is an example when using the prompt, "I prepared very seriously for the state volleyball match, but our team lost," to help students become familiar with the Six Thinking Hats technique.

- What are the facts? (white hat)
- How do you feel about your team's loss? (red hat)
- What is the positive impact of losing the game? (yellow hat)
- What is the negative impact of losing the game? (black hat)
- What is your innovative thinking about losing the game this time? (green hat)
- What is the big picture that you have seen from losing the game? (blue hat)

Apply the Six Thinking Hats technique to guide students in analyzing, reviewing, and role-playing the story of "Sàiwēng Lost His Horse." If preparing six hats of different colors is challenging, paper hats printed in six different colors can also work Students simply need to hold or wear hats of different colors, enabling them to quickly immerse themselves in the roles.

Retell the story of "Sàiwēng Lost His Horse" using the GIST activity, first in speaking, and then in writing. Students should be able to identify that they can produce richer details after role-playing the story by wearing different thinking hats.

Activity 4: Idiom Project: Reinforcing the Six Thinking Hats Technique (Periods 4–6, Estimated Time: 120 Min

Materials: Team Idiom Project Packet

- Engage in an idiom project with teams of three or four students. Each team selects one idiom from the provided list and utilizes the Idiom Project template, which includes the idiom name, its literal/implied meaning, a key vocabulary list (Chinese, Pinyin, English meaning), four pictures capturing the main idea of the story with a short description (highlighting keywords), application of the idiom in context and making text-to-text, text-to-self, and text-to-world connections (examples of how to make such connection is provided in the slide template). During the process of retelling the idiom story and making connections, apply the Six Thinking Hats technique when appropriate.

Teams present their idiom projects, and the audience learns and takes notes using: appendix 5: Team Idiom Project Packet.

- Review all of the idioms learned in context using appendix 3: Review Idioms & Idioms in Contexts.

- Vocabulary practice and structure practice are integrated into the project completion and presentation.

Activity 5: End of Unit: Review and Summative Assessment (Period 7, Estimated Time: 45 Minutes)

- Focus on vocabulary and structure review.
- Respond to six questions (Interpersonal speaking; see the following sample questions):
  - 什么是成语？
  - 请谈谈汉语成语和英文成语之间的两到三个相同点或不同点。
  - 你和你的朋友在课堂上教大家的成语是什么？成语的字面意思、寓意和成语故事是什么？
  - 除了你和你的小组同学教的成语故事，你最喜欢其他同学教的哪一个成语？这个成语的字面意思和寓意是什么？如何使用？
  - 我们在课上学到的《塞翁失马》的故事，你能给我讲一下这个故事吗？
  - 《塞翁失马》的寓意是好事可以变坏，坏事也可以变好。你是否有过或听说过坏事/好事相互转换的经历/故事？
- Reading assessments cover both "Sàiwēng Lost His Horse" and the idiom project.
- Writing assessment: Write an idiom teaching script based on the given scenario (refer to Table 8.1 Presentational Mode for the requirements of the presentational writing assessment).

The Six Thinking Hats technique and connection-making strategy (text-to-text, text-to-self, text-to-world) equip students with tools to learn the language and aid them in analyzing and evaluating both past and emerging significant events. These events include those related to themselves as well as those involving people from different cultural and ethnic backgrounds. Such skills are needed and necessary for our students to develop their intercultural communication competence, which will enable them to more effectively communicate with others.

4.4 Implementing the Six Thinking Hats Technique

All students are newcomers to the Six Thinking Hats technique. Hence, before employing it for their role-play of the fable/idiom story "Sàiwēng Lost His Horse," they are afforded the chance to familiarize themselves with the method by practicing it with topics they are acquainted with, such as: "I prepared very seriously for the state volleyball match, but our team lost," or "I did not get an offer from my favorite private Ivy League university, however, my favorite university's favorite department admitted me."

In our classes, this introductory practice was conducted for a minimum of two rounds, allowing them to grasp the essence of the Six Thinking Hats technique.

This preliminary phase effectively readies students to employ the technique when enacting the fable/idiom story of "Sàiwēng Lost His Horse" during its subsequent introduction. Allow students to work in groups of three facilitated greater practice opportunities, with each member having the chance to embody two distinct thinking perspectives by wearing different hats. During the idiom project, each group of students was tasked with wearing a minimum of two distinct hats as they presented and engaged in role-play for their idiom stories. This approach was necessary because certain stories might not allow for the incorporation of all six thinking hats.

The intricacies within the story of "Sàiwēng Lost His Horse" offer abundant chances for students to articulate their viewpoints, as they can share their thoughts following each plot twist. As students transition into the idiom project phase, they are tasked with applying the Six Thinking Hats technique to either enact the idiom itself or its connection/application. This phase of the learning journey encourages students to delve deeper into the technique's principles, enhancing their ability to approach language and idiomatic expressions through multifaceted lenses.

4.5 Assessment and Student Samples

Excerpts from students' presentational writing samples are shared here to provide insights into their language and ICC (intercultural communicative competence) development as demonstrated in their writing. While it is challenging to track students in their daily lives to determine if they have applied all four components of ICC (knowledge, skills, attitudes, and critical cultural awareness) when communicating with individuals from diverse cultures, it is possible to discern elements of their ICC "skills" (particularly relating) and "attitudes" (with a focus on "openness" in these examples), as well as their "knowledge" embedded in their writing.

In the presentational writing assessment, following the retelling of the story "Sàiwēng Lost His Horse," students were tasked with "making connections to the character, story, or the moral of the story using their own experiences or those they are familiar with, as well as connecting to texts, movies, or the world around them." The following text-to-text, text-to-self, and text-to-world connections are categorized into different groups to help readers gain insight into their learning.

The first two text-to-self connections are linked to the students' own learning experiences. These examples illustrate their ability to relate the story to their personal experiences and showcase their capacity to apply different thinking hats to analyze these experiences. This also underscores their attitudes toward such experiences. With changing attitudes compared to their initial ones, their feelings and actions adapted accordingly to facilitate better adjustment to their new environment.

Excerpt 1: "这个故事说到了一个道理，好事能变成坏事，坏事也能变成好事。这个故事让我想到了我刚来美国的时候。刚来美国读书的时候，我在一个有很多华人的学校读书，我本来认为这是一件好事，但是华人太多导致我的英语并没有太大的进步，这变成了一件坏事。"
[This story speaks to a truth that good things can turn into bad things, and bad things can also turn into good things. This story reminds me of when I first came

to the United States. Initially, I thought it was a good thing to study at a school with many Chinese students. However, the abundance of Chinese speakers hindered my progress in English, turning it into a disadvantage.]

Excerpt 2: "这个故事让我想到了我的故事，我在初中的时候，我爸爸告诉我要带我来美国上学，我原本以为会因为语言问题，还有没有朋友而成为一件坏事。但来了美国才发现，这不仅不是坏事，还是一件好事，因为学习压力没有中国那么大，相对来说比较轻松。"

[This story reminds me of my own experience. In middle school, my dad told me he was bringing me to the United States for school. Initially, I thought it would be a bad thing due to language barriers and the possibility of not having friends. However, upon arriving in the United States, I discovered that it was not just a negative experience; in fact, it turned out to be a positive one. This was due to the fact that the academic pressure was not as intense as in China, making it comparatively more relaxed.]

In the following two connections, students once again put on their optimistic "yellow hats" to scrutinize seemingly unfortunate events, drawing from both their personal experiences and those of others. Being open to exploring different perspectives of the same event enabled the students to uncover something new (for instance, how the worms in the fish tank can actually maintain clean water) and empowered them to approach apparent misfortunes with an open and positive attitude.

Excerpt 3: "这个故事也让我想到新冠病毒一开始的时候。那时，人们都需要隔离，都很孤单。但是呢，隔离也带来了家班和网络上上学，所以人们不需要花时间去办公室或者学校。这就是坏事变成好事。"

[This story also reminds me of the beginning of the COVID-19 pandemic. At that time, people needed to isolate, and everyone felt lonely. However, isolation also brought about remote work and online schooling, eliminating the need to commute to offices or schools. This is an example of a bad thing turning into a good thing.]

Excerpt 4: "塞翁失马的故事让我想到了我养虾的时候。我的鱼缸里有很多小虫子，我的妈妈说这肯定是一个坏事，要换水。但是，我后来在网上读到这些小虫子可以作为鱼的食物，也会帮我的鱼缸的水保持干净。这和塞翁失马的故事相关因为乡亲们都说塞翁丢了马是坏事，但是后来马回来了，还带回了了一匹马， 变成了好事情，就像我的虫子。另外的我的一个经历就是小时候，我从自行车上摔下来，把我的胳膊和肚子被刮伤了。因为我的肚子被刮伤了，我就不能在夏天游泳了。我觉得这是一个坏事，但是其实，这个游泳池的水很脏，所有的去那个游泳池游泳的孩子都病了。因为我没有游泳，我没有病。最后，这个坏事变成了一个好事。"

[The story of "Sàiwēng Lost His Horse" reminds me of a time when I was raising shrimp. In my fish tank, there were many small bugs, and my mom thought it was definitely a bad thing, suggesting that we change the water. However, later I read online that these small bugs could serve as food for the fish and help keep the water in my tank clean. This is related to the story of "Sàiwēng Lost His

Horse" because, just like the villagers initially thought losing the horse was a bad thing, it turned out to be good when the horse returned with another horse, much like my bugs. Another experience I had was when I fell off my bicycle as a child, scraping my arm and stomach. Because my stomach was injured, I could not swim in the summer, which I thought was a bad thing. However, in reality, the water in that swimming pool was very dirty, and all the kids who swam there got sick. Because I didn't swim, I did not get sick. In the end, what seemed like a bad thing turned into a good thing.]

The following two connections (text-to-world and text-to-self) indicate that students are capable of celebrating both for themselves and others when seemingly negative events transform into positive outcomes.

Excerpt 5: "《塞翁失马》的故事让我想到了我听过的故事。在9/11那天，有一个人要去上班，但是她的孩子那天生病了。一开始她不高兴因为她那天要照顾孩子，不能见她的同事。过了几个小时，她在电视上看到她上班的建筑被轰炸了。如果她那天没照顾孩子，她就死掉了。这个就是坏事变成好事。"

[The story of "Sàiwēng Lost His Horse" reminds me of a story I heard. On September 11, there was a person who was supposed to go to work, but her child fell ill that day. At first, she was upset because she had to take care of her child and could not meet her colleagues. After a few hours, she saw on the television that the building where she worked had been bombed. If she had not taken care of her child that day, she would have died. This is an example of a bad thing turning into a good thing.]

Excerpt 6: "这个成语故事让我想到了我妈妈跟我说的一件事。我刚出生的时候，我妈妈因为要照顾我很累。因为我妈妈很累，我的姥爷就从成都飞到美国来帮忙照顾我。我的姥爷坐飞机也不是很方便因为会觉得腰疼。他到美国以后，成都被附近的地震影响了。我的姥爷幸好没有在成都。刚开始，这是一件坏事情因为我妈妈很累，姥爷坐飞机也很累。后来，他就很幸运的躲过了一场地震。我觉得这件事跟《塞翁失马》的故事很像，因为一件不好的事情后来有好的结果。"

[This idiom story reminds me of something my mom told me. When I was born, my mom was very tired from taking care of me. Because she was exhausted, my grandpa flew from Chengdu to the United States to help take care of me. It was not very convenient for my grandpa to take a plane because he would feel pain in his back. After he arrived in the United States, Chengdu was affected by an earthquake. Fortunately, my grandpa was not in Chengdu at the time. Initially, this seemed like a bad thing because my mom was tired, and my grandpa had to take a plane. Later, he was fortunate to have avoided an earthquake. I feel that this incident is similar to the story of "Sàiwēng Lost His Horse" because something initially unfavorable led to a positive outcome.]

Students showcase their ability to connect "Sàiwēng Lost His Horse" to situations that initially appear positive but take a turn for the worse. Additionally, they demonstrate their capacity to adopt the "blue hat" perspective, allowing them to see the bigger picture of a seemingly positive event.

Excerpt 7: "这个故事让我想到了世界上很多中了彩票的人。他们本来以为天降的横财是一件好事，所以就开始没有节制的花钱。但是事实证明他们很快就把中彩票的钱给花完了，后来他们的生活还不如他们中彩票之前好。这件事说明了一个跟故事《塞翁失马》一样的道理，一个事情的性质不能靠表面来断定，因为好事也有可能变成坏事，坏事也有可能变成好事。"

[This story reminds me of many people around the world who have won the lottery. Initially, they thought the unexpected windfall was a good thing and began spending money without restraint. However, reality proved that they quickly spent all the lottery winnings, and later, their lives were not as good as they were before winning the lottery. This situation illustrates a principle similar to the story of "Sàiwēng Lost His Horse" – the nature of an event cannot be determined solely by its appearance because a seemingly good thing may turn into a bad thing, and a seemingly bad thing may turn into a good thing.]

Equipped with the connection-making strategy and the Six Thinking Hats technique, students can establish connections between more events they have learned, consequently enhancing their ability to generate more written content. This effectively addresses the challenge of students struggling to find writing topics.

5. Teacher's Reflections

Our language teachers are proficient in instructing the idiom story and its associated moral. What skills have your students learned from the idioms, aside from the idiom story and the embedded moral? Have you tried integrating idiom teaching with a life skill that students need? This idiom unit introduces the Six Thinking Hats technique while teaching idioms. Such integration benefits students in at least the following two ways. First, this integration enhances students' understanding of both the linguistic and cultural dimensions of Chinese idioms. By incorporating the Six Thinking Hats framework, students engage with the idiom "Sàiwēng Lost His Horse" in a holistic manner, better grasping the twists in the story and aiding in language proficiency improvement with a novel approach. Second, integrating idioms with Six Thinking Hats cultivates critical thinking and problem-solving abilities, elevating idioms beyond rote memorization. Students are prompted to wear different hats, encouraging diverse perspectives on the idiomatic meanings, origins, and real-life applications. This enriches language learning while also providing students with a practical life skill – the ability to approach challenges with multifaceted thinking and make well-rounded decisions. The Six Thinking Hats technique works perfectly with "Sàiwēng Lost His Horse" because of the moral and the twists in the story. This technique may still work for some other Chinese idioms or Chinese stories.

Another question is this: What approach do you use to teach multiple idioms and their stories? Allowing students to use a provided template (please refer to Google Slides 2_Idiom Project Template, which students utilized for this project) has proven to be an effective method for their work. Engaging students as active participants in the teaching process reinforces their understanding of idioms and nurtures valuable communication and presentation skills. Additionally, providing students with a structured template ensures consistency and clarity in their preparation for teaching their classmates the idiom. Facilitating this allows them to focus on conveying the idiom's meaning, origin, and usage. Encouraging collaborative learning through this method, where students take on roles as both learners and educators, fosters a sense of responsibility and pride in their language and cultural knowledge. Moreover, the act component of the idiom story teaching deepens the students' comprehension and retention of idioms, transforming the classroom into an interactive and dynamic space where knowledge is shared and co-constructed. This approach imparts idiomatic knowledge while also nurturing leadership skills and peer-to-peer learning, enriching the overall educational experience.

Finally, students often display heightened motivation for learning when they are able to discern meaningful connections. Consequently, establishing a bridge between the acquisition of Chinese idioms and the students' previous knowledge and experiences becomes paramount. The methodical approach of cultivating these connections through the employment of the text-to-text, text-to-self, and text-to-world framework offers a substantial avenue for enhancing the retention of idioms among students. For instance, the idiom 孟母三迁 can evoke a poignant reminder for students of their parents' diligent efforts in relocating to more favorable locales to access enriched learning resources. Similarly, the idiom 指鹿为马 stimulates critical contemplation of political conduct. Moreover, idioms such as 闻鸡起舞, 熟能生巧, and 半途而废 engender opportunities for profound introspection regarding their study habits and tenacity.

Appendices: Sample Teaching Materials

All materials in the appendices can be read online or downloaded using this link or QR code. Appendices 8.1 to 8.3 are fully enclosed here, while the remaining appendices are available online.

Appendix 8.1: Preview Packet

《塞翁失马》 预习作业 (Preview Packet)

1. 课文 Lesson Text

《塞翁失马》

从前有一位住在长城边上的老人，人们都叫他塞翁。他养了很多马，可是有一天他的一匹好马不见了。乡亲们听到这事，都觉得塞翁很<u>不幸</u>，都来安慰他。可是塞翁笑笑说： "<u>丢了一匹马</u>没有太大关系，还有可能会<u>带来福气</u>。" 乡亲们听了塞翁的话，都觉得塞翁的想法很好笑。马不见了，明明是件<u>坏事</u>，可是塞翁却认为丢了马还可能是一件好事。

过了几天，塞翁的好马不但回来了，而且还带回来了<u>另外</u>一匹好马。乡亲们听说塞翁的好马带着另外一匹好马回来了， 就来给塞翁道贺说： "<u>恭喜恭喜</u>呀， 马**不但**没有丢，**而且**还带回一匹好马，真是好福气呀。" 塞翁听了祝贺，没有和乡亲们一样的高兴。 他说： "白白得了一匹好马，不一定是什么福气，还有可能会变成一件坏事。"

塞翁有个<u>独生子</u>，平时就非常喜欢骑马。他发现带回来的那匹马是一匹难得的好马，就每天都骑马出去<u>游玩</u>，非常开心。 有一天，他玩得太高兴了， 就让马<u>跑得越来越快</u>。结果他从马背上摔下来， **把腿摔断了**。乡亲们听说了，又觉得塞翁很不幸。可是塞翁说： "没什么，腿摔断了，可是没<u>有摔死</u>呀，也是<u>福气</u>呢。" 乡亲们听了塞翁的话以后不明白，都在想：摔断了腿，这么<u>不幸</u>，哪儿来的<u>福气</u>呢？

不久，<u>战争</u>开始了，青年人都必须<u>入伍</u>，塞翁的儿子因为摔断了腿，所以不能入伍。入伍的青年都<u>战死了</u>，只有塞翁的儿子，虽然腿摔断了，但是却<u>平平安安</u>地<u>活了下来</u>。 这件事<u>说明</u>一个<u>道理</u>， 有时候坏事可能会<u>变成</u>好事， 好事有时候也可能会<u>变成</u>坏事。

Language Coding Key

<u>Underlined</u>: new vocabulary
Bold: useful grammatical patterns

2. 课文里的生词 New Words From the Lesson Text

	汉字	拼音	英文意思
1)	成语	chéngyǔ	idioms
2)	故事	gùshì	story
3)	老翁	lǎowēng	senior
4)	塞	sāi	frontier, fortress
5)	塞翁	Sāiwēng	the senior who lived at the frontier fortress
6)	塞翁失马，焉知非福	Sāiwēng shī mǎ, yān zhī fēi fú	Sāiwēng lost his horse, he then knew whether it was a bad thing or a blessing.
7)	从前	cóngqián	long time ago
8)	长城	Chángchéng	the Great Wall
9)	在脚下	zài jiǎo xià	at the foot of

10)	不见了	bù jiànle	to disappear
11)	回来了	huíláile	returned
12)	乡亲们	xiāngqīnmen	folks
13)	不幸	bùxìng	unfortunate
14)	道贺	dàohè	to congratulate
15)	恭喜	gōngxǐ	congratulations
16)	一定	yīdìng	for sure, certainly
17)	变成	biànchéng	to turn into
18)	好事	hǎoshì	good thing
19)	坏事	huàishì	bad thing
20)	带回来	dài huílái	to bring it back
21)	另外	lìngwài	another
22)	摔下来	shuāi xiàlái	fall down
23)	摔断了	shuāi duànle	fell and broke
24)	瘸了	què le	lame
25)	带来	dài lái	to bring
26)	福气	fúqì	happiness
27)	战争	zhànzhēng	war
28)	青年人	qīngnián rén	youth
29)	入伍	rùwǔ	to join the army
30)	当兵	dāng bīng	to serve as a soldier
31)	平安	píng'ān	peace
32)	这件事	zhè jiàn shì	this incidence
33)	说明	shuōmíng	to indicate
34)	道理	dàolǐ	principle, reason, justification, argument, basis
35)	可能	kěnéng	maybe

3. **生词练习 Vocabulary Practice**

a. Match the expressions on the left to their English meaning on the right.

1) 不见了   to bring back missed
2) 回来了   came back, returned (past tense)
3) 带来   fall and die
4) 带回来   disappeared (past tense)
5) 摔下来   fell and broke (past tense)
6) 摔断了   to fall down
7) 摔死   to bring

b. 句型练习 Sentence structure practice. Read the examples first, then create your own sentence using the structure.

3) 越来越adv/adv more and more... (马跑得越来越快。)

   a) 天气越来越热，大家都开始穿短袖了。The weather is getting hotter, and everyone is starting to wear short sleeves.
   b) 他游泳游得越来越快了。上个周末的州游泳比赛，他拿了冠军。 He

swims faster and faster. In last weekend's state swimming competition, he won the championship.

c) 她的汉语水平越来越高，可以和中国朋友流利交流了。Her Chinese proficiency is getting higher, and she can communicate fluently with her Chinese friends now.

d) (Your turn) _____

4) the "把" structure (他把腿摔断了) This construction is used to emphasize the action and its result.

a) 他把手机丢了。He lost his phone.
b) 他把家里打扫干净了。He cleaned the house very neatly.
c) 她又把项目搞砸了。He messed up the project again.
d) 她把蛋糕做坏了。She ruined the cake.
e) (Your turn) _____

4. 课文理解 Text Comprehension

a. Answer the following questions in full sentences based on the story you read:
After reading and watching the story, answer the following questions:

13) 有几次塞翁觉得发生的事情是好事情？为什么？How many times that Sāiwēng feel that it might be a good thing? What for?

14) 有几次塞翁觉得发生的事情是好事情？为什么？How many times that Sāiwēng feel that it might be a bad thing? What for?

5. Background of the Idiom Story "Sàiwēng Lost His Horse" 《塞翁失马》

The fable story 《塞翁失马》 "Sàiwēng Lost his Horse" is a well-known Chinese fable that illustrates the idea that events, whether perceived as fortunate or unfortunate, may lead to unexpected outcomes. The story is often used to convey that one should not be too quick to judge a situation as entirely positive or negative, as circumstances can change and bring unexpected results. The story is set in ancient China, although there is no specific historical context or date associated with it. The narrative centers around an elderly man named 塞翁 (Sàiwēng), who lived near the border. By comparing Sàiwēng and his neighbor's attitudes toward the loss and recovery of the horse, the story emphasizes the unpredictable nature of events. It encourages people to adopt a balanced and open-minded attitude toward life's ups and downs. The story's timeless wisdom continues to resonate with individuals seeking meaning and insight in the face of life's uncertainties.

Appendix 8.2: Study Packet

The sequence of activities below aligns with the order of student classroom activities. This unit is conducted in a high school classroom, so these activities are designed to complement the corresponding Google Slides used during class.

1. Discuss the Following Questions

1) 在什么时候坏事可以变成好事？相反的，在什么时候，好事可以变成坏事？ Under what circumstances can seemingly negative events transform into positive outcomes? Conversely, when might ostensibly positive situations take a turn for the worse?
2) 你知道好事坏事转变的例子吗？ Do you know any examples of things turning from good to bad or vice versa?

2. Watch the Video of 《塞翁失马》 and Fill in the Following Tables (https://goo.gl/oamdC8)

	乡亲们的反应	塞翁的反应
马不见了		
马回来了，还带回来一匹马		
塞翁的儿子骑马，把腿摔断了		
参军打仗的年轻人都死了。只有塞翁的儿子因为腿断了，不能参军，所以活了下来。		

3. Retell the Story Verbally Using the GIST Activity

Use the following keywords to verbally retell the story with a partner.

从前/有一天	带回来一匹马	塞翁的儿子/独生子	不幸	战死
塞翁	乡亲们	骑马	战争	好事
养了一匹马	道贺	摔断了腿	入伍	坏事
丢了马	福气	没摔死	活了下来	变成

4. Further Explore This Story Using the Six Thinking Hats Method

Table 8.2 Six Thinking Hats Technique: Thinking Hat Color and Its Representation (De Bono, 1985)

帽子的颜色 Hat Color	代表的意思 Representation	帽子的颜色 Hat Color	代表的意思 Representation
白色 white	客观事实 Objective and factual thinking	黄色 yellow	正面想法 Positive thinking
红色 red	感觉/情感 Feeling and emotions	绿色 green	创造性/创新性思维 Creative and innovative thinking
黑色 black	负面想法 Negative thinking	蓝色 blue	全局观/过程把控 The Big picture/process control

六顶帽子 Vocabulary / 生词

	汉字	拼音	英文意思
1)	帽子	màozi	hats
2)	事实	shìshí	facts
3)	情感	qínggǎn	emotions
4)	正面影响	zhèngmiàn yǐngxiǎng	positive influence
5)	负面影响	fùmiàn yǐngxiǎng	negative impact
6)	创意	chuàngyì	creativity
7)	解决办法	jiějué bànfǎ	solution
8)	结论	jiélùn	conclusion
9)	讨论	tǎolùn	to discuss
10)	问题	wèntí	question

"六顶帽子"方法/可用句型 Structures

1) 从____(新闻、数据、事件内容)中,我发现/我知道 From ____ (news, data, event content), I found/I know . . .
2) 我觉得 . . . 因为 . . . I think . . . because . . .
3) 这次事件的正面影响是 . . . The positive impact of this event is . . .
4) 这次事件的负面影响是 . . . The negative impact of this event is . . .
5) 如果要 . . . 的话,除了 . . . 以外,我认为还有更好的解决方法. If we want to . . ., besides . . ., I believe there are better solutions.
6) 我的结论是 . . . My conclusion is . . .

Role-Play the Story of 《塞翁失马》

角色: 旁白,塞翁,塞翁儿子,乡亲们 . . .

要求: (1) 一起写剧本;写剧本时, 需要什么颜色的帽子,就用什么颜色的字体写; Write the script together. When writing, use the corresponding colors when a certain thinking hat is appropriate; (2) 表演时,"戴上"颜色合适的帽子。When performing, "wear" the proper thinking hat; (3) Be as creative as you can; feel free to add more twists.

中文课奥斯卡奖

- 最佳剧本奖(Best Script)
- 最佳主角奖(Best Actor/Actress in a Leading Role)
- 最佳配角奖(Best Actor/Actress in a Supporting Role)
- 最佳小组表演奖(Best Small Group Performance)

5. Retell the Story Using the GIST Activity Verbally First, Then in Writing

*Comparing to the story retelling in Activity IV, add more details.

从前/有一天	带回来一匹马	塞翁的儿子/独生子	不幸	战死
塞翁	乡亲们	骑马	战争	好事
养了一匹马	道贺	摔断了腿	入伍	坏事
丢了马	福气	没摔死	活了下来	变成

6. 讨论 Discussion and Q&A

1) 什么是成语？
2) 《塞翁失马，焉知非福》讲的是一个什么故事？(用中文)
3) 《塞翁失马，焉知非福》这个故事的寓意是什么？
4) 中文的成语，很多都有成语故事等。英文的成语有故事吗？
5) 有没有别的跟塞翁失马比较像的故事，都是说明好事，坏事是可以相互转变的道理？
6) 你有没有过坏事变好事的经历？
7) 你有没有过好事变坏事的经历？
8) 为什么在电影《活着》以后给大家看《塞翁失马》的成语故事？
9) 在电影《活着》里边，什么时候好事变成了坏事？
10) 除了电影《活着》以外，你还知道那一部电影或者是小说里边，好事变成了坏事？
11) 请说一下汉语成语和英文成语的两到三个相同点或者是不同点？
12) 你和朋友上课教大家的成语是什么？成语的字面意思，寓意和成语故事是什么？
13) 除了你和你的小组同学教的成语故事，你最喜欢别的同学教的哪一个成语？成语的字面意思，寓意是什么？怎么用？

Appendix 8.3: Review Idioms and Idioms in Contexts

Use this review packet after the idiom project presentation and before the unit assessments.

Review Idioms and Idioms in Contexts

Warm-up Activity: Learn this Quizlet set: **4x_成语故事_2A_成语 (13 个成语)**
https://quizlet.com/792913219/4x_%E6%88%90%E8%AF%AD%E6%95%85%E4%BA%8B_2a_%E6%88%90%E8%AF%AD-13-%E4%B8%AA%E6%88%90%E8%AF%AD-flash-cards/?funnelUUID=981d0542-7416-45f3-a498-6bcd332e6856

The exercises for the multiple-choice section have not been printed here. Please refer to Google Fold to find the full text of the exercises.

"Sàiwēng Lost His Horse" 《塞翁失马》

Part 1. 成语认读

Without Pinyin, do you know how to read them aloud and their meanings.

孟母三迁	南辕北辙	指鹿为马	胸有成竹
一鸣惊人	半途而废	闻鸡起舞	抛砖引玉
刮目相看	庖丁解牛	熟能生巧	井底之蛙
孟母三迁	南辕北辙	指鹿为马	胸有成竹

Part 2: 成语的字面意思，寓意和例句

成语	字面意思 Literal Meaning	寓意 Implied Meaning	例句 Example Sentences
半途而废	在路途中间放弃，不做了 To give up halfway.	事情做到一半，就不做了；以前的努力都白费了。To abandon a task or goal before completing it, which results in wasting previous effort and time.	做事情一定要坚持，不能半途而废。 你花了很多时间在这个运动上，但现在因为一点困难就不做了，这不是半途而废了吗？ 他小时候学过很多种乐器，有钢琴，小提琴还有二胡等等。但是每次他都半途而废了，哪一个乐器都没完全学会。
庖丁解牛	厨师 chef 庖丁 name of the chef 不用看，就能把一头牛剖开。Butcher Ding knows where to cut a cow just by looking.	对某一事物非常了解以后，不费力就能做得完美。To be so familiar with a task or subject that one can accomplish it effortlessly and skillfully.	他对这个问题如庖丁解牛，很快就找到了解决问题的办法。 做事要想像庖丁解牛那么熟练，必须得长期的用心练习才行。
南辕北辙	车子向南开，车轮却向北。The carriage heads south while the wheels turn north.	说话或做事目标和行动相反。To contradict oneself, or to do things in a way that is opposite to the desired outcome.	图书馆在左边，你往右走，这不是南辕北辙吗？ 他的说话做事总是南辕北辙，让人不知道他要说什么，要做什么。
指鹿为马	指着一只鹿，说它是一匹马 Point at a deer and call it a horse	故意 on purpose 把黑说成白，把不对/对的说成是对的/不对 Intentionally misrepresent or distort the truth to deceive others.	社交媒体上很多人会不分黑白，指鹿为马，我们需要自己多注意，不要被误导 mislead。 有的政客 politician 常常指鹿为马，老百姓 civilians 需要有自己很好的判断力。
熟能生巧	经常做某件事，手就会很巧 Familiarity brings skill	不断地练习就能提高技能 skills Practice makes perfect; one becomes more skillful with practice.	只要你不断地努力练习，熟能生巧，你的排球会有非常大的进步的，更有可能进校队 school varsity。 庖丁解牛，也是熟能生巧的结果。

Part 3: 成语意思/例句

1) **胸有成竹** (xiōng yǒu chéng zhú)：这个成语的字面意思是"心里边有了竹子 bamboo的整体形象 overall image"，表示一个人对某种事情非常<u>有把握</u> confident，因为他已经准备好了。

   a) （例句一）明天你要去参加一场面试 interview，你可以花时间准备，这样在面试的时候才会胸有成竹，表现 to present/perform 出最好的你自己。

   b) （例句二）这次的考试我昨天复习了很久，已经 胸有成竹了，我相信我一定能拿到好的成绩。

2) **刮目相看** (guā mù xiāng kàn)：这个成语的字面意思是"刮一下眼睛再来看看（某个人/某件事）"，表示一个人经过了解以后，改变 to change了对某个人/对某种事情原来 original的看法，有了新的认识 understanding 或评价 comment。

   a) （例句一）我的好朋友高一的时候数学课和英文课都得了C。她今天这两门课都得了A。这是让我对她是刮目相看了。

   b) （例句二）平时不太爱讲话的小美，在中文俱乐部club面试的时候，提出了好几个非常新的想法 ideas，真是让人对她的个性有了新的了解，对她的能力 ability刮目相看。

3) **闻鸡起舞** (wén jī qǐ wǔ)："闻"的意思是听见，"起"意思是"起床"。这里的"舞"不是跳舞的意思，而是"舞剑sword"的意思，代表的是练习。这个成语的字面意思是 "听到鸡的叫声就起床舞剑"，表示一个人非常勤奋，并且每天早起工作或学习。

   a) （例句一）高中生活可忙了，为了平衡好学习和游泳训练的时间，他每天五点钟闻鸡起舞，先是去练习两个小时的游泳，然后再很快的准备好去上课，学习。

   b) （例句二）每天的时间只有24个小时了，我应该闻鸡起舞，早晨起床练习或者学习，这样才能有更大的进步。

4) **一鸣惊人** (yī míng jīng rén)：这个成语的字面意思是"第一次鸣叫就惊动了人"，表示在某种事上第一次表现就很出色，超出 to exceed了人们的预期 expectation，产生了非常好的结果 result，让人感到惊奇 surprised。

   a) （例句一）他之前一直不是很爱讲话talk，大家对他一直都没有什么印象 impression，但是他在全美的比赛中得了第一名，真是一鸣惊人呀。

   b) （例句二）我们常常看到在比赛中，新的运动员取得了一鸣惊人的成绩。可是你知道吗，在他/她们一鸣惊人以前，他/她们做出的非常多努力 effort，每天闻鸡起舞，一年如一日的勤奋练习，最后才能一鸣惊人。

References

ACTFL-NCSSFL. (2017). *NCSSFL-ACTFL can-do statements*. Retrieved May 5, 2024 from www.actfl.org/resources/ncssfl-actfl-can-do-statements

Byram, M. (2008). *From foreign language education to education for intercultural citizenship: Essays and reflections*. Clevedon: Multilingual Matters.

Byram, M. (2021). *Teaching and assessing intercultural communicative competence* (2nd ed.). Clevedon: Multilingual Matters.

Byram, M., & Wagner, M. (2018). Making a difference: Language education for intercultural and international dialogue. *Foreign Language Annals, 51*(1), 140–151.

De Bono, E. (1985). *Six thinking hats: An essential approach to business management*. New York: Little, Brown, & Company.

Wiggins, G., & McTighe, J. (2005). *Understanding by design* (2nd ed.). Alexandria, VA: Association for Supervision and Curriculum Development (ASCD).

9 "The Traveling Sonnet" 《游子吟》 (Yóuzǐ Yín)

Teaching Classical Poetry Using Total Physical Response and Storytelling (TPRS)

- **Language Proficiency Level:** Intermediate high to advanced low;
- **ICC Developmental Goals:** Open to different perspectives and values;
- **High School/AP Theme:** Global challenges – diversity issues; personal and public identities – beliefs and values;
- **Suggested College Course:** Chinese Communication and Composition;
- **Suggested Instructional Time:** Three lessons, about one instructional hour each; followed by a stand-alone week-long project

1. Introduction

In this unit, we introduce students to the rich tradition of Tang poetry. Understanding the role of poetry in both ancient and modern China is crucial for developing an awareness of cultural expressions unique to the Chinese language. In the first half of the unit demonstrated in this chapter, students learn about the tenets of Tang era poetry, including works from some of the most influential writers and their basic structure, as well as how to write their own Tang "绝句" (juéjù, 'quatrain'). In the second half of the unit, students will narrow their focus to a particular Tang poem called 《游子吟》 (Yóuzǐ Yín, 'The Traveling Sonnet') by the poet 孟郊 (Mèng Jiāo).

"Yóuzǐ Yín" is a well-known poem that depicts an ordinary scene of a mother sewing clothes for her child before he leaves home. Though the poem is only 30 characters total, it manages to express the selflessness of maternal love and the poet's gratitude for his mother's labor using simple but meaningful language. Through the mother's thoughts and actions, her love for her child is lovingly expressed, while the poet's gratitude for his mother's love can be seen most clearly in the last two lines of the poem: "谁言寸草心, 报得三春晖？" (shéi yán cùn cǎo xīn, bào dé sān chūnhuī, 'Who would say that a blade of grass could repay the sunshine of spring?'). In this metaphor, the mother's unceasing love is depicted as an immeasurable force, like the sun giving life to new spring growth. In studying Chinese poetry such as "Yóuzǐ Yín," students explore diverse ways of expressing love and emotion through comprehensible storytelling and thoughtful repetition.

DOI: 10.4324/9781003377276-9

2. Contextualizing the Topic

The lessons illustrated in this chapter are derived from a college-level Chinese foreign language course titled "Chinese Composition and Communication." This course is designed for advanced-level students pursuing a Chinese major, typically taken during their fourth year of study. It spans 16 weeks and features a two-part structure, transitioning from the study of ancient classics to modern literature.

In the weeks preceding our exploration of "Yóuzǐ Yín," we fully immerse our students in the profound world of Tang poetry. To set the stage for this literary journey, the preceding week is dedicated to the study of the article 《让孩子从小背古诗有什么用？这是我听过最美的答案》 ('Why Should Children Learn Ancient Poetry? The Most Beautiful Answer I've Ever Heard'). This thought-provoking piece serves as a window into the deep-rooted significance of Tang poetry in Chinese society. It emphasizes not only the cultural value, but also the emotional and linguistic richness that these poems carry.

Armed with this comprehensive understanding, we embark on a week-long exploration of "Yóuzǐ Yín." Our primary goal during this week is to guide students in not only decoding the poem's intricate language and vivid imagery but also in forging a personal connection with the emotions and experiences it encapsulates. We delve into the art of using poetry as a powerful medium to express profound feelings, particularly focusing on how the poem communicates a poignant sense of longing and nostalgia.

In the process, we draw thought-provoking parallels between the communication within the poem and the students' own expressions of love for their mothers. This exercise serves to instill the cherished values of "孝顺" (xiàoshùn, 'filial piety') and "回报" (huíbào, 'returning love') as portrayed in the poem. By relating the filial devotion depicted in the poem to the students' own expressions of love for their mothers, we guide them to comprehend the cultural context and values intricately woven into the text. By the culmination of this transformative journey, students not only possess a deep understanding of the mechanics of a "五言绝句" (wǔ yán jué jù, 'five-character quatrain') but are also equipped with the skills to craft their own, employing the poetic language to eloquently convey their heartfelt sentiments.

3. Methodology Highlight: Total Physical Response and Storytelling

Total physical response and storytelling (TPRS) traces its origins back to the 1980s when Spanish teacher Blaine Ray developed this innovative approach to language learning (Ray, 1997). TPRS, however, has its roots in an earlier technique called total physical response (TPR), which was introduced by James J. Asher in (1969) (Asher, 1969). TPRS builds on TPR, which improves listening skills through comprehensible input and involves associating vocabulary words with specific actions, prompting students to perform these actions in response to target language instructions, particularly well-suited for instructing poetry. TPRS allows for the transformation of abstract poetic concepts, such as metaphors and symbolism, into tangible gestures, providing students with a multi-sensory approach to grasp the meaning and recitation of poems. The inherent repetition within TPRS aligns seamlessly with the repetitive nature of poetry. This process reinforces memorization while enabling an exploration of the poem's intricate layers of meaning and symbolism, making poetry more accessible and enjoyable for learners.

The role of storytelling in TPRS plays is designed to enhance language comprehension and proficiency with scaffolded, comprehensible input. In the context of teaching Chinese Tang poetry like "Yóuzǐ Yín," TPRS leverages the structured format of Tang poetry with its regulated verse and condensed style. Each character within the poem carries significant weight, and through storytelling, students are gradually introduced to the abstract concepts embedded in these individual words. As they progress, students are guided toward a deeper analysis of the symbolic meaning behind the entire poem, enriching their understanding of both language and culture.

4. Curricular Modeling

We offer the following complete set of materials ready for use in the classroom along with accompanying activities. These materials and suggested activities support and are guided by the learning outcomes described for robust use of backward design principles (McTighe & Wiggins, 2005).

4.1. *Learning Outcomes*

The following learning outcomes are three-fold, integrated by situating language skills development in ICC skills development and vice versa. In addition to the sample course context used for illustration, "Chinese Communication and Composition," we also offer sample learning outcomes related to the macro language functions for literary understanding, communication, and composition. You can adapt the three sets of learning outcomes for your course context. The important, common consideration is how these learning outcomes, course-specific learning outcomes, language performance descriptor and ICC developing goals relate to each other and are exemplified in the class activities. The learning outcomes provide the most important Compass for backward design and assessment:

Learning Outcomes as Part of the "Chinese Communication and Composition" Course

- Identify the specific literary devices employed in the texts and analyze how these devices contribute to the meaning of a text. Students are expected to apply similar devices in their communication and composition.
- Know the plot of the target story and movements in Chinese literature, as they relate to larger themes in Chinese history and societal changes. Students are expected to read critically, think analytically, and communicate clearly both in writing and speech.
- Produce cogent written work by observing writing conventions of the target language; present information in a descriptive form in the target language. Students are expected to clearly narrate the story through writing, identifying the major characters, themes, and plot of the story.

The corresponding language performance goals are written in the "can do" format of "I can . . ." to make learners understand from their perspectives what they can achieve in this unit (ACTFL-NCSSFL, 2017).

> **Language Performance Objective (Can-Do Statements)**
>
> - I can analyze the themes and emotions expressed in "Yóuzǐ Yín" and provide interpretations based on the text. (*Interpretive*)
> - I can recognize literary devices such as metaphors and symbolism in "Yóuzǐ Yín" and explain their significance in the poem.
> - I can retell the story and emotions conveyed in "Yóuzǐ Yín" in both written and spoken forms, using organized paragraphs or spoken discourse. (*Presentational*)
> - I can engage in discussions with others about the themes and emotions in "Yóuzǐ Yín," offering insights and opinions on its relevance to human experiences. (*Interpersonal*)

The corresponding ICC development goals are written based on four aspects of ICC – knowledge, attitude, skills, critical cultural awareness (Byram, 2008, 2021; Byram & Wagner, 2018; inter alia).

> **Intercultural Communicative Competence Developmental Goals**
>
> These goals focus on developing a deep understanding of "Yóuzǐ Yín," fostering an open and empathetic attitude toward its themes and cultural context, honing skills in applying the poem's lessons to personal experiences and promoting critical cultural awareness in intercultural communication.
>
> - **Knowledge:** I can explain how "Yóuzǐ Yín" reflects the values and emotions associated with love, longing, and filial piety in Chinese culture.
> - **Attitude:** When discussing "Yóuzǐ Yín," I can approach the poem with an open mind, appreciating the cultural values and emotions it portrays.
> - **Skill:** I can relate the themes of love, longing, and filial piety in "Yóuzǐ Yín" to my own experiences and emotions, fostering empathy and understanding; I can apply the lessons learned from "Yóuzǐ Yín" to discuss and offer potential solutions to similar issues of love, longing, and filial piety that I encounter in my own life.
> - **Critical Cultural Awareness:** I recognize that different cultures may have varying approaches to expressing love and addressing family dynamics.

4.2 Materials for Teaching "The Traveling Sonnet"

A. Video Introduction to the Poem (in the Preview Packet)
   - This short video introduction (about 3–5 minutes) to "Yóuzǐ Yín" presents the historical context, poet's biography, and major themes of the poem.

B. Tang Poem Text (Chinese)
   - The full Chinese text of "Yóuzǐ Yín" for students serves as the reference including Pinyin and English word-for-word translations for better comprehension.

C. Tang Poem Text (English Translation)
   - This complete, accurate English translation of "Yóuzǐ Yín" alongside the Chinese text helps students grasp the poem's meaning.

D. PowerPoint Presentation (in Class)
   - This PowerPoint presentation accompanies the introduction including slides summarizing key points, vocabulary, and exercises in Chinese. It provides engaging visuals to enhance student engagement and understanding.

E. TPRS Activities Cards
   - A series of visual prompts or images relate to the poem's themes (e.g., images of a traveler, a mother is sewing, a distant home).

F. Vocabulary List
   - The list of essential vocabulary words and phrases relates to the poem. Include Pinyin, English translations, and example sentences to help students understand and use these words.

G. Comprehension Questions
   - This set of comprehension questions guides students in analyzing the poem's themes, literary devices, and cultural significance. Include both closed-ended and open-ended questions.

4.3. Activities for Teaching "The Traveling Sonnet"

In this section, we will outline a series of activities designed to engage students with the poem "Yóuzǐ Yín" while enhancing their language proficiency and cultural awareness. Each activity is aligned with the Total Physical Response and Storytelling (TPRS) method and includes step-by-step instructions with estimated time frames.

Activity 1: Video Introduction and Discussion (Estimated Time: 20 Minutes)

- Begin the class by showing the animation "中国唱诗班'系列动画短片《游子吟》" (about six minutes in Chinese with English subtitles).

- After watching the video, facilitate a class discussion to understand the details of the story, and make clarifications of the story.
- Encourage students to express their opinions and insights from the video.
- Summarize key points from the discussion and smoothly transition to the next activity.

Activity 2: TPRS Storytelling with Pictures (Estimated Time: 20 Minutes)

- Distribute storytelling cards to students, with each card corresponding to a key scene or character in the story.
- Explain that you will narrate a simplified version of the poem's story using these cards. While describing each scene or character, students should actively engage by mimicking the actions using gestures.
- During storytelling, emphasize repetition and clear pronunciation, pausing after each sentence to allow students to physically respond.
- Following the storytelling, encourage students to express their thoughts and interpretations of the story, emphasizing the use of vocabulary and phrases from the poem.

Activity 3: Analyzing Literary Devices (Estimated Time: 30 Minutes)

- Present the Chinese text of the poem, either on a screen or as printed copies to students.
- Guide students in identifying literary devices within the poem, including metaphors, symbolism, and imagery, while highlighting specific examples from the text.
- Engage in a discussion about the significance of these literary devices in conveying the poem's themes and emotions.
- Stress the importance of cultural awareness in interpreting the poem.

Activity 4: Creative Writing of Juéjù (Quatrains) (Estimated Time: 30 Minutes)

- Provide students with a brief overview of the structure and characteristics of Tang poetry, emphasizing the use of juéjù.
- Encourage students to draw inspiration from the themes and emotions of "Yóuzǐ Yín" as they compose their quatrains.
- Allow students time to write their quatrains individually.
- After writing, invite students to share their quatrains with the class. Discuss the unique aspects of each student's poem and how

Activity 5: Oral Presentation (Estimated Time: 30 Minutes)

- Highlight key examples of communication style used by the mother in "Yóuzǐ Yín," including specific verses or lines from the poem.

- Ask students to reflect on their own relationships with their mothers and consider how maternal love is expressed in their lives.
- Each student takes turns sharing their observations about how maternal love is expressed in "Youzi Yin," highlighting specific verses or emotions conveyed in the poem.
- Share personal anecdotes or conversations with their own mothers, emphasizing the communication style they have observed in their interactions.
- Conclude with a reflection on the impact of culture on communication style and its significance in nurturing relationships.

Activity 6: Recite the Poem (Estimated Time: 30 Minutes)

This session, we will focus on the total physical response and storytelling (TPRS) teaching method, demonstrating the teaching steps for integrating gestures into reciting the poem "Yóuzǐ Yín."

Step 1: Introduction to the Poem – Commence by introducing the poem "Yóuzǐ Yín," providing context about the poem, its author, and its significance. Ensure students comprehend the poem's meaning before proceeding with TPR.

Step 2: Identify Actionable Verbs and Nouns – Identify words from each line of the poem that can be represented through gestures (e.g., 线 – thread, 衣 – clothes, 行 – traveling, 恐 – worrying, 寸草 – small grass, 心 – heart, 三春晖 – sunray).

Step 3: Model the Gestures – Demonstrate clear and expressive gestures for each action verb identified in step 2, using hands and body to illustrate the actions.

- For example, for "sewing," simulate holding a needle and thread in your hands and make a sewing motion.
- For "wearing," gesture as if you're putting on clothing.
- For "traveling," use index and middle fingers to mimic walking or traveling.
- For "worrying," convey a concerned expression and simulate thinking and worrying.
- For "small grass" and "heart," create gestures representing these concepts.
- For "sunray," extend your arms above your head, simulating sunrays.

Step 4: Practice Gestures with Lines – Divide the poem into relevant sections based on the action verbs and practice each section with associated gestures. Encourage students to repeat after you while performing the gestures, starting with the first line, and progressing to subsequent lines as students become comfortable.

Step 5: Integration – Incorporate gestures into the recitation of the entire poem. Have students recite the poem while performing appropriate gestures for each action verb, using these gestures as memory cues.

Step 6: Repeat and Reinforce – Reinforce the association between words and actions by practicing reciting the poem with gestures multiple times. Encourage students to independently recite the poem aloud while using the corresponding gestures.

Step 7: Review and Discuss – After practice, facilitate a discussion about the poem's meaning and emotions conveyed by the gestures. Encourage students to connect the actions with the feelings and the story within the poem.

Step 8: Assessment – Assess students' comprehension and retention of the poem by asking them to recite it with appropriate gestures individually or in groups. Provide constructive feedback and reinforcement as needed.

By following these steps, we effectively employ the TPR method to assist students in reciting the poem "Yóuzǐ Yín," integrating meaningful gestures that enhance their understanding and engagement with the text.

4.4. Implementing TPRS

Though it varies from classroom to classroom, in this lesson TPRS is divided into four steps. First, the instructor introduces the new vocabulary words and phrases in a variety of formats, such as through images and gestures, providing a clear translation of the words in English. Step 1 allows the students to memorize and internalize new meanings through intentional repetition and contextualization, somewhat mimicking natural language acquisition. After the students have familiarized themselves with the new vocabulary, the instructor moves into step 2 by incorporating the new words and phrases into a short verbal story, such as "Yóuzǐ Yín." With each line or phrase spoken in the poem, the instructor should use the same gestures as in step one, as well as circling questions to check students' comprehension through the recitation.

After "Yóuzǐ Yín" has been read aloud, it is time for the students to read and discuss the poem together. In step 3, the students may be asked to translate the poem in their own words or practice reciting the poem to present in front of their classmates. The instructor should continue to ask questions throughout this step, encouraging the students to discuss the cultural themes within the poem, comparing their own experiences and perspectives. Finally, in step 4, after the class has had ample time to digest the contextualized meaning of the poem, it is time for the students to present their interpretations to the class. In the presentation, students should be able to clearly define the beginning, middle, and end of the poem, exemplifying their comprehension of the new vocabulary and their understanding of the poem's deeper significance.

4.5. Assessments

Formative assessment throughout this unit is in the format of speaking and writing checkups assigned in the Preview Packet and the Study Packet. Toward the end of the Study Packet, students are engaged to writing a 七言绝句 (qī yán jué jù, 'seven-character quatrain') to express their feelings during the pandemic time using the symbol of a flower serves as a multifaceted assessment. Firstly, it evaluates students' comprehension of the structure and conventions of classical Chinese poetry, including the specific requirements of the qī yán jué jù form. Secondly, it assesses their ability to apply abstract concepts like emotions and symbolism within the context of poetry, fostering creative expression. Thirdly, the use of the flower as a symbol demands students to engage in critical thinking, as they must choose and interpret the symbol in a way that effectively conveys their feelings. This homework assessment not only tests linguistic and literary skills but also encourages introspection and artistic expression, making it a meaningful and comprehensive evaluation of their understanding and creativity. Here is a student's writing sample:

Title: 吾感心伤
First line: 我最幸生时,
Second line: 命却飞花絮。
Third line: 隔离无尽期,
Fourth line: 只望幸福世。

In addition, for the final speaking assessment of this unit, students are evaluated to delve deeper into the expressions of maternal love as seen in the Chinese poem "Yóuzǐ Yín" and compare them with the communication styles used by their own mothers. The goal is to understand and analyze how language and communication play a crucial role in conveying affection and nurturing relationships. Here is a student's writing sample:

在《游子吟》中，母亲为孩子缝衣服到很晚，也表达了对离开家的孩子深深思念和等待。她等孩子很长时间，即使她知道孩子可能不会回来，她也静静地等，给孩子温暖和舒适。我觉得这和我的妈妈很像，每天的生活中，妈妈常常给我做饭、洗衣服、支持和帮助我。可是我觉得《游子吟》里的妈妈更传统和含蓄，比如我的妈妈常常和我说她爱我，她也常常会抱我和亲我直接表达她的爱。

还有，我觉得《游子吟》中表达了很重要的中国传统文化中 孝顺和回报父母的观念，这是中国文化中的一种核心价值观。孩子常常被教导要孝顺和尊敬父母，常常有责任感去回报。在西方文化中，也有对母亲的深厚感情和回报的想法，可是没有中国文化中那么强调。西方社会更加注重个体的独立，孩子不会觉得被要求回报母亲，而是被鼓励健康、亲密的关系，在需要的时候帮助就可以了。

[In "The Traveling Sonnet," the mother stays up late sewing clothes for her child, expressing deep yearning and anticipation for the child who has left home. She waits for the child for a long time, even though she knows the child may not return. She waits quietly, providing warmth and comfort for the child. I feel a strong connection to my own mother. In our daily lives, my mother often cooks for me, does my laundry, and supports and helps me. However, I think the mother in "The Traveling Sonnet" is more traditional and reserved. Unlike my mother, who often tells me she loves me and directly expresses her affection by hugging and kissing me.

Furthermore, I believe "The Traveling Sonnet" conveys important concepts of filial piety and repaying parents, which are core values in Chinese traditional culture. Children are often taught to be filial and respectful to their parents, with a sense of duty to repay them. While Western culture also emphasizes deep affection for mothers and repaying them, it is not as strongly emphasized as in Chinese culture. Western society places more emphasis on individual independence, and children are not obliged to repay their mothers but are encouraged to build healthy, close relationships and offer help when needed.]

This sample work demonstrated the students' ability to compare and apply to their own lives after their study of the Chinese Tang poetry. Here is also a student's comment in the course feedback:

> Studying Chinese Tang poems has been an enriching experience that has allowed me to delve into the rich cultural and literary heritage of China. These poems offer a window into a bygone era, providing insights into the thoughts, emotions, and values of people who lived centuries ago. Through the study of Tang poems, I have not only improved my language skills but have also gained a deeper appreciation for the beauty and complexity of the Chinese language. These poems often explore universal themes, such as love, longing, and the passage of time, which resonate with people from all walks of life. Moreover, studying Tang poems has broadened my cultural awareness, allowing me to understand the historical and social context in which these poems were written. Overall, delving into Chinese Tang poems has been a journey of discovery, offering a profound connection to the past and a deeper understanding of Chinese culture and language.

5. Teacher's Reflections

We've found inspiration from our experiences with haiku poem instruction, which has informed our approach to teaching Chinese Tang poetry. While haiku and Tang poetry may differ in form and cultural context, the fundamental principles of brevity, imagery, and emotional depth are universal. This realization sparked a unique perspective on how to make Tang poetry more accessible and engaging for my students.

Incorporating the simplicity and concise nature of haiku into teaching Tang poetry has allowed me to break down the seemingly daunting task of writing classical Chinese poetry into manageable steps. We encourage students to select a single vivid image or emotion as the focal point of their poems, akin to the essence captured in a haiku. This approach not only simplifies the creative process but also facilitates a deeper exploration of individual words and characters, a hallmark of Tang poetry's condensed style.

Teaching Tang poetry as a meaningful practice for Chinese students goes beyond just literary exploration. It is a profound journey into the roots of our language, culture, and identity. By composing Tang poems, students connect with the voices of ancient poets, gaining insight into the emotional and philosophical landscapes of their ancestors. This practice fosters a sense of continuity and belonging, reinforcing cultural heritage while honing language skills. Moreover, writing Tang poetry encourages creativity within the constraints of a structured form, a skill that is invaluable in modern academic and professional contexts. It challenges students to express complex ideas and emotions concisely, refining their language proficiency and critical thinking abilities.

We strongly recommend that Chinese language teachers explore foreign language teaching methods as a source of inspiration. Drawing from the instructional techniques used in teaching haiku has profoundly transformed my approach to teaching Tang poetry, making it a vibrant and purposeful experience for both teachers and students. This approach not only enhances students' linguistic proficiency but also enriches their cultural awareness, fosters their creativity, and establishes a profound connection to a literary tradition that plays a pivotal role in shaping their identity within our ever-evolving world.

Appendices: Sample Teaching Materials

Additional supplemental materials, such as PowerPoint slides, can be requested by scanning this QR code.

Appendix 9.1: Preview Packet

《游子吟》预习作业 Preview Sheet

1. 课文

《游子吟》
(唐)孟郊
慈母手中线，游子身上衣。
临行密密缝，意恐迟迟归。
谁言寸草心，报得三春晖。

2. 生词 Vocabulary

   1) 孟郊　　　Mèng Jiāo　　a famous Chinese poet in Tang Dynasty
   2) 游子　　　yóu zǐ　　　man travelling or residing in a place far away from home.
   3) 吟　　　　yín　　　　chant
   4) 慈母　　　cí mǔ　　　loving mother
   5) 线　　　　xiàn　　　line, thread
   6) 临行　　　lín xíng　　before leaving or traveling
   7) 密　　　　mì　　　　dense

224 *"The Traveling Sonnet"* 《游子吟》

8) 缝 féng sew
9) 意 yì mind, heart
10) 恐(怕) kǒng pà be afraid of
11) 迟 chí late
12) 归 guī to go back, to return
13) 寸 cùn inch
14) 报(答) bào dá pay a debt of gratitude
15) 晖 huī sunshine

3. 汉字练习 Hanzi Practice

Use the following words to make sentences in Chinese:

1) 临行:
2) 缝:
3) 归:
4) 回报:
5) 恐怕:

4. 句子练习 Sentence Practice

After you watch this video, please write down the meaning of the poem in Chinese: www.youtube.com/watch?v=ny9ZahYhKso

Line 1:
_____
Line 2:
_____
Line 3:
_____
Line 4:
_____
Line 5:
_____
Line 6:
_____

5. 回答问题 Short Answers

1) 你觉得在这首诗里作者想表达什么感情？
2) 他是怎么表达自己感情的？
3) 你常常怎么表达感情？
4) 你读这首诗的时候，你会想到谁？
5) 你读这首诗的时候，你有什么样的感觉？

Appendix 9.2: Enrichment Guide
《游子吟》 Enrichment Guide

1. Why Should We Study Chinese Tang Poetry?

Chinese Tang poems have left an indelible mark on the modern Chinese mindset, shaping perceptions, values, and artistic expressions in profound ways. The influence of Tang poetry on contemporary Chinese society is multifaceted and can be observed in various aspects of life:

1) **Cultural Identity:** Tang poetry embodies Chinese cultural values, such as Confucian ideals of filial piety, respect for nature, and the celebration of beauty. These values continue to resonate in modern Chinese society, contributing to a sense of cultural identity. For example, poems like Du Fu's "春夜喜雨" (Chūn Yè Xǐyǔ, 'Spring Night, Joyous Rain') celebrate the beauty of nature and continue to inspire an appreciation for the environment.
2) **Language and Literature:** Tang poems have significantly enriched the Chinese language, influencing modern Chinese literature and fostering linguistic creativity. Many idiomatic expressions and literary references in contemporary Chinese writing have their roots in Tang poetry. These references serve as a bridge between generations and enhance the depth of modern literary works.
3) **Artistic Inspiration:** Contemporary Chinese art, music, and film often draw inspiration from Tang poetry. Renowned painters, composers, and filmmakers have been influenced by the imagery and emotions conveyed in these poems. For instance, the film *Raise the Red Lantern*, directed by Zhang Yimou, reflects the themes of love, power, and tragedy found in Tang poetry.
4) **Spiritual Reflection:** Tang poetry encourages introspection and philosophical contemplation, fostering a reflective mindset in modern Chinese individuals. The introspective and philosophical nature of Tang poetry, as seen in Li Bai's "将进酒" (Jiāng Jìn Jiǔ, 'To the Tune of Taking Leave of a Friend'), encourages deep introspection and a pursuit of meaning in contemporary life.
5) **Social Commentary:** Some Tang poems offer insights into social and political issues of their time, which resonate with modern societal concerns. For example, the social critique in Bai Juyi's "秋夕" (Shūseki, 'Autumn Evening') reflects on the plight of the common people, a theme that continues to be relevant in discussions of social justice and inequality.
6) **Emotional Expression:** Tang poetry's profound exploration of human emotions continues to provide a vocabulary for expressing feelings and relationships. Contemporary Chinese love songs and literature often draw on the emotional depth found in poems like Wang Wei's "相思" (Xiāngsī, 'Yearning') to convey complex feelings of love and longing.

The enduring influence of Tang poetry on the modern Chinese mindset lies in its ability to bridge the past and the present, offering a reservoir of cultural richness, linguistic depth, and emotional resonance that continues to shape contemporary Chinese thought, creativity, and identity.

2. Tang Poetry Background and 三教

Under the intellectual influences of Confucianism, Daoism, and Buddhism, poetry in the Tang Dynasty developed to encompass what is often considered to be the Golden Age of Chinese literature. With Confucianism, poets like Du Fu can be seen emulating themes of benevolence, righteousness, moral responsibility, and service to the state. Through poems written by Li Bai, the influence of Daoism shows a different view of life, with themes of abandoning worldly affairs and seeking harmony in the natural world. While Confucianism and Daoism are indigenous schools of thought in Chinese culture, Tang poetry was also influenced by Buddhism, brought to China from India during the Han Dynasty. As a result, Chinese Buddhism is also seen in works written by poets such as Wang Wei, including ideas that depart from the mortal world, emphasizing the suppression of desire and the impermanence of life. As the Golden Age of Chinese literature, influences from all three of these schools of thought can be found in some of the most famous poems written during the Tang Dynasty.

3. Eminent Poets of the Tang Dynasty: Li Bai, Du Fu, and Wang Wei 盛唐三杰: 李白、杜甫和王维

Li Bai (李白) is one of the most renowned poets of the Tang Dynasty. His verses celebrate the joys of friendship, the beauty of nature, the pleasures of drinking, moments of solitude, and more. Throughout his life, he immersed himself in Daoist practices, choosing to remain at a distance from the Confucian civil society. Despite his remarkable talent that could have secured him a respected position at court, he shared a kinship with the earlier "Seven Sages of the Bamboo Grove" (竹林七贤), preferring to avoid the entanglements of court life. Li Bai's life and poetry together exemplify a commitment to the unadulterated expression of the human spirit, free from the constraints of convention, a legacy that endures to this day.

Du Fu (杜甫), another notable poet of the Tang Dynasty, served as a civil servant for much of his life while occasionally exploring Daoist hermitage. His dedication to the intricacies of Tang poetry is one of his defining features, as is his portrayal of the daily challenges faced by common people. Despite his deep knowledge of Confucian classics, Du Fu initially struggled to advance in his civil service career. Eventually, he formed a friendship with Li Bai, embracing a Daoist lifestyle for a time. Later in life, Du Fu returned to his Confucian roots and pursued an official position. His poetry reflects the interplay of his Confucian, Daoist, and Buddhist perspectives, mirroring his diverse life experiences. He earned the title "Sage of Poetry" (诗圣).

Wang Wei (王维), a musician and a pioneer in monochrome landscape painting, is another highly respected poet of the Tang Dynasty. While none of his original ink paintings or musical compositions survive, his poetry has endured for centuries, earning him the reputation of a master poet. Influenced by Buddhism, Wang Wei often composed verses about humanity living in harmony with nature, embodying his belief that poetry should mirror the simple elegance of traditional Chinese ink paintings, and vice versa. Wang Wei's poetry embodies Chan Buddhist ideals of peace and detachment from the mortal world, evident in his works through the absence of human attributes and his frequent use of natural elements like water and mist. He is referred to as "Poet Buddha" (诗佛).

4. Tang Poetry Form: 五言/七言绝句

One of the prominent characteristics of Tang poetry, which often celebrates a liberation from human limitations and revels in the spontaneous beauty of the natural world, is the notable adherence to strict poetic forms expected of poets during that era. Unlike English language poetic forms, which generally include rhyme, meter, and genre type, Tang poets conformed to numbered grids that resulted in a set word-syllable count. While the oldest works of Tang poetry might be composed of four characters per line, with every alternate line rhyming, eventually this style was adapted to accommodate five-to-seven-character quatrains (五言绝句、七言绝句). In addition to the numbered quatrains, Tang poems also require a rhyme scheme, and certain "tonal" constraints that are sadly often lost in translation. The structure of Tang poetry evolved from the natural rhythm of the Chinese language, which is syllable-timed and tonal. Here is an example:

Original Poem (by Li Bai): 静夜思 (Thoughts in a Tranquil Night)

床前明月光， (The bright moonlight before my bed)
疑是地上霜。 (I suspect it to be frost on the ground.)
举头望明月， (I raise my head to gaze at the bright moon,)
低头思故乡。 (Lower it, and my thoughts turn to my hometown.)

In this classic Tang poem, each line adheres to a five-character structure, creating a succinct and harmonious rhythm. The poem vividly captures the essence of a tranquil night, with the moonlight casting a serene glow before the speaker's bed. However, this moonlight is so bright that it is mistaken for frost on the ground, which beautifully portrays the idea that nature's elements can be mysterious and deceptive. The central theme of homesickness and nostalgia is then expressed through the last two lines, as the speaker, while contemplating the moon, finds himself yearning for his hometown. This poem exemplifies the precision, economy of language, and the art of conveying profound emotions within the constraints of the 五言绝句 form, a hallmark of Tang poetry.

These structured quatrains offer a unique insight into the profound literary heritage of China, where creativity flourishes within the confines of strict poetic rules.

5. Translating Chinese Poetry 《游子吟》

Much of the work of translating Chinese poetry involves adding words for context, fleshing out ideas that are usually only implicit in their original form. This is because the audience for these poems was often of similar social and educational backgrounds, so many of the unspoken ideas deduced from Chinese poetry could be understood without need for explanation. When translated into English, the lack of context makes for a puzzling combination of words. When read in Chinese, the impressions of the individual characters leave a story within the audience's mind, filling in the gaps of what is lost in translation.

Chinese Hanzi	Literal Translation	English Translation
《游子吟》	[travel] [child] [song]	"Song of the Wanderer"
慈母手中线，	[compassionate] [mother] [hand] [in] [thread]	Thread in the hand of a compassionate mother –
游子身上衣；	[wander] [song] [body] [on] [clothes]	clothes on a wandering son;
临行密密缝，	[just before] [travel] [close] [close] [sew]	just before his departure she sewed closely,
意恐迟迟归。	[think] [fear] [late] [late] [return]	in her mind worrying about his late return.
谁言寸草心，	[who] [speak] [inch] [grass] [heart]	Who would say that the heart of inch-high grass
报得三春晖？	[repay] [achieve] [three] [spring] [shine]	could repay the sunshine of deepest spring?

From this short poem alone, you may be surprised how complex and impactful the story within "游子吟" is in the minds of Chinese readers. After reading the poem and its different versions of translation, watch the short animation below to better understand the implied meaning of a mother's love as expressed in "游子吟."

6. Other Resources

"中国唱诗班"系列动画短片 《游子吟》 www.youtube.com/watch?v=DaO28aa4qNc&t=2s

Appendix 9.3: Study Packet

《游子吟》学习作业 (Study Packet)

1. 背诵和录音 Recitation and Recording

Recite the poem 《游子吟》:
Listen to the provided link:
www.youtube.com/watch?v=xZFpdkQnTGs
Memorize the poem individually, paying attention to pronunciation and tone.
Recording:
Record yourself reciting the poem. Ensure clarity and fluency in your delivery.
   Submit the recording along with your study packet.

2. 回答问题 Answering Questions in Chinese

1) 作者觉得妈妈的爱像什么？你觉得你的妈妈的爱像什么？
   Reflect on the poet's portrayal of a mother's love in 《游子吟》. Compare it to your perception of your own mother's love.
2) 在诗里，作者和妈妈的关系怎么样？(At least four sentences) 你和妈妈的关系呢？(At least four sentences)
   Analyze the relationship between the poet and his mother as depicted in the poem, providing at least four sentences. Share insights into your own relationship with your mother.
3) 在这个故事里面妈妈用了什么方式表达她对孩子的爱？你们的家人是怎么样表达她们对你的爱？你觉得有什么相同或者不同？(At least six sentences) Examine the ways the mother expresses her love in the poem. Compare it to how your own family members express love toward you. Discuss similarities and differences, providing at least six sentences.
4) 你想过要回报家人对你的爱吗？你想怎么做？Reflect on whether you have considered reciprocating the love shown by your family. If so, outline your thoughts on how you would like to express your gratitude and love.

3. 视频 Watch and Narrate in Chinese

View the video to gain a visual understanding of the poem's narrative. Summarize the story portrayed in the video using at least ten sentences. Capture key events and emotions conveyed in the animation.

4. 唐诗欣赏 Poetry Appreciation

After you read or do more research about the poems, please write down each poem's author, meaning, and the feeling to express:

床前明月光，疑是地上霜。	作者： 表达： www.youtube.com/watch?v=82jcwYdKPTY
空山不见人，但闻人语响。	作者： 表达： www.youtube.com/watch?v=y1ldmPOXEPo www.youtube.com/watch?v=R7IXfiop6_0
国破山河在，城春草木深。	作者： 表达： www.youtube.com/watch?v=Sm0lziolZyM&t=859s

5. 写你自己的诗 Create Your Own Poem

Poetry Creation Practice:

Reflecting on the theme of familial love, create your own poem in Chinese. Consider the emotions, experiences, or memories you wish to convey. Aim for at least four lines. This is an opportunity to express your feelings creatively. Before you start your poem, choose an emotion you want to express and perhaps a symbol you want to use to express that emotion. If you'd like to challenge yourself, you can even make the poem rhyme.

Here are some prompts to consider for your poems!

- Write a poem about a moment when you felt overwhelmingly joyful. Try to convey this emotion by depicting images and symbols.
- Sadness is a deep emotion that has inspired some of the greatest works of art in the world. Write about a time or memory that makes you feel nostalgic.

Submission

Submit your original poem along with the study packet. Include the Chinese and English translation. Feel free to also share the inspiration behind your poem, adding a personal touch to your submission.

English

Line 1: _____

Line 2: _____

Line 3: _____

Line 4: _____

中文

Line 1: _____

Line 2: _____

Line 3: _____

Line 4: _____

References

ACTFL-NCSSFL. (2017). *NCSSFL-ACTFL can-do statements*. Retrieved June 1, 2022, from www.actfl.org/resources/ncssfl-actfl-can-do-statements

Asher, J. J. (1969). The total physical response approach to second language learning. *The Modern Language Journal, 59*(1), 3–17. Retrieved from www.jstor.org/stable/322091

Byram, M. (2008). *From foreign language education to education for intercultural citizenship: Essays and reflections*. Clevedon: Multilingual Matters.

Byram, M. (2021). *Teaching and assessing intercultural communicative competence* (2nd ed.). Clevedon: Multilingual Matters.

Byram, M., & Wagner, M. (2018). Making a difference: Language education for intercultural and international dialogue. *Foreign Language Annals, 51*(1), 140–151.

McTighe, G., & Wiggins, J. (2005). *Understanding by design* (2nd ed.). Alexandria, VA: Assn. for Supervision & Curriculum Development ASCD.

Ray, B. (1997). *Fluency through TPR storytelling*. Command Performance Language Institute, Blaine Ray Workshops.

Index

ACTFL Assessment of Performance toward Proficiency in Languages® (AAPPL) 22, 49, 70, 74, 104, 138, 140, 168, 191, 192, 193
activity types for language acquisition 145
anime 4, 13, 112, 138–139
authentic materials 6, 13–15, 48, 101, 103, 148

backward design 1, 15, 16, 21, 49, 72, 104, 140, 167, 177, 192, 215
Ballad of Mulan 161, 182
bias 9, 137–138, 140–141, 152, 172, 174, 188
Bloom's Taxonomy 4–5

Chinese classic stories 1, 3–4, 11–12
Chinese literary masterpiece 23, 46–47, 60, 62
cognitive challenges 5, 13
cognitive styles 112, 190
comparative analysis 47, 195
critical thinking 4–5
cultural authenticity 184
cultural capital 2
cultural insights 3, 15

dramatic inquiry 20–21, 25–27, 54
Dream of the Red Chamber 46

emotion expression 214
etiquette 47
experiential learning 46–48, 53–54

favorable timing, geographic location, and human factors 70, 75, 79, 81, 84, 94–97
feedback cycles 27
feminism, global 161–164

Festival, Mid-Autumn Festival, Moon Festival 99, 101, 105, 107, 115, 125–127
Filial Piety 163, 214, 216, 221
folklore 2, 161, 163–165, 168–182, 189

gender roles 3, 102, 103, 105, 167–168, 172, 183
GIST (Generation Interaction between Schemata and Text) 75, 79–80, 196, 209

identity 4, 63, 138–140, 161, 163–166, 183–184, 223–225
idioms 104, 163, 188, 190–199, 210–211
integrative model for using classic works to connect ICC with language proficiency 11–12
Intercultural Communicative Competence (ICC); definition of ICC 7; domains of ICC 7–9; integration of ICC with Can Do statements 7–9
interdisciplinary approach 15
International Working Women's Day 173, 176

Journey to the West 1, 19–23, 34–39

KASA: knowledge, attitude, skills, and critical intercultural awareness 73
key cultural concepts 55

literature in the world language classroom 5–6
love and fate 54

mental health 115
Monkey King II 25
moon iconography 105–106, 110–112, 124–125

multi-sensory approach 214
mythology 34, 71, 99–102, 107–109, 112, 121–129

names in Chinese culture 90–91
Nézhā 137, 193; Nézhā and Sūnwùkōng 153; *Ne Zha* (movie) 1979 vs. 2019 153–154; Nézhā movie character chart 150; Nézhā movie five themes 139; Nezha movie quotes 155–158

Over the Moon 99, 102–103, 107, 109, 110–111, 115–116, 132–133

podcast 167, 169, 177

Question Formulation Technique (QFT) 70, 72, 75, 77–78, 81, 83

real-world application 57
Red Cliff II 70, 72; Battle of Red Cliff, Library Guide 76, 77; Battle of Red Cliff, Quick Facts 89; *Red Cliff II*, Main characters relationship chart 85; short introduction of the film *Red Cliff II* (Chinese) 75
Right Question Institute 70, 72, 78
role play 42, 48, 54, 55, 57, 66
The Romance of the Three Kingdoms 69

scaffolding 14–15, 27, 178
semiotics, social semiotics 102–103
Shanhaijing 101, 103, 105, 107, 121–122
Six Thinking Hats Technique 191–192, 197–198, 208
storyboard 110–112, 132–133
Sun Wukong's Three Bouts with the White Bone Demon 19
symbolism 215

Tang Juéjù (Quatrain) 218
Tang poetry 213
text-to-text, text-to-self, text-to-world connection-making strategy 139–140
thinking outside the box 71, 79
To Borrow Arrows with Thatched Boats 69
Total Physical Response & Storytelling (TPRS) 213
transcultural identification 4
translation 62–63, 186–187, 217–218, 227–228

visual literacy 56
visual storytelling 25

The Window, Mirror, Door Metaphors 71, 139, 147, 199–202
Women's History Month 162, 176

Yóuzǐ Yín (The Traveling Sonnet) 213

For Product Safety Concerns and Information please contact our EU
representative GPSR@taylorandfrancis.com
Taylor & Francis Verlag GmbH, Kaufingerstraße 24, 80331 München, Germany

www.ingramcontent.com/pod-product-compliance
Lightning Source LLC
Chambersburg PA
CBHW061346300426
44116CB00011B/2014